PLANE HEALING

M000249737

"*Planetary Healing* offers a strategic plan to more effectively redefine the path of human evolution. The book's guided shamanic journeys induce a state of calm consciousness expressed as α-EEG brain activity. Its informative and nurturing insights offer readers an opportunity to actively manifest new positive and empowering futures that benefit humanity, Mother Earth, and all of life."

BRUCE H. LIPTON, PH.D., CELL BIOLOGIST AND
BESTSELLING AUTHOR OF *THE BIOLOGY OF BELIEF*

"One can't even begin to turn the opening pages of *Planetary Healing* without becoming fully engaged. The storytelling alone is magnificent, as Nicki and Mark share their personal journeys into the realm of alchemical healing. Their intention for their readers is 'nothing less than transformation at the deepest level.' And they deliver on this promise, giving tools and practices to foster a deeply personal and planetary healing journey for each individual willing to be a catalyst of change. They've created a true wisdom book, fabulously interesting, inspiring, and utterly transformative."

ROSEMARY GLADSTAR, HERBALIST AND AUTHOR OF
ROSEMARY GLADSTAR'S FAMILY HERBAL

"Nicki Scully and Mark Hallert give us tools and resources to take a quantum leap in our evolutionary intelligence as we collectively move through the narrows of planetary challenges. It especially lends itself to joining with others in going through the visualizations together."

JUSTINE WILLIS TOMS, COFOUNDER OF NEW DIMENSIONS
RADIO/MEDIA AND AUTHOR OF *SMALL PLEASURES*

"*Planetary Healing* is a treasure trove of teachings and spiritual practices for transforming ourselves and the planet. Nicki Scully and Mark Hallert reach in to the wealth of their life experiences with great passion to share with us vital information for our survival. Great work!"

SANDRA INGERMAN, AUTHOR OF *MEDICINE FOR THE EARTH* AND *AWAKENING TO THE SPIRIT WORLD*

"*Alchemical Healing* opened the gateway to individual work in shamanic healing. Now, in *Planetary Healing*, Nicki and Mark offer visionary processes to heal Gaia and move the planet and its spiritual transformation."

NORMANDI ELLIS, AUTHOR OF *AWAKENING OSIRIS*

"Grab your paintbrush and set up your easel. This book is more than a museum of the past and a fantasy of the future. It is a call to action, to co-creation. Its message—'Don't despair; create a new reality'—goes beyond the usual ways of approaching the current ecological crisis. It skillfully guides us to effective ways to enhance our relationships with ourselves, others, and our planet. Come! Add your strokes of love and healing, joy and yearning, to the canvas. Dream a future perfect. Weave a web of wholeness."

SUSUN S. WEED, AUTHOR OF *WISE WOMAN HERBAL* SERIES

"*Planetary Healing* brings to life the tapestry of the inner realms as a path to conscious evolution and transformation for the self and the planet. Nicki Scully and Mark Hallert provide a rare opportunity to look into the inner workings of their spiritual journeys, sharing personal stories, rites of passage, and practical tools that inspire and invite the reader to awaken the healer, visionary, and mystic within."

DANIELLE RAMA HOFFMAN, AUTHOR OF *THE TEMPLES OF LIGHT*

"Nicki Scully and Mark Hallert are authentic loving examples as true planetary healers and visionaries. Their fierce compassion and loyal dedication to their work together has carried them through many powerful shamanic journeys on the 'path' and has led them to an ultimate truth that permeates the pages of this book. . . . Their Spirit Medicine is a soothing balm for a troubled world that is finally ready to remember that the healer lives within all of our hearts."

LINDA STAR WOLF, AUTHOR OF *VISIONARY SHAMANISM* AND *SHAMANIC BREATHWORK*

PLANETARY HEALING

Spirit Medicine for
Global Transformation

NICKI SCULLY and MARK HALLERT

Bear & Company
Rochester, Vermont • Toronto, Canada

Bear & Company
One Park Street
Rochester, Vermont 05767
www.BearandCompanyBooks.com

Text stock is SFI certified

Bear & Company is a division of Inner Traditions International

Library of Congress Cataloging-in-Publication Data
Scully, Nicki, 1943–
　Planetary healing : spirit medicine for global transformation / Nicki Scully and
Mark Hallert.
　　p. cm.
　Includes index.
　ISBN 978-1-59143-130-5 (pbk.) — ISBN 978-1-59143-943-1 (e-book)
　1. Spiritual healing. 2. Shamanism. I. Hallert, Mark. II. Title.
　BF1623.S63S38 2011
　299'.93—dc23

2011027135

Printed and bound in the United States by Lake Book Manufacturing
The text stock is SFI certified. The Sustainable Forestry Initiative® program
promotes sustainable forest management.

10 9 8 7 6 5 4 3 2 1

Text design by Virginia Scott Bowman and layout by Priscilla Baker
This book was typeset in Garamond Premier Pro with Warnock Pro and Myriad
Pro used as display typefaces

To send correspondence to the authors of this book, mail a first-class letter to the
authors c/o Inner Traditions • Bear & Company, One Park Street, Rochester, VT
05767, and we will forward the communication.

For Luke Scully,
A planetary healer of cosmic proportions

October 14, 1967 – December 26, 2004

We choose to believe that Luke faced the tsunami
with fearless wonder, which is how he embraced
all of life, and how we will remember him.

SPECIAL NOTE TO READERS

Although this book suggests experiences that can result in healing, it is not meant to give exact recommendations for specific illnesses, either physical or emotional. This book explores a variety of alternative possibilities that are meant to be used as adjunctive approaches to conventional modalities and are not intended to replace recognized therapies or medical diagnosis and treatment. It is suggested that readers approach these guided journey meditations with caution, for they, as with any deep explorations of the psyche, can sometimes catalyze emotional states of intensity.

The accompanying CD includes a guided journey that begins with the Heart Breath practice. Listening to this practice prior to reading the book will be a great help in performing all the exercises contained herein. See pages 273–74 for a guide to working with the CD.

Contents

Preface

We are living on a planet in crisis. Never before in recorded history have so many people walked the surface of Earth, and never before has the human species achieved the power to destroy life on such a scale as we have reached today. As more and more people awaken to the co-creative power we share with one another and with Spirit, the potential to become active participants in determining the future of our world grows with the overall population. The potency of our thoughts, intentions, and actions exponentially increases as people in growing numbers consciously combine forces—we can now redirect and reinvent our evolutionary trajectory.

Tools, practices, and processes in this book are designed to foster new ideas and increase creativity in solving problems. Our intention for our readers is nothing less than transformation at the deepest levels. The urgency we feel has motivated us to seek immediate and efficient solutions; and the primary arenas of our research include alchemy and shamanism. Both require deep commitment and presence and a willingness to step outside the comfort zone of more traditional doctrines such as science and religion.

Shamans have been crossing the veils between worlds for millennia. From their travels in altered states they bring back information, wisdom, and power for their communities. Their path is difficult, and rarely one that is intentionally sought. Rather, it is one to which a person is called, often after traumatic illness, visions, and dreams, or having been struck by lightening, or having been recognized by the elders of their tribe or community. Their training is rigorous, and despite the fact that no religion or specific doctrine is associated with shamanism, true shamans live a life of service, almost always accompanied by a more ordinary way of making a living.

Most shamanic traditions that we have investigated include the use of sacraments, psychoactive plants used both as medicines and for communion with Spirit, or God. Many countries worldwide, in their attempt to solve a very real problem of drug abuse and dependency, have lumped all uses of mind-altering substances together, labeled them dangerous, and made them illegal. Consequently, most Western cultures have been generally dismissive of shamanism, and there has been little support for people who have spontaneous shamanic experiences or initiations with no appropriate guidance or interpretations available.

This book is not meant to be confused as a primer for shamans. We offer techniques that are shamanic in nature, requiring practitioners to travel and explore other dimensions during their ongoing quest for solutions. Readers are responsible for their own experience. Although we are experienced in, and have been inspired by our psychedelic explorations, it has always been our intention to bring to the world shamanic methods that do not require the use of mind-altering substances of any kind.

We are striving for a quantum leap in consciousness that allows access to information and wisdom from a higher source of intelligence than the collective stream that has brought us to this brink. Perhaps the invocation of a new "smart gene" is in order. It is our hope and desire that you will find inspiration in these pages. Life on planet Earth is a collaborative painting, ever a work in process. We are all artists who continue to contribute with our thoughts, our insights, and our love. May your journeys bring you wisdom and joy, and may your efforts bring healing, peace, and harmony to our world.

Acknowledgments

Mark and I give blessings and gratitude for each other every day of our lives. We are deeply appreciative of each other and of the amazing process of creativity with which we have been gifted.

First we would like to give thanks to Inner Traditions, Bear & Co., and especially Jon Graham for holding space and giving us continued encouragement for this project ever since *Alchemical Healing* was published in 2003.

Deep gratitude goes to our editors, Mindy Branstetter and Jaya Walsh. With your care and thoughtful attention to details and clarity, you have transformed our rough-cut stone into a lustrous jewel.

During the twenty-five-plus years we have compiled material, there were countless people who helped and supported us in the creation of this book, including students all over the world, other Alchemical Healing teachers who contributed, our staff over the years, and our family and friends who tended us and gave us space to do the writing during times when their attention could have been spent on other, equally pressing matters. This includes (but is not limited to) Jeya Aerenson, Roland Barker, Anita Bermont, Gloria Taylor Brown, Bo Clark, Normandi Ellis, Christine Fehling, David Groode, Steve Harter, Charla Hermann, Julie Knouse, Liisa Korpela, Dea Lisk, Tanya Priest, Kathryn Ravenwood, Chris Tice, Kay Cordell Whitaker, Imani White, and many other of our friends and cohorts.

Particular thanks to David Groode and Gloria Taylor Brown—your keen vision ever on the ball—you kept reminding us of the importance of this book. Toward the end, it was Gloria who showed up and helped us put our records in order, a task that required way more skill in organization than either Mark or I possess. Thank you again, Gloria.

Indigo Ronlov responded when I called for help, my back too impaired to continue at the computer, and became my scribe for several months, assisting me to prepare the first draft to send to Inner Traditions International. Thank you.

When Diana Wells came to work for us, little did we know how much her skill and experience as an editor would help us to prepare and format the manuscript. Thank you Diana.

Once the first draft was completed, I tentatively showed it to Joan Borysenko, Normandi Ellis, Drs. Mitch and Lori Stargrove, Elizabeth Emmons, and Dr. Reuben Paul Wolff. I offer gratitude to them for their comments, suggestions, and enthusiasm.

Bruce Lipton, Ph.D., graciously discussed Intelligent Evolution with us in chapter 18 and offered additional information, explanations, and studies cited, helping to bring our DNA and cell biology science up to date. Thank you.

When I needed a song to go with the Making Spirit Medicine ceremonial journey, Alexa MacDonald wrote the music and lyrics, went out on the road with me to perform it, then recorded it for the CD that appears with this book. The music was produced and created by Roland Barker. Deepest appreciation for the fine work you both did.

We wish to give our extra special heartfelt thanks to all the spirit guides, animal totems, plant allies, ancestors, and deities that gave their gifts and guidance in support of this book. And finally, to Thoth, our primary teacher and muse, we say, "Thank you."

Introduction
Our Stories

This book is written for those who are motivated by love and compassion to engage with the events and situations that cause suffering on our planet. Such engagement, when played out in the spiritual arena, results in the potent release of energy, creation, and healing.

We believe in our ability to create change. It begins with any heartfelt response to events and situations, and grows when fueled by a passionate commitment to serve in creating a better future for ourselves and for future generations.

We started researching this book when we were looking for new tools for our students of Alchemical Healing. Our aim was to find spiritual techniques that would help us both envision solutions to the current challenges on our planet and make the fundamental changes necessary to adapt to and survive these challenges.

There are some survivalists who think that colonizing space will give us a place to which we can escape. Personally, we would rather keep our precious planet, return it to the Garden of Eden on a massive, all-encompassing scale, and still send ships to the planets and the stars for the adventure and the intellectual thrill of it.

While visiting Peru recently, we learned that the astonishing structural creations of the Incan civilization—their temples, stone cities, terraced gardens, irrigation channels, and marvels of agricultural achievement—were all designed and built in a span of a hundred years.

The many designers involved applied a shared vision of enhancing human life while working in a spiritual and harmonious balance with nature. It was a group effort that has yielded tremendous inspiration toward sustainable development.

When we compare this with what our own industrial revolution has produced during the past one hundred years, a divergence in priorities becomes garishly obvious. We started out with a keen sense of aesthetics: early engines, iron buildings, and pieces of furniture were works of art and beautiful to behold. But then something began to change as science and technology began to evolve and progress at an astounding pace: utility replaced beauty, and we conquered and expended the gifts of nature rather than honor her with the respect and appreciation she deserves. In the name of progress, technology has become our religion, and arrogance the limiting lens through which we relate to our world.

Some obvious questions come to mind: How can we bring forward the lessons learned and lived by the ancient civilizations, and fold the best of them into our way of life while avoiding the pitfalls and cruelties that often accompanied them? How can we spur the pace of change without opening the process to threats of violence and misdirection? And if a major step forward in human evolution is required for us to survive, what will that global transformation look like and how will it come into being?

It is unlikely that we can change our direction fast enough to avoid certain consequences using ordinary means, such as revolution, war, the voting process, or the judicial system. We simply do not have enough time. Even a fundamental shift in our paradigm—the way we view and interact with our environment, one another, other life forms, and the earth itself—though necessary and important, will come too late unless we can change not only our minds, but our physical attributes as well. Only a quantum leap in our evolution, in our intelligence actually, will position us to realize the possibility of the glorious and harmonious future that has been the promise of the Golden Age.

The number of people who have explored, expanded, meditated on, and otherwise altered consciousness is growing, to be sure. Many of us have had moments of experiencing the oneness, the All, the full presence by which we align individually with the mind of God. However, most of us cannot yet sustain such states over time.

Perhaps now we must learn to jump-start our dormant sensibilities, or even create new ones. Yet we cannot really know entirely what capacities and techniques we will need in the coming reality.

Further challenges await us if and when we enter this new dimension of awareness. Cultural, societal, and survival pressures work like gravity to pull us back into the old paradigm.

Our quest is to enter a dimension of utter wholeness, where the entire encyclopedia of all knowledge is available to our consciousness— a true wisdom book that can be read forward and backward throughout time. In this dimension, an amplified intelligence would be the medium of our existence. What can be known must be experienced with a new set of tools for sensory comprehension so that we can articulate that for which we currently have no words. Actually, were we to achieve this goal in the numbers that it would take to make an evolutionary shift for our species, I doubt that words would be necessary.

ALCHEMICAL HEALING

Planetary Healing: Spirit Medicine for Global Transformation is an extension of our work in Alchemical Healing. It can be the next step, or the first step, depending upon where you enter the path. Alchemical Healing is a continuously growing body of work that is sourced in ancient Egypt and inclusive of many ancient traditions. At its core it is an art form that empowers the person being healed to participate in and engage with their healing process.

In my (Nicki's) previous book, *Alchemical Healing: A Guide to Spiritual, Physical, and Transformational Medicine,* I invite readers to learn and experience a wide range of information and processes that generate self-healing, personal spiritual growth, and the ability to assist others in healing. Alchemical Healing initiations and techniques provide ways to weave spirit and matter, to develop communications between divinity and humanity, to transform experience into wisdom, and to skillfully influence physical reality to achieve healing and transformation. It is a form that honors the accumulated wisdom of the Earth and humankind, both in written and oral traditions, and also accesses the magical realms of intuition and limitless knowledge.

Many techniques offered in *Alchemical Healing* are best applied to individuals and small groups. The material in *Planetary Healing* offers a new, expanded expression of alchemy. Although similar in many ways, it allows readers to dip from a broader collective well that serves larger groups and global issues, while still addressing individual needs. In this book we share some of the newest teachings that we have been exposed to post-*Alchemical Healing,* along with others that started coming into our awareness shortly after Mark and I got together in 1985. Our intention is to help guide our readers to get their own teachings directly from the source through the experiences catalyzed by the practices and journeys we provide.

Whether responding to global issues or specific personal needs—whether for physical healing or for spiritual growth and development—our inherent ability to recognize and utilize available intelligence is often underestimated and overlooked. Alchemy is the process of turning the base substance of who we are—the dark mystery of our subconscious—into the alchemical gold of knowledge and enlightenment. Like carbon that undergoes tremendous amounts of heat and pressure in order to become a clear, hard, exquisite diamond, we master our lives and achieve clarity and brilliance through the management of pressure and our adversarial conditions.

Alchemy, by its nature, is inclusive of everything. It turns mud into food and food into energy—it is the spiritualization of matter. The process leaves the alchemist unfettered as she moves seamlessly between dimensions and across time and space. Modern alchemy is emerging as one of the most powerful tools for transforming our reality, and Alchemical Healing is an important vehicle for those who would heal themselves, and others.

Upon completion and publication of *Alchemical Healing* (2003), I

(Nicki) felt that the Great Work in my life was accomplished. By my sixtieth birthday, the prime material had been transformed, and the universal medicine had been extracted and infused with light. The seven stages of alchemy had revealed a "stone" of truth, and the unofficial, but equally important, eighth stage, sharing the knowledge with the world, had begun.

Alchemical Healing had barely been born when Mark and I realized that *Planetary Healing* needed to be published. This should not have come as a surprise—a body of knowledge, these teachings, had been growing throughout our time together.

OUR STORIES

When I was writing *Alchemical Healing,* my publishers asked me to include a brief biographical history so that people would know more about me and how the work originated, and to give it the credibility it deserves. In response, I wrote a thorough survey of the salient points of my life, including my family of origin, my transformation from "nice Jewish girl from Beverly Hills" into the world of psychedelics and the Grateful Dead, my years as a back-to-the-land hippie, two of my three marriages, my introduction to Native American spirituality, Egypt, Thoth, and cancer. I do not feel the need to repeat those stories, however interesting they might be.*

What is more relevant to this book starts when Mark and I came together, and the magic with which our relationship and this work are entwined. With our very different backgrounds and personalities, we are as alike as rockets are to dragons, yet we found each other through the same inexplicable synchronicity that permeates our lives and this book.

Before I met Mark I saw his eyes in a vision. I had been separated from my previous husband, Rock Scully, for nearly five years and was

---

*See Nicki Scully, *Alchemical Healing* (Rochester, Vt., Bear & Company, 2003), 17–42.

definitely ready to share my life with another. My teacher at that time, Nadia Eagles, suggested a ceremony that I could do to call in my future partner. The ceremony required a list of the attributes I was looking for. My list was long and detailed, and I was not surprised when I was told I would have to wait a bit, but he was coming. Later, after the ceremony, I did an exercise with the class during which I was shown the man in my future; Mark's bright, blue eyes appeared quite clearly, and I was content with the knowledge that I would soon have a partner.

Meanwhile, up north in Seattle, Loa and Kathy were plotting. "Mark and Nicki—Nicki and Mark, it is just too perfect." Loa was one of my closest friends and knew me well, and she knew and admired her only brother Mark. And Kathy knew all of us. The two of them gifted Mark one of the Huna classes I was teaching at the time. There were sparks that weekend, but the girls were going to have to work a little harder. Kathy kept dropping hints to Mark; "Nicki needs a deer fence, you should build her one . . ." and Loa was talking up her brother to me. I had not yet looked closely at his eyes.

It all came together just before winter solstice in 1985. My car had been stolen, with my most important possession, the *Cannunpa* (sacred pipe, pronounced Cha-n̲ü-pa) that I carried for the Grateful Dead, in the trunk. I was devastated, and set about trying to get at least the sacred pipe back using all means at my disposal, including putting ads in the newspaper offering a fat reward, setting the wards ceremonially, praying in the sweat lodge, and anything else I could think of at the time.

To make a long story short, Kathy sent Mark to support me through this tough time, and he never left.

In Mark's words: "I did not have much experience with ritualized spirituality. That became apparent when Nicki, just within a few minutes of my arrival, told me that there was going to be a solstice sweat lodge. I did not know what solstice was. I did not know what a sweat lodge was, either, but I imagined it must be something like a Swedish sauna and it sounded like fun. I had already fallen for Nicki when we had met during her class, and the Swedish sauna sounded pretty good to me. I had no idea I would be crawling around in the mud in a Native American ceremony that was way too hot, with no light and lots of prayer and chanting.

"The crisis Nicki was in required her full attention. It was as if her entire property was in ceremony. There was something really appealing about the confidence she expressed; there was an emergency and we were dealing with it through a form of prayer and ritual and somehow, although it was entirely new to me, I resonated and worked with it. I felt no cynicism or doubt; there was an emergency, and, through prayer and ritual we were dealing with it. Once the crisis was passed, the sense of spirituality did not go away. Eventually, about six weeks later, the police found the gutted and trashed car, but the medicine bundle and the sacred pipe were still there. It was amazing; the one thing we had been praying for was the one thing that had not been molested.

"I found myself immersed from the beginning in something bigger—no matter what was going on in our personal lives, no matter what was going on in the world, there was the sense that we could participate and help. There were unseen forces at work, there were traditions to be respected, and there was new knowledge to be gained. No matter if it was about the radiation from Chernobyl or a stolen car, there was always something that we could do spiritually that could have an effect.

"Our histories are so different, it is a wonder that we have come to similar personal truths. My background included divorced parents (a rarity in the fifties), two foster families, eight homes, nine schools from first grade through eleventh, and a short stay in juvenile hall by the time I left to explore the world at age sixteen. There was one crucial thing Nicki and I had in common that bridged our divergent backgrounds: we both became hippies as soon as we left home.

"My adventures in California hippiedom ended abruptly with a trip to boot camp on the way to Vietnam. This exercise in extremes and opposites—going from love-ins and riots for peace to panic and boredom in war, for instance—became an unintended theme that has recurred throughout my life. I have lived in a cloud forest high in the Andes south of the equator and worked at 400 feet below sea level in the North Sea as a diver. I studied aeronautics landlocked in Oklahoma, and worked on ships crossing oceans and seas. The time spent connecting these dots included a lot of travel—thirty-six countries that I can remember and at least one that I have difficulty remembering—the month I spent in an opium den in Afghanistan in 1972.

"The pendulum started to swing toward settling down on my twenty-fifth birthday when I met a German woman in Costa del Sol in Spain. We married in Mexico, tried living in Germany, and finally settled in Washington State.

"Ahh, the peaceful life: while I worked overtime building ships for an airplane company (I am not making this up), Brigitte gave dressage and jumping lessons, and we hosted equestrian competitions and shows. My spare time (like there was such a thing!) was spent building, repairing, and maintaining our arenas, jumps, and fences. Two great kids became part of this story, and they were six and seven when the marriage failed. Two years later, they met Dad's new girlfriend, Nicki Scully. That was twenty-five years ago at this writing—twenty-five years of a very different kind of growth and adventure."

Among Mark's many talents is that of working inside the dream world. One night shortly after his arrival, I had a dream during which I glimpsed the face of a certain teacher of mine, and then felt a dagger enter my back. I was instantly fully awake. I can still feel the violation when I remember the moment. I had such a sinking feeling. My spine tingled and the tissue around the wound seemed to cave inward; I had no physical pain, but the vulnerability and loss were palpable.

I woke Mark and he became immediately alert, although he moved as if in a trance. He spontaneously leaned over and began to gently suck from the place where the dagger entered my back. I could feel a distinct pulling sensation as the blade was removed. He then got up and took it outside where he disposed of it appropriately. As Mark returned from his trancelike state, he told me that he had dreamed this event at about age seventeen. It was because of this dream that he knew what to do and had no fear of doing it.

That was not the only dream Mark had that portended our life together. He vividly remembers a lucid dream he had when he was about twenty-one: He was in an ice field, completely barren and inhospitable, with no apparent way out. Way off in the distance, Mark could see himself sitting in a rocking chair on a wooden deck, with flowers and green vines growing all around. From the ice field, he had to yell through his cupped hands to reach himself on the deck: "How do I get there?" he cried. His future self yelled back from the rocking chair, "If you can't get here, we don't want you." He had been at my home for a short time before he recognized my back deck as the one in his dream.

That Mark was a visionary came as a wonderful surprise one day as we were driving down the I-5 corridor on our way from Eugene, Oregon, to San Francisco, early in our relationship. I was off-handedly calling out the names of the Egyptian deities, musing to myself about Egypt. Mark was driving, and suddenly veered to the shoulder of the highway, stopped the car, and jumped out, backing away. "You had better have a good reason for calling them," he admonished me, "because they're all here."

I calmed him down and talked him back into the car, and our ensuing conversation revealed that Mark could, indeed, see and hear and even feel the presence of these beings.

This was an unexpected turn-on for me, and a great boon. It happened not long after I had connected with my primary mentor and teacher, the Egyptian god Thoth, and had discovered that people around me could connect with him more directly than I could. That one of them lived with me—the possibilities were exhilarating. Before I continue our story, an introduction to Thoth would be helpful so that you will understand my excitement.

Thoth represents the highest concept of mind, and is widely respected as the god of wisdom, communications, healing, science, language, magic, and more. He is also the mediator of the gods. As god of the moon, he is associated with the wisdom of deep reflection. He is most often seen as a man with an ibis head, however he also appears as an ibis or a baboon. Thoth is considered by many to be the source of Hermetic wisdom and Western mystical and magical traditions.

I had first encountered Thoth in a shamanic journey during a transmission of teaching authority from Nadia, and was aware that he was already in many ways directing my progress and helping me to develop my own unique work and healing form.

Once I discovered that Mark had ready access to Thoth, I used him like a telephone to get information, guidance, and direction. It was an arrangement that worked well for us—I would ask the question and Thoth would show or give Mark an image or experience that Mark would relay to me. Sometimes the answer was obvious, sometimes not. It was up to me to interpret the image; if Mark tried, his rational brain would influence the imaging. He learned early on the importance of "getting out of the way" and letting the images flow without his input. Often Thoth would give us information about things we had not yet realized we needed to ask. Sometimes what he gave us would not make sense for a couple of days, and then something would happen and it would all fall into place.

As my classes grew, so did the requests from my students for more tools and practices. Early in 1987, Mark and I did ceremony to request new teachings for my advanced healing students, and things shifted radically. While wonderful and exciting information was still pouring in from other sources for other projects, including animal totem journeys that would eventually be published in *Power Animal Meditations,* Thoth, Mark, and I were hard at work. Our visioning sessions were producing detailed instructions as to what these teachings would be, and we set up a class for the week before Harmonic Convergence, which was to happen August 17, 1987. Our intention was to give our students more new tools to work with for that occasion.

Approximately twenty students came to that first Planetary Healing class, and the pressure was on for us to deliver this brand-new and very complex body of work. We were running to our room between processes, consulting with Thoth, and trying to get it right. By the time the workshop was over at the end of the weekend, the students were enthusiastically sated, but Mark was wrung dry from over-sight. . . . It would be many months before he would vision for me again.

The issue of boundaries has been one that we had to revisit a number of times in the twenty-five years we have been collaborating. I have struggled with a desire to rely on Mark, Thoth, and other visionaries in my life. As I share these tools and the process by which they came to us, I am reminded that all devices can become crutches, and can ultimately weaken our ability to see for ourselves if we overuse or abuse them.

Once we were back on track, Planetary Healing, alchemy, and the Egyptian Mysteries started to shape themselves in new ways in our minds and in our lives. I began taking tours to Egypt in 1989, and since then have led more than fifty groups. Over time, my participants urged me to offer more destinations, and Shamanic Journeys Ltd. came into being. Soon the list of tour offerings I would arrange and lead included Mexico, Tibet, Peru, and Greece. Besides Egypt, it was Peru that most captured my interest; the magic of the high mountains, the jungle, and the ever-present and still-current living culture of shamanism lured me into a magical relationship with the country, her people, and her sacred divine plants. After about ten tours to Peru, and when I took a moment to realize that I was visiting five continents per year and was away far more than I was at home enjoying my garden, I decided to bring my focus back to my first love, Egypt. Since then I have been organizing tours for other teachers, and fulfilling my wish list of teaching partners by co-leading tours to Egypt with the spiritual teachers I most admire.

Meanwhile, Mark and I continued to set aside time for special ceremonies in order to vision for each new class or program. I scribed every session and extracted from the transcriptions the teachings, rites, and journeys, then offered them in my classes and later on in phone bridges (tele-web conferences). The transcripts were loosely organized in my computer, but it was the ceremonial work and the teachings themselves that set and maintained the spiritual vector of our lives and our work together. These sessions provided the magical underpinning of our relationship and the alchemy that is catalyzed by our partnership.

The idea to get married occurred to both of us simultaneously during the New Year's Eve Grateful Dead concert following the death of Mark's sister, Loa, four days prior. For us, this was her wake, yet it was during this intense time that we were magically shown that marriage was part of our destiny together.

Our wedding was a festive event, witnessed at our home by about three hundred of our friends in August of 1990. Our garden provided a vast array of flowers in full bloom, and all the amenities (floral arrangements, food, and decorations) were offered by our talented and generous friends; although it was completely home grown, the ambiance, food, and entertainment were over the top—belly dancers and sword swallowers and copious amounts of music and laughter, oh my!

Yet the hint of the full potential of our union came during our honeymoon, for which we were lent a beautiful home on the edge of the ocean near Puna, on the Hilo side of the island of Hawaii. The bedroom of our beautiful, gas-lit home had a wide and far-ranging view of the sea on three sides. We could see where the fresh lava from the ongoing eruption of Kilauea volcano poured into the sea, sending up a fountain of steam during the day, and a fiery light show at night, giving us a constant reminder of the temporal nature and vulnerability of this part of the island.

Expecting a "normal" honeymoon, we started out early in the afternoon in the bedroom, but were drawn inexplicably outside, and down to the peninsula of lava that jutted out from the main house. As we neared the edge where the waves were flowing toward the sharply defined lava coastline, we found a natural seat where we could take turns sitting with our back toward the oncoming waves, each of us guarding the other to allow the experience. Although the waves were breaking about ten feet to the side, it felt as though they were crashing through, as well as around us, and the effect was of a cleansing or purification at the deepest levels of our beings.

Mark surveyed our surroundings and decided it was safe to venture further out, although it would require his full attention to be sure we would not be swept away. The lava was sharp and jagged, and formed pools that we explored as we carefully picked our way further out on the edge of the finger of lava to where the ocean swells seemed to be forming immediately at the side of us. Each pool we investigated had an entire ecosystem of tiny, tropical fish and other unique and enchanting life forms. When the waves rolled by just right, the water was refreshed, but the fish stayed in the pool. The entire adventure was exquisite.

We could not go out much further without endangering ourselves from the waves that were now moving parallel to us, just a few feet away, but there was one more pool, even more colorful and lively than any we had seen that was compelling us forward. We could see lots of small crabs skittering out of the way before each wave would crash into it, then run back as soon as the water receded. I crouched down to get a closer look. Mark was being extra-vigilant in order to allow me to observe this fascinating pool. As he watched the waves developing beside us, he noticed a large sea turtle riding the swells, and called it to my attention. I stood up and looked where he was pointing, but became a bit disoriented because I thought I was seeing double. I saw two turtles, and told Mark so. The two turtles were locked together, riding the waves, and looking directly at us. As soon as Mark realized what we were seeing, he went into guard mode to allow me my moment, just as I melted into the female turtle. It was as though I became the turtle, and as the female turtle I received the full orgasmic experience of the copulation, and the insemination that was taking place.

Although Mark and I did not fully understand the relationship between this magical encounter and the future work we would be creating together, it became apparent as time went on that the spiritual eggs that were fertilized during this unusual consummation bore fruit in our creative partnership.

The sea turtle was already a totem in our work and published in *Power Animal Meditations.* Her attributes include service and giving, and her clutch of eggs can number in the hundreds.

After publication of *Alchemical Healing,* there was more of a sense of urgency to complete our planetary healing compendium. I was still on the road, touring to promote *Alchemical Healing* when the next round of new teachings entered, and the ball was rolling again. A few months later we did a nine-day retreat on the Greek island of Santorini, specifically to explore our newest tools for planetary healing. There, perched on the rim of an exquisite natural caldera, we delved into the Communal Cauldron (Making Spirit Medicine), and found ourselves drinking deeply of its medicine while practicing the Wave in ceremony during a summer solstice sunrise atop the volcanic cone in the center of the caldera, next to the vent of an eruption that blew in 1944 and is called—Nikki's Crater.

The core practices of *Planetary Healing* came in the first burst of the unique creative process that Mark and I were gifted by Thoth, who continued over the years to be generous with his guidance and to let us know how important this work was.

Over time the lessons became more obscure, like riddles or enigmas. They required more deep thought to interpret. At a certain point we had to confront the difficulty Mark had differentiating between receiving information from an external source, Thoth, and his own Higher Mind. I was reticent initially, and it took some time for me to accept that Mark had made his transition to being able to tap directly into the High Self, which is the ultimate goal of the practices in this book.

Mark and I have had an ongoing discussion that occasionally becomes heated—Is Thoth inside or outside of us? Mark, having a highly developed inner sight, knows himself. He also knows and can recognize the essence of truth, which is a true measure of wisdom.

For me, as my relationship with Thoth developed over time, I found a deep and abiding trust that continues to this day. The unconditional love I have felt from Thoth is profound. He has helped me to learn that as a mature adult I am capable of making my own decisions, ascertaining my own direction, and recognizing my own distinctly original ideas. That said, I honor the power and magic in my relationship with Thoth and will continue to seek his wise council when necessary. It is my joy and honor to introduce others to him, knowing that each person will have her own evolving relationship.

The completion of this book represents a graduation for me—no gold star, no diploma—just growing up. I am ready to move on to the next as yet, unimaginable arena of being and magic.

The story of Mark and me and our muse is one of a unique and magical creative process, one for which we are boundlessly grateful, and one that is still fresh and new and constantly changing, even after all these years. Our ability to grow and learn new things together is a measure of our love—we are endlessly interesting to each other.

Throughout all our years together, Mark and I have been dedicated to creating tools for the healing of our Mother Earth and All Our Relations. This collaboration represents the most current fulfillment of this shared mission.

How to Use This Book

This book is a *do,* rather than a *read.* We suggest that you start from the beginning and work your way through, chapter by chapter, engaging in the processes as you come to them. It is best to practice and begin to integrate each piece before going on to the next one. Some readers will want to read through the book before actually taking the journeys. That is fine; however, we still highly recommend that you do the work consecutively and in the order given. Many of the processes build upon previous chapters that develop the skills and awareness for what comes next.

BASIC INSTRUCTIONS

There are two things to keep in view to maximize the safety and efficacy of these techniques: follow the instructions carefully, and be in a place of heart-centered presence every time you practice.

In the optimum scenario, you would have a place to practice without distraction as you learn how to use these tools. You would also have someone with you or nearby with whom you can process with as soon as you complete each journey, especially the first time through.

This book lends itself to working with friends, taking turns reading to one another. One of the best applications is to have a circle of people that are interested in spiritual activism, personal transformation, and/or planetary healing, and meet on a regular basis, with each person taking a turn as the reader. When working with a friend or in a circle or group, it is important to allow time for sharing. When people share their experiences, it helps the others to better understand their personal journeys, and is often a source of inspiration in a way that is provocative and gives breadth and depth to everyone's experience. We are all in this together; and with mutual support and encouragement, we can collectively make a difference.

We realize that the need for healing often arises spontaneously, and that there will be times when you will be called upon to enter into these rites while traveling or at work. As you get more grounded in the various techniques offered in this book, you will be able to transition in and out of them more quickly. The more you practice, the more confidence you will gain using these powerful tools.

Lightness and play can be incorporated into much of this work, bringing levity to very serious situations. We can get into trouble when we take ourselves too seriously.

You will be drawn to the causes, people, situations, and events that resonate for you, and we include exercises for many specific problems, such as cancer, war, and air pollution. Some of the processes we offer here will allow you to engage with the creation of conscious, intelligent evolution. Others offer opportunities during which you can invite and, hopefully, witness spontaneous healing and miracles.

Think of these processes as maps you can follow, not necessarily to land in specific destinations, but to see where they lead you as you seek solutions to the situations that are important to you, and consider how you will serve.

Many people are able to follow the guided visualizations as they read, however others prefer to make a recording and play it back, using the pause button to allow yourself time to follow each instruction. You will find that journaling your experiences with these practices is both gratifying and important. Many of your adventures, although quite vivid in the moment, will fade like dreams in the hustle and bustle of life. When you take the time to write them down, especially when the experiences are fresh, you will be able to review them later and find recurring themes and teachings that might not otherwise be apparent. You will learn more this way, and also find unexpected inspiration and insights. We suggest you keep a special book, a magical diary that you reserve specifically to keep track of your Planetary Healing adventures.

Throughout the time you spend reading and practicing Planetary Healing, and as you encounter the many allies you will meet along the way, please remember that gratitude is the time-honored way we show our appreciation for the help, guidance, and teachings we receive. Whether you are communing with other people whom you meet in the spirit realms, ancestors, deities, or other spirit guides or totem allies, it is important to express your gratitude in some way. Sometimes it will simply be acknowledgment or thank you, and others you might find yourself committing to an act or gift of generosity and kindness as your contribution to whatever situation you are dealing with.

ALTARS

A small altar dedicated to this work can be helpful. Make it as elaborate as you choose, or as simple as a candle. Smudging with sage, juniper, or any organic incense each time you begin is useful for clearing the space. If you are sensitive to smells, you can sprinkle water on yourself with the intention of purification. Intention is sufficient on its own when the items are not practical or available in the moment. Since you will be breathing the Heart Breath in preparation for every process and journey, you can infuse a breath or two with the specific intention of self-purification, thus clearing emotional toxins and negative energies that may be within or around you. (We will teach you the Heart Breath in detail in the next chapter.)

I used to carry an altar with me wherever I went. I have spent considerable time studying traditions that use altars, mesas (indigenous Peruvian portable altar wrapped in a woven cloth), or other kinds of touchstones to support my connection with Spirit and to remind me of what is important. For various reasons, I have mostly let go of portable altars. Airport security checks can be disrespectful, so I have found other ways to tie into and honor Spirit. It is a personal choice what you will want to travel with to sustain you in this spiritual work; play with it. Remember that everywhere you walk upon this planet is sacred, and you can honor that sacredness in many ways. What matters is your sincerity.

Mark and I are fortunate to live in a beautiful garden sanctuary. From the beginning and throughout our time here, we have participated in many, many ceremonies. The sweat lodge was first built with the help of a traditional Native American medicine man in 1985; we have hosted several troupes of Tibetan monks who have offered their blessings to our land; and been honored with ceremonies from shamans from Peru and Mexico, and others of diverse traditions and disciplines. The sense of the sacred grew like our garden, and when I began teaching the Egyptian Mysteries here, the rituals included the laying of the foundation of and eventually the consecration of an etheric Egyptian temple, invisible yet strongly present. Our Egyptian Mysteries retreats have been gatherings during which we honor the temple with a procession that pays tribute to the *neteru*, the family of the Egypt pantheon to whom the temple is dedicated. Over time, retreats and workshops, sweat lodges and other ceremonial events developed the sacred space and strengthened the foundation with intention and purpose.

Our garden is one of the primary altars on our land. I started developing it when I moved here in 1981 and it was dedicated to Kuan Yin during a time when I was going through treatment for cancer eleven years later. (This story is recorded in chapter 20, "The Pandemic of Cancer.") I watched Mark as he tended the plants throughout my healing process while I snuggled in the hammock strung between two apple trees. Each year our garden expands a bit more. It has secured our connection to the sacred, and it travels with us wherever we go.

Whenever sacred space is created and honored, it becomes a part of the physical landscape of its creator. The sanctity of our land and our connection to it has strengthened and deepened over the years with our attention and our love.

PROTECTION

We, who are doing this work, are explorers of the inner planes. We cannot always know where we will wind up or what we will encounter along the way. We take care of and respect our physical requirements, honor our allies, set and hold clear intentions, and maintain a great deal of trust for the magic that supports us. We try to stay present and focused, and employ discernment in our choices. Beyond that, we look for meaning and teachings in the encounters we have and in whatever happens on our journeys. As in life, we venture out into the unknown every time we travel.

When we ground and center with the Heart Breath,* we connect to love, to our sacred Mother Earth, and to the entirety of the universe, we call on that power, vitality, and intelligence to awaken us, to make us present and aware, and to be one with us in our travels. We are brought into equilibrium—in our rightful place—centered between Earth and Sky, between spirit and matter. Then as we practice the work in this book, we will meet new allies and build relationships that will keep us in good stead, supporting and protecting us as we move forward.

Our greatest protection is in our heart-centered loving presence, and in the relationships we make. Awareness, strengthened by our willingness to give and receive love, is a force to be reckoned with, a fortification that draws the goodness of the universe while repelling the darkness.

There are very few "rules" in this work. Taking the time to become present when you begin each exercise, and to fully ground and center yourself upon completion are crucial to your well-being. This will also help you achieve the full potential of the practices. It is also essential to honor the sacredness of the magic and the mystery you are entering into, without expectation that the fullness of the mystery will ever be revealed. It is a mystery, after all.

There are no doctrines or rulebooks in shamanism. Most indigenous shamanic traditions have at their base the requirement that the medicine person is journeying for the benefit of their communities. Integrity,

---

*See chapter 1.

or the lack of it, can be found anywhere, and again, your presence and discernment are your greatest protections.

Many years ago, while leading a tour to Peru, I had an interesting incident occur with a shaman who saw me as an opponent in a struggle for power. At the end of the tour, after the participants had left for home, I confronted him for behaving inappropriately toward one of my charges during a medicine ceremony. He was enraged, and threatened to harm both the other person and me. At this point in the journey I had become quite ill and was running a high fever. I missed my flight home.

The following day the shaman was doing a medicine ceremony with another group at one of the sacred power places on the outskirts of Cusco. I was sure that he intended to attack me during that ceremony. Terrified, I called Mark to ask what I could do to protect myself. He suggested that I place myself in a bubble, so that any thought I might generate would stay contained within the bubble and simply reflect back on me. If I had a fearful thought, I would feel the fear amplified. But if I was able to stay in love, that love would be the medium of my existence, and nothing could harm me.

As he finished describing the process, Mark and I were disconnected, and I was unable to reach him by phone for the duration of the ordeal. I steeled myself in the room where I was staying; besides, I was too sick to leave and had nowhere to go.

I set about building the bubble around me with my imagination, formulating it in my mind, and settling myself into this transparent container with a reflective surface that would give all my thoughts back to me. I quickly learned that fear did indeed magnify itself. I willfully focused on love. I kept the bubble around me, generating as much love as I could muster. Although my terror was initially palpable, I somehow moved away from thoughts of fear and kept generating love inside my bubble.

The day passed slowly. By dinnertime I was able to sit up in the kitchen for a while. During that time the shaman returned, hissing in my ear as he walked past me, "I did not feel a thing." I was stunned to realize that he had assumed I would either be attacking him or countering his attack, notions that had never occurred to me. That is also when I took in how well the bubble shield had protected me. I was unscathed and getting stronger by the moment. I called the woman and was assured that she, too, felt protected.

When we shine our light like the beacons we are, the processes in *Planetary Healing* are self-filtering. In the same way that music draws like-minded people and repels others, we draw in forces from the light to support us.

We hope that you will be inspired to travel the inner planes on your own to find new and unique tools to use as you face life's difficult challenges. In doing so, you may bring forth new ideas and contribute to what we hope is an ongoing dialog among the practitioners. As we chart new territory in creating global transformation, we must report back to one another and discuss our findings. We can link to a template or matrix of commonality and unified intention. We have set up a website, www.PlanetaryHealingBook.com to provide a forum for discussing the processes, and where we can work together to respond to the needs of the moment. We invite you to participate.

PART I

Introducing Planetary Healing

1

The Heart Breath

In order to be most effective in any intentional act of healing, co-creation, or transformation, all Planetary Healing work starts from and is threaded through the heart center. True wisdom is perceived from the heart. Every process, every meditation, and every act of healing and conscious creation you will encounter in this book starts with the Heart Breath: you get centered and focused in the heart space, and develop and direct your intention from the heart. This process will allow you to quickly and easily bring yourself into alignment with the higher purpose of this work. Initially published in *Alchemical Healing,* the Heart Breath has been employed by thousands of practitioners around the world. It is efficient and effective, and its value accrues with use.

The Heart Breath practice will help you to establish a direct connection with the intelligent source of our universe. You can use it as part of a daily meditation practice or any time you need to bring yourself back to center; returning to the Heart Breath will allow you to maintain center as you function throughout your day. It can serve as a beacon with which to call forth appropriate guidance to help you meet your needs at any time. We employ the Heart Breath often, and have found that it restores clarity of thought during times of emotional upheaval or crises. Consistent practice of this process, however you use it, will result in a saner, more balanced awareness that you can sustain.

The Heart Breath is the nexus point between the grounded, dense, and solid energy of earth (matter) and the radiant, complex intelligence of the stars and the universe that enfolds and surrounds us (Spirit). In this breathing practice, we connect the powers of Earth and Sky within our heart center while nourishing the sacred, central heart flame. In the space of the Heart Breath, the energy and intelligence of source is transformed into accessible information and power, and fosters our perspective of the wisdom of the heart.

Although you will start out breathing Earth and Sky individually, you will soon find that you can connect with both simultaneously, while continuing to hold your attention and add your love to the equation. Your personal capacity for love grows as you activate feelings of love and direct them into your heart breath. It can help to connect with the love that you feel toward your family, your friends, your allies, and the Earth, or whatever stimulates the love in your heart and the love for your self.

As you become proficient in the Heart Breath Practice, develop it, live with it, play with it. The practice itself will become smoother and easier and will eventually integrate so that it becomes second nature—only a matter of focusing your attention to bring yourself into centered and balanced equilibrium. Still, you need to remain vigilant so that it does not become a rote formula. In order to keep the Heart Breath vital, it is important to stay conscious of the sources of energy, including the love component, that feed this practice and keep it alive. Without your heart-centered presence, it could become devoid of the spirit and intelligence it is meant to invoke, and disconnected from the spontaneous magic that initially inspired it.

The Heart Breath can also be used as a way to direct healing to any part of your body. Simply breathe in the powers of Earth and Sky, mix with the love you are adding to your heart flame, and direct your exhale to any place in your body that is in pain or in need. Likewise, it can be used with other people to develop and foster a strong, heart-centered connection. The Earth Breath, the first part of the Heart Breath, can be used separately, apart from the combined Earth and Sky breaths. There are occasions in this book where we recommend it to give additional grounding as needed.

EXERCISE

Heart Breath Practice

Relax. Close your eyes, and take a couple of deep, calming breaths. . . . Focus on your heart. Look within and find the eternal flame of your being that dwells in the sanctuary of your heart center. . . . This flame is the spark of your soul that endures throughout time. . . . As you bring your heart flame into focus, access whatever inner senses are available to you—sight, hearing, feeling, knowing, imagination. . . . When you perceive your heart flame in whatever way it presents itself, feed it with love. . . . Activate feelings of love in your heart and use those feelings to feed your heart flame. . . .

Love is the fuel. As you continue to feel love in your heart and pour love upon your flame, it brightens, it intensifies; it spreads warmth and light throughout your being. . . .

As your heart flame brightens within you, breathe as though you are drawing power and vitality from the heart of the Earth up through all the strata of the Earth, drawing from all the elements, minerals, and plants. . . . Pull the energy that comes with your in-breath up through the Earth's crust and into your body, all the way up to your heart center. . . . Hold your breath for a moment while the power and intelligence of Earth mingles with the love that you continue to pour on your heart flame. . . . As you exhale, the charged energy radiates out from your heart center, igniting every cell of your body with life-force energy and love. . . .

Take several deep, slow, strong Earth Breaths. . . .

While you continue to breathe the Earth breath, simultaneously extend your consciousness upward toward the heart of the cosmos. As you inhale the power of Earth, you are also inhaling from the sky, drawing down power, vitality, and intelligence from the billions of stars and all the heavenly bodies, and the intelligence that permeates the universe. As the power of Sky joins the power of Earth in your heart center, see-feel-know-imagine the further nourishment of your heart flame. . . . Hold your breath for a moment as these energies combine with your love. . . . With each out-breath, experience the growing life-force energy, intelligence, love, and radiance that extend throughout your body and beyond. Notice how the Heart Breath works like bellows, fanning the fire until you are sitting within the bright glow that radiates from your inner heart flame. . . .

When you feel yourself in that perfect place of equilibrium between Earth and Sky, you are ready to move forward with whatever process or exercise is before you, or simply meditate quietly within this glow until you are ready to open your eyes. . . .

2
Love and Fear

What does the word *love* mean? The variety of responses in the dictionary indicates a complexity rarely found in a single word. The concept includes any affection between people; the tireless caring parents extend to their children, a heartfelt devotion for God, and the passion that accompanies the sexual drive. Love is the glue that holds the universe together, or at least makes it work in a more sane and pleasurable way.

Mark and I have found that love is an essential element in the Planetary Healing work, because love is its primary motivating force, as well as the single most important ingredient. We strive to sustain a connection to love throughout this work. To put ourselves in the position of creator would be pure arrogance; however, in this work, we step boldly into the position of co-creator with Spirit. Entering this journey in full recognition of our relationship with love gives us strength and protection, and aligns us with our High Selves, and with the perspective of the heart.

Without love, Planetary Healing is an abstract concept that can be discussed, but not necessarily experienced. The invocation of the Heart Breath as we enter each process, rite, or exercise helps us shift our perspective to the heart center, where the experience of love is naturally available.

Some of the processes in this Planetary Healing work may bring up unresolved issues that can limit the experience of the journeyer. The most common obstructions, whether seemingly based in indoctrination, judgment, or constrictions of the heart, can be traced back to fear.

Mark and I decided to put this chapter early in this book. We want to equip you to meet fears that may be more or less quietly lurking in your shadows, and transform them if they arise by providing you with tools and abilities to deal with them and make more space in which love can reside and radiate.

Fear is real. It is also an important survival tool that we all employ to keep us out of harm's way. Many of our fears no longer serve us. They have often been laid on us by others sometime during our life, especially in early childhood, or they are sourced in events that are no longer a threat. Yet the fears linger, and, until they are dealt with, they will continue to have an impact on our lives as well as our peace of mind.

The influence of fear on our planet is profound. It is a powerful and all-too-common tool used throughout history for governmental and religious dominance and control, and is also pervasive in personal and family relationships. Although we recognize that fear is at the core of many human-caused planetary challenges, we cannot deal with the depth and complexity of the subject in a single chapter in this book. Many fears are deeply rooted and evolve into syndromes and disorders that require extensive therapy. That said, we have had some powerful results from the practice we offer here—an alchemical solution that we have found helpful in our healing practice with many fear-based situations.

It takes courage to heal fear, and it is well worth the effort: remember that any clearing of fear makes space for more love.

THE ALCHEMY FOR TRANSFORMING FEAR

Following the ceremony during which Mark and I concluded that love and fear need to be addressed early in this book, I found myself participating in an Alchemical Healing session that arrived at my door like a gift from the universe.

Joan came all the way from Delaware to see me here in Oregon. The synchronicity surrounding this session was evident; Joan desperately needed help with the same issues we had just committed to for this book.

Joan told me she was done with traditional therapies for the time being. The years spent with various therapists and medications had not helped, and the source of her depression had yet to be identified. Joan was clear and determined: she was looking for spiritual support and self-empowerment. After reading *Alchemical Healing,* she hoped that a face-to-face session with me might help her.

I carefully explained that I am not a therapist. In fact, I do not consider myself to be doing anything beyond experimenting with spiritual tools that may or may not be of assistance. She accepted this. We began the session as usual, with the Heart Breath. While breathing the Heart Breath with Joan, I had the idea that I would start by attempting to find a time before the depression set in, a time when she was truly happy in her body and not questioning *Why am I here?* and *What is the point of living?*

As we mentioned earlier, the Heart Breath is a powerful breathing exercise that shifts your perspective directly to the heart. Occasionally some people initially have trouble with this, but Joan could not do it at all. Whenever she tried to focus on drawing the power of the Earth or Sky into her heart, she encountered a physical sensation as though her heart muscle was clenched, closing off access to the experience of the love.

Usually the Heart Breath offers a gentle reminder of the existence of love within, as well as the love we can draw from the universe. Joan's heart was closed to this. When she tried to breathe in love, power, and intelligence, she instead felt fear. The fear was firmly entrenched and seemed unmovable.

When I regressed Joan back through time, I was forced to conclude that the fear constricting her heart had been present since she was conceived. She then told me that she was the eighth of nine children, and before she was born, her mother had experienced two full-term pregnancies that ended in stillbirths.

It occurred to me that Joan's mother carried her to term with a staggering amount of fear. Joan had been exposed to her mother's fear from conception and throughout her time in the womb. Even with all that fear, Joan held the belief, at least intellectually, that the medium of our existence is love and that the intelligent force of the universe is love. We had to find a way to move her from abstract knowing to tangible, deep feeling. In order to do this, we would have to deal with the fear.

For the purposes of the session with Joan, I chose to use sulfur as the ally and catalyzing agent to assist in the process.

Sulfur is an element of the earth, bright yellow in color. Although some compounds utilizing sulfur may be toxic, sulfur itself is essential for life, and also an essential ingredient of our bodies. It is not to be confused with sulfa, or the sulfonamide compounds that were used as antibacterial drugs before the discovery of penicillin. Sulfur is also called brimstone. The odor it emits in certain compounds, such as those naturally occurring in volcanic emissions and in many mineral hot springs, evoke a smell reminiscent of rotten eggs, and we can all relate to the familiar acrid odor of a freshly lit match. Our olfactory sense is a powerful instrument in this kind of work; it stimulates our deeply held memories and brings them into our awareness. You do not need any physical sulfur to experience this process, however you do need to be familiar with its smell; it is the smell that will catalyze the alchemical process with which you will engage. Sulfur also has a very low flashpoint, which is particularly advantageous in our process.

In traditional alchemy there are three classical principles, or heavenly substances: sulfur, salt, and mercury. Sulfur is the most active principle, related to the sun and fire, hot and dry, and representing the spirit of life and our eternal aspiration to reach enlightenment. It is the active principle of transformation.

In this alchemical process, the person journeying breathes the sulfur into his or her body to the place where fear resides. The sulfur ignites the fear, and the ensuing fire activates the transformation. It is the task of the person to stand in that fire and witness as the fear is consumed.

Fear was so deeply engrained in Joan that it seemed to reside all through her body, although it was primarily located in her heart. I suggested that she focus on her fear, remember the smell of sulfur, and then breathe the stench of the sulfur deeply into her body, directing it first to the source of the fear in her heart. While she was engaged in that part of the process, I connected with the spirit of sulfur and asked for its help.

I knew Joan was entering a state of receptivity when she began to relax into the sense of safety that was provided here. She recognized that she was in the presence of love. Surrounded by love, she was able to begin to breathe in and direct the sulfur to the tightness within and around her heart.

As the sulfur connected with the fear in her heart, it ignited. I instructed Joan to sit with the process of the fear burning inside her, witnessing the transformation. She kept breathing the sulfur and focusing on her fear, sitting with the alchemy of the burning of the fear within. Sometimes the fear is layered, and hides deep within. Joan was determined and vigilant in seeking out the fear and breathing sulfur into it. Eventually, when she breathed in the sulfur, no new fires were lit, and the ones that were burning died down.

As soon as the accessible fear was gone, I used the earth element (in Alchemical Healing we work with five specific elements, and can direct them for various functions) to ground the change, bringing the transformation from the etheric field into her physical body. Then I suggested that she see herself swimming in the clear waters of the Caribbean, which was her favorite swimming sea. She imagined the water flowing through her and cleansing any remaining debris from the fire, the sulfur, and the fear that might have been left in her body.

The results from this process were immediate. Joan was able to connect with the Heart Breath. She felt a sense of happiness that was new to her experience. Perfectly at peace, and without any fear, she could now experience, feel, know, and express love. It was a remarkable transformation.

As of this writing, it has been several months since the session. Joan reports that as a consequence of our work, she has had very little recurrence of the fear, and in most cases any fear that she finds, she has been able to release through reengaging with this practice. She considers our time together a pivotal moment in her healing.

The following journey can be a great help for anyone who feels limited or constricted by his or her fears. It was initially inspired by the vision of Margrit Meier, a member of the Thoth lineage living in Switzerland, in the late '90s, and has since been used extensively in my sessions and in classes on Alchemical Healing, Egyptian Mysteries, shamanism, and Planetary Healing.

In this guided shamanic journey, you will meet the Egyptian god of the underworld, Anubis, known as the Opener of the Way. Anubis is usually seen with a man's body and a jackal head, and sometimes as a jackal. He is the elder half brother of Horus, the son of Nephthys and Osiris,

Anubis, the god of the underworld

and was raised by Isis. Among many other functions, he is the god who looks after miscarried and abandoned children, and guides the souls of the dead. He guards and protects equally in the day and the night, and knows all the pathways that lead from the darkness into the light. His keen senses and watchful eye assure that no outside forces will endanger you while you do your inner work.

We have found Anubis to be a trustworthy guide, teacher, and protector, and are honored to share this important process with you.

As you prepare for this journey, determine the fear you wish to work on. You may choose to work with fear that has recently shown up for you, a long-standing fear, or one that surfaces on occasions. Whatever it is, bring it clearly into focus when you are ready to begin. Allow yourself to taste that fear. Notice where you feel it in your body. Once the flow of the alchemy in the journey gets moving, it will be easier to find the deeper fears hiding within your body and being.

Describe to yourself the feelings that the fear invokes in clear and simple terms. Sit with this description, sit with the feeling and look at the fear objectively like a scientist with a microscope.

The fear you seek to transform may have served you well at some time in your life; it may have been an ally. Are you ready and willing to release the fear that no longer serves you? This is important. Make an agreement with yourself that you are ready to relinquish your insupportable fears. Your willingness and determination are important elements of the process.

We suggest that you read this journey through before taking it for the first time. Instead of doing it from memory, have a trusted friend read it to you or make a recording in your own voice, leaving ample space between instructions or using the pause button while you do the work.

Anubis is the shaman priest in the Egyptian pantheon who awakens the healing power of the heart. If ever you feel the desire or need, you can call on Anubis in future meditations by invoking his presence through the Heart Breath. He is a wonderful teacher with a wide range of gifts he is willing to share.

JOURNEY
Transform Fear

Ground and center yourself with some deep, grounding breaths. . . . Look within and find your eternal heart flame. . . . When it enters your perception in whatever way it does, feed your heart flame with love, and notice how it grows. Continue feeding your inner heart flame as it intensifies and sends warmth and light throughout your being. . . .

Engage the Heart Breath, increasing your connection to the intelligence and vitality of both Earth and Sky. . . . As your heart fire continues to expand, notice how you become filled with light as the radiant glow expands within and around you. . . .

Take a moment to recall the fear that has been compelling you. . . . Allow yourself to feel it in your body. Where is it most noticeable? Bring it to the surface of your consciousness so that it is more easily available for transformation.

You will become aware of the presence of Anubis just outside the light of your heart flame. He watches you from the darkness beyond with glowing eyes. You can see, feel, hear, know, smell, or simply imagine his presence. As your awareness sharpens, he comes more fully into focus. . . . He leads you into the darkness, looking over his shoulder occasionally to be sure that you are following him. Anubis guides you through the darkness, deeper and deeper, until you come to a river between you and what appears to be, on the other side, a dark, rough-hewn land flickering with fire. You must find your way across this river. As you focus on your strong intention to complete this transformation, you will discover how to make the crossing.

When you find yourself on the other side of the river, it seems darker than before, although you still see flickering flames farther in the distance. As Anubis leads you forward, strange sounds come out of the darkness. When you arrive at the entrance to a large cave, you are struck by the reeking smell of sulfur. With a great force of will, you enter the large, stifling cavern. He positions himself outside as a sentinel while you find your place within and allow your fears to surface. . . .

As you focus on your fear, breathing in the rank sulfuric odor, the sulfur reacts as iron to flint, and your fears immediately ignite. You must stand in the fires of your own fear as the transformation takes place. Consciously breathe in the acrid smell of burning sulfur and stay with this process as you witness the transformation of your fears. . . .

Sometimes fear hides beneath layers within you, and so you keep going, allowing for deeper layers of fear to reveal themselves. Be attentive to what memories come to the surface. Do not dwell or get stuck in them—simply note them, and respect and honor yourself for the work you are doing—then let your fear be consumed by the fire. Keep doing this until, when you breathe in the sulfur, there is nothing further to ignite. . . . [*Long pause.*]

Anubis appears when the work is complete and guides you deeper into the cavern, to a far crevice with a small opening. Crawl through this and into a spacious underground grotto. A shaft of light brightens the cavern and shines upon flower blossoms protruding from a ledge, nourished by the spray from a waterfall that feeds a sacred spring with clear, sweet water.

Enjoy some time bathing and swimming in the cool, clear waters, rinsing away every last remnant of the sulfur and fear. . . .

Anubis will show you where steps have been cut into the rock along one side of the cave, and you climb upward until you emerge once again into the bright dawn of a new day. Notice how much lighter you feel. . . .

Offer your gratitude to Anubis, and receive any further messages or instructions from this powerful ally and guide. . . .

Bring your attention once more to your physical body and ground and center yourself, re-engaging the Heart Breath as needed. . . .

Take time to record your experience in your journal.

UNIVERSAL LOVE

Whether or not you are dealing with issues of fear, it is likely that you are not always able to sustain awareness of universal love or heart-centered perspective. Mark and I have been working throughout our quarter century together to develop our ability to stay in love, more or less successfully, as we go through the roller coaster of life. We have had our epiphany moments, and have developed many tools and practices to assist in love maintenance, yet flawless consistency on a daily basis is sometimes elusive. We consciously bring ourselves into resonance through ritual and our spiritual practices, such as our sacred pipe ceremonies, the water altar, my healing practice, Mark's sense of humor, our visioning ceremonies, and day-to-day spontaneous moments of feeling deep love and being at one. We believe it is reasonable and worthwhile to strive to continuously direct our lives from a place of love and the wise perspective of the heart.

Meanwhile, we continue to reconcile opposing forces within us, and between us. This is a constant balancing act—it goes on and on. Over time, we have discovered that our challenging situations—whether within ourselves, in this relationship, or in our relations with any other human being—are truly opportunities for learning, personal growth, and deepening love. Rather than seeing such challenges as conflicts and becoming adversarial, we accept whatever has come up and pay attention to when and how we are participating. When the occasional tug-of-war comes up, love and respect help us listen and be heard. It has become more about finding and using the strengths of each side than about digging our heels in and pulling.

September 11, 2001, marked a pivotal moment in world history. The horrific events of that day set off a chain of events from which our country and other parts of the world are still reeling. They also inadvertently catalyzed a personal epiphany for me that has reverberated throughout all our subsequent work.

I am writing this from memory, which always alters the actual experience. I remember the moment of death, when I turned on the TV and felt sure I was watching some bad movie about planes crashing into buildings. I remember the shock, the paralyzing numbness, the overwhelming grief; then there was the slow return to life, each new sunrise bringing a renewal of sense and strength. I cut off my hair and sent it to Locks of Love. (They take ponytails of at least ten inches to make wigs for children undergoing chemotherapy.) That was the start of my return. But to heal this in myself completely, I would have to delve way deeper for some understanding, for some positive outcome, for some new path. The old way was not going to work anymore.

It was only a week or so after the event that I entered the sweat lodge with the mindset of a spiritual warrior. I was sure that my vision quest would make a difference; that it would somehow truly contribute to making things better. My intention going in was to pray for the people who lost their lives and their families, and for a positive future. My plan was to stay in for only twenty-four hours, because I was participating in a wedding a full day's drive north the following weekend. Sometimes a short quest is more intense because the experience is condensed. Such was the case for me: my challenges were exacerbated because I had difficulty practicing the teachings and using the tools I had been taught to carry me through even this short time of no food, no water, and no light. The result, by the time I left the lodge late the next afternoon, was a sense of inadequacy and failure. It was a very humbling experience.

Looking back I realize I had set myself up by thinking I could, or should, or would somehow make a significant contribution in the aftermath, and that I would bring back something for my community that would help in the healing so needed at the time. The integration process took weeks longer than I thought I was committing to at the outset as I struggled to come to terms with what I perceived as my failure in the lodge.

Confusion often precedes clarity, and so it was in this story. Even a couple of weeks after the actual quest, my senses were still heightened, and my consciousness remained altered. I could not shake the feeling that the ceremony of the quest was not yet complete. My confusion manifested as self-absorption and my dissatisfaction affected how I viewed what was going on around me. I tried to understand surrounding events through the filter of my personal journey. I could tell I was getting frayed around the edges of my psyche. I was engaged in a struggle I could not win—as though I was arm wrestling with myself. Only complete surrender—giving up any vestige of expectation or preconception of outcome, of my role in that outcome, of my ego itself—would achieve movement. I had reached the point at which my rational mind did not have the resources to know what was right and true.

I remember when I finally got it—when I felt myself drop from relentless mental anguish to a heart-centered perspective. We were on the way home to Eugene from a trip to Orcas Island, when Mark turned off I-5 for a meal. I did not want to get out of the car, because I felt a shift was coming. I sat in the parking lot while he went in. I knew I required stillness and quiet to manifest the needed change. Somehow, in that moment, I finally stopped struggling and allowed myself to relax. I had no idea what would happen. The highway noises and the people passing by became part of my inner world, then everything got quiet. I seemed to float in the stillness without an agenda. There was nothing to do but be. Allow. Surrender. . . .

And then it came—the shift from my will to my heart, from ego to essence. It came with the help of a life-long friend who had died some years before. Peter was a poet who had lived in India for a time in the '60s and studied with a master who had initiated him into a practice and way of knowledge that he held throughout his life, although he had difficulty reconciling what he knew to be true with what he saw around him and around the world. He had been at the births of both of my daughters, and we shared a deep bond of friendship. He appeared in his usual quiet manner, reminded me that I was a true seeker of truth, and worthy of the life I was striving to create and the wisdom that was within reach. He then reached into my heart and touched something deep inside. It was as though he gifted me with a treasure that could not be named. The shift occurred instantly.

I barely had time to express my gratitude before he passed back across the great divide, leaving me in wonderment, and joy. I joined

Mark in the restaurant; I am sure he was relieved to have me back.

Although I had tried for weeks to get there, when I finally slipped into my heart center it was as though I had been there all along—my mind had been blinding me. Everything was different, though nothing had changed but my perspective. Peter has never returned, yet the magnificence of the state of total presence in the heart remains, though I cannot always sustain it. It is a place I have learned to revisit when I recognize I have strayed: if I relax fully, if I surrender completely, I am back, totally present, held in the soft caress of the compassionate heart, connected to everything and everyone, with respect and admiration for every living being. There is such comfort in being part of the larger tribe of all life rather than being a separate, isolated individual.

Since then, I have made it a large part of my practice to develop the ability to enter into heart-centered presence and sustain this as much as possible. The exercise below gives us the recognition of the difference between the old and new paradigms. It is about the distinction between what serves us personally and what we serve—between our personal will and divine will.*

My experience of surrender instigated a spontaneous leap into heart-centered awareness. Although powerful and transformative in nature, that initial revelation was only the beginning of a deeper exploration of the movement from will to heart. The inevitable tests that followed forced me to consider the tools I already had that I had not been using, such as certain relationships I had developed in my work with animal totems and spirit guides, and other empowerments, rituals, and techniques. Regardless of how you get there, sustaining the level of presence required to stay in your heart demands vigilance and attention.

It was a guided visualization journey with Giraffe that catalyzed my next experience of entering the pure heart space of unconditional love

---

*The initiation that came from that experience is published in *Alchemical Healing*, in chapter 20, "The Wisdom of the Heart." The initiation is called "From Will to Heart," and "is an empowerment that helps you return to and remain in your heart. It is a rewiring of the energetic circuits that elevate your center of power and wisdom through a movement from Will to Heart—from ego to essence."

and compassion. In this journey I was transported to the veld in Africa, where I met Giraffe, the animal with the biggest heart (a large heart is required to pump blood up its long neck). Looking into the eyes of Giraffe in the visualization, I could see the loving network of light that connects us all in the dimension of the heart. In this journey you have an opportunity to strengthen the ties in your special relationships, and to nurture the entire web of life with your love. I recommend the giraffe journey here because it provides a simple, effective, and joyful way of tuning in to and maintaining heart-centered awareness, and is also a delightful planetary healing experience.*

I cannot say enough about practicing the Heart Breath to cultivate and sustain presence in the heart center. This breath can be used to rekindle your heart flame as well as to align your current emotions or ambient surroundings with the energies of love and compassion.

When we feel the need to invoke universal love and seek to be in harmony with it, we are acknowledging that we have stepped out of love. The reconciliation of opposing forces within us is part of what keeps us in balance. In life we seem to oscillate from one state to the other, back and forth and back again. . . . The following exercise is a further refinement of our work toward gaining and maintaining our balance and our connection to universal love—the love that permeates the universe.

JOURNEY
Universal Love Practice

Allow yourself some time and space where you will not be interrupted. Smudge or light incense to clear the air and turn off your phone. Take pause from everything happening inside and around you, so that you can gain a fresh perspective.

---

*For the full transcript of this journey see Nicki Scully, *Power Animal Meditations* (Rochester, Vt.: Bear & Company, 2001), 235, or go to www.shamanicjourneys.com/ articles/giraffe.php.

Kindle your heart flame and breathe the Heart Breath. . . . Be fully present. Take stock of everything that has been going on inside you and around you so that as you continue to focus on your heart, you can begin to remove yourself from that turmoil. Find peace within, and as you focus on it notice how your breath naturally responds. Feel the calming.

Use the Heart Breath as needed to assist you in finding and sustaining this calm, centered state.

When you enter this peaceful state, the chaos begins to retreat from within and around you. . . . See yourself as a sphere of blue calm water and air. . . . Notice any changes in your feelings. How does your body feel? How does your mind feel? Where do you still feel tension or excitement in your body? Relax further, releasing tension in each place that you feel it. . . . Notice how letting go of tension and excitement allows the calmness to grow.

The edges of your sphere dissolve outward into something beyond the issues that are happening in your life. . . . It extends beyond the situations of concern on the planet. . . . The sphere extends outward beyond the atmosphere of Earth, incorporating more and more of the planets. . . . As it expands further, encompassing the stars, you begin to feel a growing sense of compassion, and something else. . . . Universal love becomes the primary frequency, the essential medium of your existence in this expanded state. Focus on this rich sensation that feeds you and become aware of the natural reciprocity involved. You are nurturing the universe as well as receiving its nurturing; you are giving and receiving love in perfect balance. Feel the harmonics as you add your tone to that one universal tone, the one that has always been there. . . . As you sit in the resonant harmonies of Universal Love and become familiar with them, you can begin to distinguish the unique frequencies of other conscious contributors to it. . . . There are other beings at any given moment who are also tuning in as you are. Notice the similarities in the broadcasting of this tone, as if it were being generated from one unified heart. Notice how this connection to universal love strengthens your heart, while you are simultaneously contributing to it. Sit with this feeling of connectedness and love. . . . [*Long Pause.*]

As you prepare to come back into your body and rejoin your surroundings, breathe the Heart Breath, feel your attention return to your physical body. Notice how you perceive your surroundings from this place of connectedness with universal love.

As you feel yourself coming into completion with this journey, ground and center yourself. . . . Wiggle your fingers and toes, and breathe the Earth part of the Heart Breath to help you connect back to the physical plane.

Take a few moments to journal your experience to help integrate the feelings you have experienced.

Allow this heartfelt perception of universal love to be prominent in all the actions in your everyday life. Each time you practice this exercise, notice how much longer its influence stays with you. You will find that the more you practice, the more it becomes a way of being.

You will know that you are in alignment with your heart center and universal love when you are aware of the fullness of being, the perfection of creation, and your integral place in it, and the deep compassion and love you feel for all of life—particularly for those around you. In my own experience, self-absorption simply vanishes in the light of the perfection of the moment, and I become receptive to inspiration beyond my personal imaginings.

Now is the time to embrace your practices—whatever they are—diligently, prayerfully, and with intention. When we make the shift from ego to essence and our hearts become the source of our guidance, we will be tuning forks that others can resonate with. The stronger we resonate from our hearts, the easier it will be for others to find compatibility and resonance in theirs. We then carry that reverberation of love into the world wherever we are and whatever we are doing.

Regardless of how you go about it—no matter what tools you choose to use or what discipline you choose to practice—the movement to a heart-centered perspective is a powerful tool for improving the quality of your life, both individually and for those around you.

It can take time and attention to keep your practices fresh. Although this exercise may introduce you to or remind you of the omnipresence of universal love and how it feels, you can reinforce your experience and develop consistency by remembering the things you are grateful for, by integrating the Heart Breath into your ordinary activities, and by varying your practices. The next chapter provides a unique and quite different exploration of Universal Love. Although love and heart-centered presence cannot be forced, the good news is that you might just get there and stay there the next time you try.

3
Thoth's Magic Diamond

I was first introduced to the Egyptian god Thoth during a shamanic journey with Nadia Eagles in 1984, as part of the transmissions that authorized me as the first of her students to teach the advanced levels of her work. It took awhile for me to comprehend the magnitude of the mentoring Thoth offered. It was through the vision of one of my students that I was reminded that Thoth is ever present, waiting for me to extend the requisite attention. Once I took notice, the connection solidified, and our relationship grew and deepened until there was a level of trust that allowed me to receive and act on his wise guidance, which has remained the most significant rudder for the course of my life.

Mark was already living with me when this transition occurred, and when he described some inner imagery that had started to come in, I realized that I had a way to access Thoth! I would imagine or vocalize a question and Mark would describe the images and feelings that spontaneously arose. Then it was up to me to interpret the images and find my answers and guidance. As Mark learned how to "get out of the way" and how not to anticipate or direct the show, I started using this connection more frequently. Too frequently, in fact. Mark started to get jealous of my relationship with this "other man" and at one point dumped a glass of water on him (in the imaginal realm). Fortunately, Thoth has a good sense of humor, and it was water off an ibis's back.

As mentioned in our introduction, Mark became comfortable with his newfound gift, I learned restraint and the importance of framing my question and holding focus, and we had a new tool that has served

Thoth

us well over the years. As we gained experience and confidence with our new tool, little "miracles" began to appear. Along with the basic guidance I was seeking, some of the answers were to questions that had not come up yet, or our attention would be drawn to something we had been unaware of but needed to know.

The work Mark, Thoth, and I were doing began to show up in my professional life in classes, talks, and publications. Thoth is the architect behind most of what is presented in this book. He has a way of making his lessons interesting, often with a great deal of humor. He would sometimes show up with a chalkboard and a pointer, drawing diagrams to explain the teachings as they were coming in. Other times he would appear as a cigar-smoking gambler, wearing a visor and blowing smoke rings. When I needed to learn a particular lesson, he might take me fishing in a dinghy, and when a fish was caught, I would know that I had gotten it right.

Thoth's Magic Diamond was one of the first teaching tools he gave me, and this is one of the few journeys that I developed without the help of Mark or any other visionary ally. It was inspired by my kahuna friend, Henry, a shaman who was working with me around the time Thoth started giving us the teachings that would be presented in this and my previous books.

Once you have received Thoth's Magic Diamond, you can use it to explore the many facets on the diamond to receive new and different experiences and teachings each time. We highly recommend that you return to visit Thoth whenever you have questions about the work in this book. Following this introduction, it is up to you to develop your own relationship with Thoth and see where it leads you.

In the following exercise, Thoth's magic diamond takes us on a journey into ourselves to remind us of our divinity, and of the responsibility we have as stewards not just of our planet but of our bodies and the miraculous and magnificent universe within. Use this whenever you wish to renew yourself, and when you wish to reconnect to the awesome power of love.

JOURNEY

Thoth's Magic Diamond

Close your eyes, relax, and breathe deeply, using the Earth Breath to ground and center yourself. . . .

Focus your attention on your heart center. Activate feelings of love in your heart. Direct love to the eternal flame within your heart and observe how it grows. Feel as the radiance from your heart flame expands to fill your entire being. . . . Breathe the Heart Breath, inhaling the power, vitality, and intelligence of Earth and Sky. . . . Within the glow of your heart flame you will perceive first the eye of Thoth, and then his countenance, looking at you. He may appear in his ibis-headed man form, his human form, or in another of his guises. . . .

However he appears to you, Thoth is a wise guide and mentor for this work. He is pleased that you have invoked his presence, and has a gift for you. Thoth hands you a magic diamond, a large, sparkling stone with many facets. As you hold it between your forefinger and thumb, take a moment to take in its clarity and beauty and its brilliance. Each facet of this diamond is a window, each providing a different view. As you slowly turn the diamond, look through it to focus upon your physical body, as though the diamond was a microscope, revealing a different depth of field with each rotation. You begin to perceive your body as a landscape. As seen from above, its surface textures look like geometric forms. As you continue rotating your diamond, still focused on your body, you pass through starburst patterns of energy, discovering yet deeper fields of focus, until you find yourself gazing into the night sky, spangled with stars.

As above, so below: you recognize yourself and the universe within you. Each star, each cell of your body, is a sun with its revolving planets, peopled with abundant life forms. You are God or Goddess of your own universe, and it is your responsibility to enlighten all life within you. Begin to radiate unconditional love energy through your magic diamond, into the field beneath you, infusing every cell with all the colors of the rainbow, charging all life within with the radiant light of love. . . .

This energy, this love that you have sent forth, is reflected back to you, magnified by the magic diamond, and you experience waves of bliss and shivers of joy as that which you have sent out returns to you. Feel as it tingles and awakens every cell of your being. . . .

Begin to reverse the rotation of your diamond, observing your body becoming solid once more, window by window, as you return through the different levels of perception. . . .

If a part of your body is weak, in pain, or in need of healing, focus on that place through the lens of your diamond. Notice the pattern that appears. As you concentrate your attention on this pattern, become aware of what is needed to promote healing and restore harmony. Allow yourself to offer forgiveness to yourself or others as appropriate to this process. . . .

Notice that the area in question has already been healed in the dimension of the diamond. Be open to receiving information and knowledge of changes you can make to manifest this transformation in your physical body. . . .

As you continue to focus your intention toward healing, a new pattern begins to emerge. Experience this pattern of health and vitality with all your senses. . . . Now generate a beam of light through your diamond, directing love, light, and color into the new pattern, noticing the changes as they occur. Continue to see, feel, and experience the results as the new harmony is reinforced with your attention and focus. [*Pause.*]

Now spend a moment exploring another window, another facet of this magic diamond. [*Long pause.*]

Take some time to receive any further message Thoth has for you at this time. . . . Perhaps you will want to arrange another meeting soon in order to deepen your connection with this significant and invaluable guide. . . .

When you are ready, make an offering to Thoth in gratitude for this valuable healing tool. Attention and acknowledgment would make appropriate gifts, along with a expression of interest and desire to develop a deeper relationship.

Be sure to take a few grounding breaths to assure that you are fully connected with and centered in your physical form before opening your eyes. . . . Then spend a few minutes journaling your experience.

PART II

Basic Planetary
Healing

4

IT BEGAN WITH
A DISASTER...
Chernobyl

On April 26, 1986, the devastating nuclear power accident occurred at the Chernobyl Power Plant in the Ukraine, then part of the Soviet Union. This information was initially suppressed by the Soviets, and became known to the world several days later. The amount of fallout was four hundred times the amount released from the bombing of Hiroshima.

Unaware of this occurrence, Mark and I were preparing our home and property for a weekend event with Lutie Larson, a world-renowned teacher of radionics. Radionics is a healing modality that studies and identifies frequencies. It is based on the premise that all matter is vibration, and that vibration is created by thought as well. In radionics, healing at a distance is achieved by using a simple machine to find and generate missing and harmonious frequencies in order to restore health and harmony. The class was to start on Saturday. Students would be arriving from all over the country to study with this excellent teacher.

Another friend, Kickapoo medicine man Fred Wahpepah, had asked to use the sweat lodge that he had helped build on the back meadow of our property the previous fall. He wanted to use it for a vision quest, beginning on Friday with a sweat lodge purification ceremony.*

Since we have more than three acres, I believed that there would be plenty of room for the two events, without conflicts. I thought I could handle both spiritual and organizational responsibilities simultaneously. I also thought I could participate in the Friday evening sweat lodge and still be available to greet Lutie and the other participants when they arrived. Because the person questing would be engaged in a traditional vision quest, she would be without food or water for several days; I anticipated a fairly mild lodge.

Wrong! The lodge was much hotter than I expected. The slightest movement produced searing pain. I felt caught in the grip of something beyond my control, held by a source that was also holding and directing my thoughts, forcing a laser-sharp focus on the present, from which I could not stray. I sat quietly in the pitch black, paralyzed, yet calm in the knowing that I was safe—providing I did not resist the force that seemed to be in charge.

Our personal prayers are offered during the second of four rounds. When the door was pulled shut and the lodge was resealed for the second time, I was not sure I would be able to speak, yet when my turn came, and I opened my mouth a song came out. It was a familiar Native song dedicated to Grandmother Moon. As I began to sing, I felt a gush of liquid, originating from inside my uterus, pooling around my thighs. There was no room for my thoughts to follow my concern that I was bleeding in the lodge, a taboo I had learned to respect.

Compelled by the song and whatever else was directing me, I found I could also witness myself while I sang, as though observing from a different vantage point. I experienced the song changing in tone and

*The traditional Lakota sweat lodge or *inipi* ceremony that we are familiar with is a purification ceremony where rocks are heated in a fire, and brought into a covered, igloo-shaped lodge. Water is poured on the rocks, creating steam and heat. Songs and prayers are offered during the four rounds when the door is closed. We have kept the lodge with great respect for the tradition it came from, honoring all the rules as they were taught to us. We have made it available for use by many traditional elders who have passed through our area.

becoming the shrieks of a woman in labor while I felt the onslaught of labor pangs, which then increased in intensity. I also felt an expansion in perception that included past and future visions, as if looking through a strange and multidimensional tunnel.

I could feel every detail as if I were physically giving birth as the baby's head crowned and the spirit child was delivered. The silence in the lodge was palpable. In the timeless pause, I was just beginning to feel some relief when a new song started, this one unfamiliar, with a very different energy. It was accompanied by a second gush of liquid, along with another wave of shame for bleeding in the lodge and also a sense of wonder. My voice, screaming in the agony of childbirth, was so loud that I was sure I would be censured, but again there was only silence all around me. A second spirit was born in an equally visceral birthing experience. This spirit felt more masculine, although not quite as strong as the first, more feminine presence. I managed to mutter "Mitakuye Oyasin," (Lakota for "All My Relations") and the personal prayers continued as if nothing extraordinary had occurred.

I had no idea at the time what happened to the spirit children who were delivered. It was many years before I would put together the rest of the story, including an understanding of the conception that preceded the birth, and the function of the spirit beings who were delivered.

The *Cannunpa*, or sacred pipe, was smoked inside the lodge while the door was open between the third and fourth rounds. Although I was still in an altered state, I remember feeling concern about taking hold of the pipe while I was most surely drenched in blood. Despite feeling as though I was being held in a vice, I was compelled to take my turn, drawing deeply of the sweet smoke and offering my prayers on the exhalation. Although I cannot parse out or articulate the visions that continued to emerge during the remainder of the lodge, so many profound aspects of my work and identity were simultaneously projected: my relationship with the sacred pipe; who I had been and who I was becoming; a number of rites of passage and pivotal moments that led up to this time; my purpose and destiny; and the journey of my soul. There was no room for doubt or confusion in those moments. There was only truth.

When the last round was over, I pulled myself together and made an intentional decision to stand strong and tall, even though I would be dripping blood in front of everyone. I stood. I was surprised to discover it was not blood, but water. It was the amniotic fluid that manifested physically from the psychic birth.

I realized at once that I was still too altered to be with people, especially a houseful of strangers. As I breathed the cool, brisk air and saw the steam pouring out of the lodge, I was given a very clear message: I needed to go back into the lodge and steal away from all the people who were gathering at the house, because I was too elevated in my consciousness; I would have gone crazy trying to chat, and I could never have explained myself—not even to myself.

When I told the medicine man, he suggested I ask Shawno, the woman who was questing, if she was willing to share the lodge with me. When I put forward my request, she said she already knew. So, after gathering two sacred pipes and two vision quilts, we entered the lodge together, where we stayed, sealed in, through the night, holding our *cannunpas* and praying. The next morning, I knew that I was complete and it was time to come out. I had needed that night to assimilate my experience and restore my ability to be with people. Little did I know that this event's wondrous, sacred magic marked not only the birth of spirit twins, but also the beginning of a new round of healing work from which would emerge many of the new Planetary Healing tools and spirit medicine for personal and global transformation that appear in this book.

Rumors that something had happened and was still happening at the Chernobyl nuclear reactor had been picked up by Western observers, but the USSR was trying to keep a lid on it. It was not until radiation reached Sweden that the magnitude of the meltdown was revealed. We noticed a correlation between the timing of the nuclear meltdown and our lodge, however the significance did not become clear for several days. Meanwhile, the class continued, and so did the magic.

Radionics is all about frequencies. Since the material world resides in the intersection of light and sound, everything emits a frequency that can be measured. In the radionics class we learned how to read our general vitality index (GVI) on the black box used in that system to measure frequencies. We would turn the dial on our radionics machine and find out at what level we were functioning.

Saturday afternoon I visited the medicine man at the lodge, where he was tending the fire and holding space for Shawno as she continued her quest. I sat with him for some time, and we shared a medicine brew that he had made for fortification. Afterward, when I checked my GVI, I noticed that my numbers were rising so rapidly I could not track them. I called Lutie over to see what was going on. As she tuned in and turned the dial, the numbers rose off the scale and continued rising. By the next morning, when we returned to class and I checked my GVI again, it was so high that even the students sitting close to me had higher than normal readings. I felt very energized, and strong, but otherwise normal.

So many astonishing things had been happening, I was hardly surprised on the following day when Kay Cordell Whittaker, a friend and colleague who was participating in the class took me aside to tell me she had received guidance to give me a particular initiation. She had earlier received an implantation of etheric quartz crystals, one in each of her palms, and she had now been instructed to give a set to me. While others had lunch, we went upstairs. During the ceremony that followed, Kay drew the invisible crystals out of the air. I connected to the experience immediately when she inserted them, and felt quite clearly as one entered each palm, my hands filling with energy.

Kay gave me detailed instructions on how to begin using the crystals, and soon I could control the energy flowing through them and focus it to a point or spread it across a large area. I found myself working with a grid-like structure that gave me even more control when I perceived it as inclusive of the entire universe. Kay also explained to me how I could heal more than one person at a time, extending the energy with these crystals to cover a wider range. This was very exciting to me because I had this sort of experience quite unexpectedly, shortly before receiving the implants: I was doing a healing for a person with a back problem, and someone nearby in the same room had a spontaneous healing of an old knee injury, apparently utilizing the same energy.

This new method, using the crystals and establishing the grid, allows me to do this intentionally, extending the life-force energies to make healing available to anyone or any situation within its range, providing I could hold my focus and direct my intention clearly.

I decided to try the crystals out a few days later when I was speaking at a Healers' Breakfast meeting in Portland. With sixty people present, I wanted to see if I could combine psychic surgery with the new work involving the crystals. My aim was to perform a simultaneous healing for everyone there. Standing in front of the group, I closed my eyes and extended the sphere of the grid to include the entire restaurant and all the people in it. I did the technique as I had been instructed. I could feel a tremendous surge as the power of the energy poured through me into the people. Later, during the reception, while people were sharing their experience of the healing with me, I looked down at my hands and was stunned to see that the blood had risen to the surface in my palms. They had swollen slightly and the skin turned purple-blue. It was many hours before the discoloration and puffiness gradually wore off.

Meanwhile, the radiation from the nuclear meltdown in the Ukraine had been picked up by the jet stream and was heading in our direction.

During the drive home from Portland, my friend Mary, a very powerful and sensitive psychic, saw what appeared to be a pink shield forming over the region. We wondered if it was in some way connected to the approaching radiation that was still two days away.

On that Friday morning, I woke up feeling exhausted, even though my GVI was still off the scale, suggesting that I should have had plenty of energy. I told Mark that if anybody wanted to see me, they would have to visit me in the bedroom.

Shawno was the first to drop in. We talked about her vision quest and what it was like to share the lodge that night and about Chernobyl. Just as she was about to leave, we noticed a weird haze out the window. On closer inspection, it looked as though a strange pall was spreading across the land, as though a curtain was being drawn. I phoned Mary, who lived on a hilltop just above me. As soon as she looked out her window, she began to receive information. She interpreted this as the first sign of radiation coming onto the land. I could feel the hackles rising on the back of my neck as Mary began to give me instructions for what I was to do. First, we needed to build a sacred fire at the lodge.

Shawno left, and I started looking around for Mark. I found him down at the sweat lodge, standing before a sacred fire he had just built. Before announcing my presence, I quietly watched as he reverently offered his prayers along with the tobacco ties that held Shawno's prayers for her vision quest into the small fire. Mark was not aware of Mary's instruction—this was further evidence magic was afoot and Mark was tuned in.

Once the fire was built and proper offerings made, I was to touch the tips of my crystals together to turn them on and then envision a grid circulating out from the faceted crystals while holding them steady with their points upward. The grid was to encompass a large portion of Eugene and Springfield and some of the surrounding area. When the grid was set, I was to hold space, get out of the way by getting out of my body, and allow the radiation to funnel down into the fire pit. It seemed simple enough, but as I prepared the grid and started to call for the work to begin, Mary, who was back on the phone directing me, stopped me. "You have to protect yourself, get yourself together, and GET OUT OF YOUR BODY! This is big work."

I was not sure what else I needed to do, as I thought that whoever was calling the shots would not send me unprotected to do this work. I was not sure how to protect myself anyway. I decided to simply ask for the protection of my guides and allies, then I called for white light to surround me, and grounded and centered myself as best I could. By now I was feeling a sense of urgency, but no fear. I finished building the grid and did my best to get out of my body, or at least out of the way. When I thought I was ready, I said to Spirit, "Okay, give me all I can handle. . . ."

I have had considerable experience with what I thought was power, but nothing I have encountered before or since has equaled the power of what transpired next. Nor have I ever seen such vivid colors. I had no sense of time; it felt like an infinite moment that lasted forever, and at the same time it felt like no time at all. In that suspended pause, I witnessed a vortex of brilliant Day-Glo energy swirling down from above like a tornado running in reverse down into the fire pit. I felt an instant "knowing" that recent unexplainable events had occurred in preparation for this moment. I was also swept through with a sense of fulfillment, as though I had accomplished my reason for being alive at this time.

My initial elation knew no bounds; for I had been catapulted beyond any previous expansion of consciousness, experienced or imagined. One remarkable effect that lingered for some time was that I now could see through people and things, as though I had X-ray vision. In my naiveté, I quickly convinced myself that this new gift was Spirit's response to my service—I did something to help the Earth, and I was given the gift of sight. Almost immediately, I noticed that with this new sight came new abilities. I could direct healing for people at a new level. I focused on a physical problem one of my daughters had—it was a small growth on her skin, and I saw it clearly and, just as clearly, I saw it disappear. Although it would be some time before I could verify this, I knew it was done.

And then came the onslaught. . . . Perhaps I had not sufficiently gotten "out of the way" after all. I was suddenly overwhelmed with the realization of suffering and misery on the planet, and tried to turn away, but could not. I tried to shut off the new gift of sight, but it was as though my inner eye was sewn open. And then the pain hit. My head felt as though it would burst. This new vision came without a filter! I had no way of shutting out anything I could see and feel. I seemed to be tuned in to all the pain and suffering in the world. So much disease and despair. . . .

Light became unbearable. We found a small purple silk scarf and used it to cover my eyes. Although it made a physical blindfold, it did not shut down the new sight. The throbbing continued. Mark tried to help, but he did not know what to do. This was all very new to him, and my own distress and pain made it more difficult for him to grasp. To make matters stranger and more confusing, when he came close to me, he could feel my pain. He finally gave up and lay down next to me anyway, hoping to provide some comfort with his presence.

Fortunately, Mary, who was keeping a psychic eye on me from her house further up the hill, felt the disturbance and gave us a call. When Mark expressed his concern, she gathered her tools and herbs and came down to help. She put hot and cold fomentations on my hands and my face. By then I was so far out of my body that I could not distinguish hot from cold. Eventually, I felt and described waves of purple and gold radiance pouring over and through me. Mary recognized this as the presence of her spirit guide and felt that she had done all she could. For the first time, I felt as though my body might return to normal. I was unaware of the passage of time.

At some point later, my dear friend Kathy Wilkins arrived. While she sat with me, it occurred to me that I might actually die. *Here we go again.* I had experienced shamanic death before. My mind shot back to the first time I thought I was dying, long before I had any understanding of the shaman's journey. I had held myself together so tightly. And I also remembered that when I had relaxed and let go, it was not death that took over, nor even stayed in my memory; it was the glorious rebirth and attendant beauty and love.

I began to realize that the only way I could keep my body would be to surrender. An opportunity was presenting itself here, and I had to willingly and knowingly relinquish myself to it and hope for the best. I told Kathy that I had to go on a journey, and I asked her, please, no matter what happened, not to let anyone or anything touch me. And then I let go.

I did not die in the way I expected. I seemed to swirl down into darkness, and soon found myself deep within the crust of the Earth. As the internal landscape of the Earth came into focus around me, a woman appeared. She brought to mind a Russian peasant woman, wearing a babushka and greeting me with a kindly expression. She led me carefully through a narrow crevasse within the Earth to an area that was made of clay. Scooping the clay from the walls, she patted it thickly all over my entire body. The clay began to absorb the poisons inside me. The woman remained with me while the clay was drying and pulling the toxins from every part of my body.

Meanwhile, there was a point when I became vaguely aware of Kathy's fear as she held space for me. She later confessed that at one time she did touch me to see if my heart was beating. She even used a mirror to check my breath.

When the clay became dry and crusted, my guide led me out of the Earth and I found myself in a beautiful sacred pool, being washed clean of all radiation, toxins, and poisons in the torrent of a waterfall. To my great relief, it occurred to me that this journey was similar to an element initiation that I had previously received from my teacher Nadia. I was convinced that we would be visiting all the elements to receive their support in this healing process. Instead, I suddenly found myself back in my body. Earth and water were all that was needed for this particular purification.

My first tentative normal breath was accompanied by a shot of pain. My body was not yet functioning properly and I felt as if certain internal organs had shut down. My third eye still burned, and I did not have to test it to know I could not yet tolerate light. I immediately dropped back into a trance and continued the process of directing the energies to heal myself and participate in the reconstruction of my body.

When I finally surfaced, Kathy almost cried with relief. And so did I—I was amazed to be alive; although I was not sure I was out of the woods yet. The searing pain was gone from my third eye, but I was still hypersensitive and was not yet ready to remove the blindfold.

Mark came back to look after me, and Kathy reluctantly went home. After summing up the current situation, he determined that I needed a bath. He carried me downstairs to the bathroom and, while I soaked in the tub, scrubbed me thoroughly. He then helped me to stand while he showered me, washed my hair, and gave me a final rinse with cold water. I stayed blindfolded throughout—even candlelight was too bright.

When I woke up the next day, I was stronger. Sometime in the afternoon, we removed the blindfold. My next call was to a friend who had a cabin on the coast, asking for the keys. We gathered up every crystal in the house, carefully packed the sacred pipe, and drove to Yachats, where the cabin sits on a cliff above the churning Pacific. When we arrived, it felt like we walked into an oracle temple. Almost immediately, information began pouring into Mark about what was happening to us, although we were not told much about what the devastating Chernobyl meltdown was about. We also learned that when we are committed in service, we may be called upon to act at any moment in surprising ways. This is part of the function of a spiritual warrior. At this level of participation, information is given to us on a need-to-know basis. I asked whether others had been involved in the redistribution of the radiation; I was told that, yes, there were a few.

Mark and I slept deeply that night and woke up feeling refreshed. We made our way down from the cliff to the beach below. We washed all the crystals we had brought and cleaned the pipe in the ocean before we connected it and offered a ceremony of prayers and gratitude, after which we felt complete. We then returned home to Eugene.

Every person that associated with me during the time I was working with Chernobyl got sick to varying degrees. Mary was hit the hardest. Mark went to her home and literally gathered her up off the floor to take her on the journey into the Earth. Even Lutie, the radionics teacher who was monitoring what was happening from afar with her machines, required the healing journey. The cure was always the same—to go into the element of the earth and be packed in clay and then go into the water to be fully cleansed. We had each person shower and scrub thoroughly afterward and drink lots of water.

I did not speak of this for more than a year, and then a most remarkable thing happened. The first person that I felt compelled to tell this story to had had a similar experience with Chernobyl.

Understanding that I needed to give her the crystals, I learned how to give that transmission. After that, I knew I was to tell the story and transmit the crystals during my Planetary Healing classes. This entire event stands out as one of the most sacred of my personal rites of passage.

5
Making Spirit Medicine

DISCOVERING THE COMMUNAL CAULDRON

Throughout history and in many cultures and traditions, the cauldron has been a symbol of nurturing, magic, and healing. Here we use the Cauldron for the making of spirit medicine—a profound and potent process through which individuals and circles co-create solutions with ancestors, spirit guides, totems, plants, and other spiritual allies.

above	LI	THE CLINGING FIRE
below	SUN	THE GENTLE, WIND, WOOD

The six lines construct the image of Ting, THE CAULDRON; at the bottom are the legs, over them the belly, then come the ears (handles), and at the top the carrying rings. At the same time, the image suggests the idea of nourishment. The ting, cast of bronze, was the vessel that held the cooked viands in the temple of the ancestors and at banquets. The head of the family served the food from the ting into the bowls of the guests.*

---

*The I Ching or Book of Changes, The Richard Wilhelm translation (New York: Bollingen Foundation Inc.,1950). New material by Bollingen Foundation (Princeton, N.J.: Princeton University Press, 1967), 193.

Mark and I were falling asleep when the visions came. It was the night before a day-long intensive class on Alchemical Healing at the Women of Wisdom conference in Seattle, in February of 2004. Mark spontaneously entered that space where we most love to live, connected to the source of the teachings. I struggled to stay awake long enough to get the instructions he was receiving: There would be an egg and a cauldron. Who knows what else came in? When Mark and I awoke in the morning that was all we could remember from our foray into the subconscious. I shook off sleep and prepared for class, invigorated by a sense of anticipation. Something new was about to happen: I could feel it.

There were about sixty-five women in the circle that day, most of them new to me. My good friend and staunch ally Kathryn Ravenwood sat beside me. I knew I could count on her for clear vision during uncertain moments.

We opened the circle with an invocation and honoring of the directions. As we first entered meditation, Raven called my attention to Nekhbet-Mother-Mut (pronounced Moot), the ancient alchemist goddess of protection, who appeared in her vision as a vulture soaring above the room. This was my cue that the new work coming in would be big medicine—life changing and transformative.

Mut is the Crone. As in *Power Animal Meditations,* she is represented here by the watchful, soaring vulture who is also the ancient alchemist, guardian of the sacred Communal Cauldron. Mut's presence often indicates a juncture, a crossroads in our sacred journey when our ascent signals the death of the old and makes way for something new to happen. This felt like such a moment, and I became alert to the possibility that a new path was revealing itself.

Mut's arrival was, for me, an announcement of the magnitude of the upcoming ceremony. She had shown up twenty years earlier at the inception of the original Cauldron Alchemy, a new body of work that changed my life and eventually evolved into *Power Animal Meditations* and *Alchemical Healing.* She is also the number one card in *The Anubis Oracle* deck, the Alchemist. Before her initial appearance, I had been teaching a form of Huna (a traditional Hawaiian philosophy and healing modality), and soon after my connection with Mut I was teaching an empowering and intuitive healing form from which my life's work has poured forth. Mut appeared in order to witness and oversee the death of one way of life and the birth of another.

Now, as I sat with this wonderful circle of women in Seattle, I felt joy at Raven's words, "Mut is here." And true to Mark's words the night before, there was also an egg and a cauldron.

As with all Alchemical Healing work, we started with grounding and centering ourselves, and honoring both the seen and unseen dynamics of our circle. It is within the glow created by our united heart flames that we were able to distinguish the images of gifts brought forward from other dimensions. The first etheric symbol that appeared, the purple-black egg speckled with gold, represented creation itself. It was also the *prima materia,* or the first matter—the potential from which the new teachings would come, and the body of the work would develop. We energized this egg by feeding it with our love and the energies of Earth and Sky through breathing the Heart Breath simultaneously. Thus, we transformed it into a Cauldron. With our intentional, focused breathing, we were able to build a multidimensional holographic image of a Cauldron in our midst. Each of our perceptions added to the richness of the image and to the brightness and solidity of its form.

As we continued to direct the Heart Breath toward this image, it began to fill with love in the form of the primordial waters of life. Although each person's perspective and means of experience was unique, the resulting reports were consistent for all of us, and soon the Cauldron was glowing in the center of our circle. Although it was an etheric symbol, it became the altar that is the focus of this new body of work. In subsequent circles I have often placed a physical cauldron to represent the etheric one in the center. When I am forced by the way the room is set up to do this ceremony theater style, I have the people imagine they're sitting in a circle, with the egg/Cauldron in the center.

Instructions for Entering into Participation with the Communal Cauldron

In *Alchemical Healing* we explored ways of accessing and generating energy, and of including the intelligence of all forms of life in our healing work. In this new level we are participating in a collective dynamic that exponentially increases the power of the work. The flow of the energy we are tapping into strengthens because of the combined attention we bring to it.

In *Planetary Healing,* we are using this guided ceremonial journey to initiate readers into the Universal Live Force energy, the same current of energy used in most healing forms. Once this infinite source is accessed, you will be able to call upon it any time you use the Heart Breath, and it will always be available to you. You can direct it into almost every aspect of your life: into your food, your garden, your loved ones, your works of art or other creations, and anyone or any situation in need of healing.

The original Cauldron, to which we connect in this ritual, has been in existence for eons. Each time a person or circle invokes the Communal Cauldron, they connect to the energies of every person who has made Spirit Medicine in this way over time. What we brewed on that day at Women of Wisdom is nectar that is vital and alive. Its potency is renewed every time a person from the circle remembers that she holds this medicine within, and the circle continues to grow and strengthen with each new practitioner.

You can connect to the Communal Cauldron initially by reading the following journey as a meditation or by listening to the CD included with this book. Once you have participated, if you choose to become a carrier of this medicine, it will remain accessible to you at any time. This magic lives—only a Heart Breath away.

JOURNEY

Making Spirit Medicine

We are about to take a journey—a journey into a timeless way of healing. Relax, close your eyes, and breathe deeply as you ground and center yourself. . . .

Bring your attention to the inner sanctuary of your heart, wherein dwells your soul's eternal flame. As you bring your heart flame into focus, use as many of your inner senses as you can to observe your flame. . . . When it comes into focus in whatever way you perceive it, activate feelings of love within your heart center, and use those feelings to feed your flame with love. Love is the fuel. . . .

As you continue to pour love upon your flame, it brightens; it intensifies. Notice how it spreads warmth and light throughout your being. Keep pouring love upon your flame and feel its warmth radiating throughout your entire body. Bask in the light of your inner heart flame. . . . As you look within the glow of your heart flame, you may be aware of the presence of a vulture circling high above you. . . . In the center of the radiant light, a purple-black egg appears. This etheric egg of creation is the prime material that begins the process of alchemy in which we are all engaged.

While this etheric egg holds part of your attention, begin to breathe the Earth Breath part of the Heart Breath, drawing in energy from the heart of the Earth with each in-breath. Feel it rise from the very core of the Earth, moving the power and intelligence that dwells within all the layers of the Earth, through all the minerals and the roots of the plants and trees, up through the crust of the Earth and into your body. The energy rises. It rises with your breath and enters into your heart. Its power mingles with your heart flame. As you exhale, express this energy out from your heart. It passes through every cell of your body as it radiates out in every direction into the world. . . .

Continue to inhale from the heart of the Earth and exhale from your heart into the world.

To the Earth Breath, you now add the Sky Breath: Place your attention on the heart of the cosmos. Pull energy down with your breath; imagine you are inhaling from the very center of the universe. Feel the breath enter your body through your crown, carrying with it the energy and intelligence of the stars . . . the sun . . . the moon . . . and cosmic consciousness itself. With each in-breath you pull it in through your crown, this energy moves down through your body to your heart, and there it mingles with the Earth breath and the love you continue to pour upon your heart flame. Then with each exhalation, express the energy and power that has gathered within your heart out into the world in every direction. . . .

When you breathe the Earth and Sky breaths simultaneously, you are breathing the Heart Breath. Continue to focus on the purple-black egg that is in front of you as you breathe from Earth and Sky in this way. The continued Heart Breath works like bellows, increasing the intensity of your heart flame. As you focus on the egg before you, it transforms into a vessel, a cauldron. . . . The energies from the Earth and the cosmos, combined with your own heart flames, will further empower this ancient Cauldron into existence in this plane.

When the Cauldron is fully developed, and you have perceived it with as many senses as you can engage, return your attention inward.

Continue breathing the Heart Breath, and on your next in-breath, focus your intention toward connecting with the source of the energies of Earth and Sky, and feel this force as it fills your body and enters into your heart. . . . As you exhale, put your focus and attention on your hands and feel the energy that has mixed with the love within your heart radiate outward through your shoulders and down your arms. . . . This Universal Life Force energy pours out through the palms of your hands like great rays of light. . . . Keep your attention focused on your hands as you draw the next in-breath, continuing to build the energy from Earth and Sky, and your love. . . . On your next out-breath, the newly awakened current of energy that is the universal life force continues to pour down your arms and out through the palms of your hands, and it also flows out your fingertips like sunbeams or moonbeams. . . .

Hold your hands up so that your palms face the Cauldron. Pay attention as the current continues to grow and then smoothes out into a strong, sustained force. Continue to stay focused as this current carries the power and intelligent energies of Earth and Sky, the universal life force, through you and into the Cauldron. . . . As you continue to pay attention and breathe in this way, directing the light from your hands, the Cauldron fills with liquid light. . . .

Once the Cauldron is filled, it begins to expand. . . . If you are part of a circle, it will grow larger and take up more of the space within.

It is time to further empower the Cauldron by invoking your spirit guides and allies. Invite totems, deities of any pantheons, spirits of plants and minerals, ancestors, and any other intelligent support you wish to include in your circle. As you invoke these allies, they gather around the Cauldron. With your mind's eye, see their images or the symbols that represent them etched upon the outside of the vessel. Some spirit allies may peer over the rim from within the brew. The medicine you are creating is enriched by the energies of all these spirit guides. As your ancestors and the ancestors of all those connected with this work join you around the vessel, you see that the Cauldron has once again become larger. It continues to grow as you continue to empower it.

It is important to know that your energies and your circle's energies are connecting to the integrity of a Cauldron that has already been created by all who have put their energies into this process. The brew it contains continues to strengthen and gets more potent with each addition. An Elder steps forward from the circle that surrounds the Cauldron. She is a wise sage who is the spiritual guardian of the medicine. This Elder may appear as one of your ancestors, or one of the ancient crones or sages connected with this Communal Cauldron. Greet this Ancient Wise One with respect.

The Old One steps up to the Cauldron, checks the contents, smells it, stirs it, nods, and steps back. Now, it is time to add your personal power to the medicine that is brewing. Consider your strengths, your skill, and your intention. What do you have to contribute?

See yourself step up to the Cauldron and stir your medicine into the brew. Offer sacred prayers from your heart. Offer your hopes and dreams for this medicine and what it will do for all who will ever draw from it. Using your voice gives you another way to empower your contribution to the Cauldron. Speak your intention and any additional attributes you wish to include out loud. . . .

As your prayers and your personal skills and power enter the Cauldron, the brew begins to bubble. . . . Focus your attention into the medicine as you imagine all of the qualities that are contained in this brew—the healing power, the strength and clarity, joy, love—all the healing attributes that have been added over time in a sincere and heartfelt way are now bubbling before you. . . .

The Elder steps forward to check the contents of the Cauldron again, noting the alchemy that is taking place and how it is progressing. There is a time of waiting while the ingredients integrate. . . . As the various elements are drawn together, they gradually transform into the potent spirit medicine that you are creating. [*Pause.*]

Now when the Elder approaches the Cauldron once again. She stirs and tests the nectar; she smells the fragrance of the vapors, studies the consistency and texture, and nods. The medicine is now ready. . . .

The Old One uses a crystal ladle to pour just enough liquid for three sips into a tiny crystal cup. She hands this cup to you.

Receive your portion and hold it in your hands while you gather and focus your intention. Engage the Heart Breath once again and notice how the energies from your Heart Breath pour through your hands and continue to invigorate the elixir. Feel the energetic connection between you and the cup of spirit medicine. . . .

The first sip that you will take is for yourself. First, imbue the cup with a strong intention for whatever physical, emotional, mental, and spiritual healing you need. Feel your intention enter the medicine in your cup as you focus on the areas of weakness, illness, or pain in your body. . . . When you are ready, bring the cup up to your nose and smell the fragrance. . . . Feel the vapors enter your body even before you taste the brew. . . .

Now take the first sip. . . . Feel it on your tongue and roll it around in your mouth.

Taste the brew and feel its texture and viscosity. It is important for you to physically swallow this sip. When you do, you will feel it move immediately throughout your entire body, giving you strength and healing. Observe how it radiates through your body, your mind, and your emotions, and how it spreads throughout your being to fulfill your intention to heal yourself. Feel as the medicine enters your places of weakness and begins the work of transformation, alchemy, and healing.

The second sip is for your family, your friends and coworkers, and those in your most intimate circles. Take a moment to think about and connect with those in your community who need healing, those to whom you wish to send this medicine. . . .

Once again, feel your connection to the medicine as your intention moves through your hands and into the cup you hold. . . .

Again, lift the cup to smell the aroma of the elixir. You may be surprised to notice that this sip has a different fragrance than the first. Let the vapors enter your body, and then take the second sip into your mouth, tasting and feeling the new flavors and textures. . . . Be sure to physically swallow this second sip as well, and stay aware as it moves through you and out into the world to reach those for whom it is intended. . . .

The third sip is for the world. Your intention now is to direct the healing power of the medicine to all aspects of our precious Mother Earth: all her people, her environment, our world situations, and all creatures that walk, swim, crawl, and fly around her. . . . Focus your intention on the medicine left in the cup toward all of life and the healing of our planet. As you smell the fragrance of this third sip, feeling the vapors move through you and out into the world, know that the healing begins on a larger and wider scale. . . . As you take in and swallow your third sip, feel the power of the medicine course through you, out through your heart, through your family and close community, and out to all the places in need. Follow it with your attention as it weaves together for the web of life all the healing intentions, including those from the past and from the other elders and allies. . . . Follow the medicine as it spreads out through the land and reaches all the people and species in need, and all the situations in need. . . .

Once you have swallowed your three sips, you will notice that the Cauldron has expanded so that you are now a part of its rim, its shape, and the integrity of the whole. You are both the Cauldron itself and the medicine within. You are the medicine and the medicine maker. . . .

Now you have an opportunity to be a carrier of this sacred spirit medicine. To work in this way, simply reach out your arms to surround as much of the Cauldron as you can. Slowly pull your extended arms together, as though grabbing hold of the entire vessel, and pull it into yourself. It shrinks down to a size that fits perfectly within your belly. And yet, the original Cauldron maintains its full size. . . .

This smaller replication of the Cauldron will remain safe in your belly until the next time you need to call on this potent medicine.

Anytime you wish to use this medicine for either yourself or another or the Earth, ground and center yourself, then tune in to and feed your heart flame. Breathe the Heart Breath and focus your intention as you pull the Cauldron out of your belly and place it in front of you once again. Then call in your allies and guides. Continue to feed the Cauldron with your Heart Breath, your love and intention, and your personal power. Take this medicine for yourself as you need it, and give it to others when you feel called. Anyone who receives this medicine must physically swallow each sip. Finally, if you find yourself giving and giving to others, take this medicine for yourself as well.

Now take a moment to honor and give gratitude to all who have assisted in creating this nectar of love: all of the medicine makers, the allies and spirit guides, the totems, the ancestors, the pantheons, the plants and tree beings, the minerals, the energies of Earth and Sky, and the Elders who continue to steward this Communal Cauldron filled with the spirit medicine that you helped to create. . . . You will continue to develop your relationships with these guides. Always remember to give thanks.

With practice, you will feel more and more that you are becoming the Cauldron. Our greater circle shapes it and gives it integrity. This Communal Cauldron and the medicine it contains are fed and renewed by your attention, your intention, your energy, and your love. What we create here does not end just because we have completed this meditation. You will put what you will into this Cauldron, and it continues to exist so that whenever you feel the need, you can reach in and take another sip.

6
Becoming a Beacon

The basic rite of passage to what we call the Beacon provides a road-map to finding our power place in air. Perhaps another school of sha-manism might call this the Upper World, the Imaginal Realm, or the Dreamtime. By whatever name you call it, our experience as the Beacon is found outside of time and space as we ordinarily experience them.

The elements are fundamental to everything that we do and cre-ate; much of the work in this book can be viewed elementally. We are choosing this particular map because air is the realm of the mind and the intellect. It is the medium of communion and connec-tion. Our voices move through air, as do music and fragrance, and because air is so light, there are fewer barriers and obstructions found in it.

From the new vantage point that you will discover here, you can access other dimensions and other intelligences without the distrac-tions and obstacles inherent in our earthly experience. The power in the Beacon experience is pure air, pure mind, with nothing in the way. In order to get there, we must first be grounded and centered, leaving our corporal bodies securely anchored in a safe and sacred place.

The first step is to choose the place that will serve as your altar. It can be any power place that is sacred to you, preferably one in nature or at least outdoors. You need to be familiar enough with this location to be able to recognize neighboring landmarks and find it from great heights above when you visit it mentally. This power place will become the altar upon which your body is held safely during your journeys. I have used specific consecrated spaces where I have done ceremony in my garden at home, sacred springs or waterfalls, and the flat area at the top of the Great Pyramid in Egypt.

JOURNEY

First Beacon

Make sure you are in a comfortable space, and that you prepare it appropriately for sacred ceremony. It is a good idea to smudge with incense or sage, perhaps light a candle. It is up to you how elaborate you wish to make your home altar, the place from which you orchestrate this rite. It is always appropriate to honor the directions, the elements, and any spirit guides, totems, and other allies you engage to witness and hold space for you while you journey.

When you are ready to begin, start by grounding and centering. . . . Find and kindle your heart flame with love. . . . You might want to remember and utilize your experience of universal love. . . . Take your time practicing the Earth Breath before engaging with the Sky, then move into the Heart Breath. Once you create a strong internal heart flame that radiates out from the center of your being, you can begin to perceive the place that you have chosen for your altar. . . . Familiarize yourself with the surrounding landscape and bring it into your awareness with all of your senses. Imagine what it would look like from above, then shift your awareness higher and notice what you would see if you were looking down from there. . . .

Ground your awareness back at the altar and place yourself at the exact spot that, for you, represents the power of the place. From there, orient yourself to the directions. Use all your senses to perceive your surroundings. What does it look like? What does it feel and smell like? What is the nature of the ground? Is it stone or sand or a soft carpet of forest mulch? Take a moment to honor the place and the spirits that inhabit it. Ask the spirits to uphold you and guard you as you journey. . . .

See your body as sitting cross-legged, or if it helps you to relax, lying down on the ground of your sacred altar. Notice in which direction you place your head or face. It always helps to orient yourself to the directions, because you are naturally at the center of your universe. Breathe deeply. A grounding breath is really important any time before you journey in this way. As you exhale, feel your body sink just a bit into the ground of the altar. Do this until you reach neutral buoyancy, about half in the ground and half out above the surface. Notice how secure you feel, as though nothing could move or dislodge you from your place on this altar. . . .

Focus your attention on the luminosity of life. Every cell of your body emits light, and the more you focus on this light, the more your body is transformed into light.

As soon as you feel as though your body is made of or filled with light, intentionally draw your light body up and into your head. As a result of your intention, the light of your body is pulled upward from your fingertips and your toes, from your entire body, drawn into your head, into the center of your consciousness. The dense body that is left behind has no grasp on your light body. Your consciousness loosens its grip on your physical form. . . .

Your light body becomes free and lifts away from your head, already spherical in shape. It looks like a balloon, or a bubble—like an orb of light. You might also notice a golden cord that shimmers. This cord is attached to your physical body and reels out easily to keep you connected. Notice if there is any color to your balloon. It floats above your body, and you can look down from the center of your consciousness upon your body, where it is safely parked in your sacred place, half submerged.

Your desire for self-preservation is a form of love. When you acknowledge that love, a whitish shimmer covers your body. . . . This creates further protection.

Your bubble floats upward and is caught by a gentle breeze, which lifts it further. As you drift upward, gently buffeted about by breezes and currents, you soon look down from a height of about fifty feet, recognizing the landmarks that you imprinted on your mind earlier, the familiar terrain that surrounds your sacred place. If your altar is indoors, you will have floated right through the ceiling and will be looking down upon your material body within the structure where you started.

You will be subjected to the conditions of the moment. Experience what it is like to be blown with the wind, perhaps even bumping into branches or snagging on trees. Feel out the drafts and notice how pockets of heat cause you to rise rapidly. As you become more comfortable floating in your light-body orb, discover the aerodynamics of being a light balloon; develop a sense of your own potential to move about at will. Experiment with your ability to go against the wind or otherwise define your direction. Notice how the balloon streamlines while pushing into the wind. . . .

It is the power of your will from inside the balloon that is the driving force. Because you are continually subjected to the elements, you get better and better at dealing with them. The more adverse the conditions, the more you will be forced to control your own movements.

It is your goal and intention during this first flight to establish your place of power in the air, somewhere above your sacred altar.

Practice moving up and down along the column of air that extends up from your material body, along the golden cord that connects you to your dense body until you feel your place of power. You will recognize this place because of the resonance that will occur. You might feel something like surges of electricity, sparking like a broken wire. You might feel drawn to the spot as to a magnet, or you might be riveted there.

Hold your position when you find it. . . .

Notice how balanced and centered you feel. The puffs of air do not dislodge you here. It becomes a point of strength—your power spot. Nothing can dislodge you. With your increasing strength comes the ability to transmit energy as light; you can radiate it outward in every direction from this power spot in the air. . . . Explore the feeling of your own radiance. . . .

Now notice what happens when you set your intention to communicate your presence to other intelligent beings who might also be exploring the universe this way. Your transmission of energy intensifies with your intention, and your light glows brighter. . . . Now, try altering your intention into an appeal for help. We do need help, and any intelligence we encounter at this level may have something to contribute, perhaps even answers or solutions to our problems. The challenges we are facing that require help may have been resolved elsewhere in the universe, so be attentive to ideas that come to you; they might hold answers to your concerns. Notice that you continue to brighten until you become a beacon, a searing blue-white light. . . .

The interconnectedness of light and sound becomes apparent to you as your Beacon is established. Notice the sound emissions you generate. The brighter your Beacon becomes, the louder the sound it emits, and the deeper the sound gets. It is as though your intention itself becomes the light. The combined forces of sound, light, and the power of your intention begin to feed and strengthen the whole of your transmission. . . . As this new force becomes greater than the sum of its parts, spokes of light radiate out in every direction. The form solidifies and the energy becomes denser, more controlled and contained. The more strongly your message is broadcast, the brighter the core of your beacon becomes. . . . Once the fullness of the Beacon is established, the sound grows softer and quieter. . . . Now there is more a wave of feeling and warmth than a sound.

Notice the unique emotion of your appeal. . . . Listen for a response. . . . *[Pause.]*

When you feel the time is right to begin the process of closure, look down at your dense body. It is covered in a veil of shimmering light. The cord that connects you to your body is giving it life force. Bring yourself slowly back down along the cord, noticing the changes in feeling and sound as you move farther away from your power spot. . . .

Stop a few inches above your body and blast it with love and light before entering your physical head. . . . Become aware of the feeling in your head as you reenter. Allow this feeling to spread through your head and shoulders as your light body reincorporates, into your torso and arms, down through the rest of your body, and into your legs, feet, and toes. . . .

Your body seems looser, less compact, with more space for you to fit into. You may feel tingly. You will almost certainly feel a great sense of revitalization and empowerment from this exercise.

Thank the spirits of the altar where your body remained safe. . . .

Begin to ground and center. . . . As you return fully into your body and the light from your beacon moves through it, your body is gently eased up and out of the Earth. . . . Complete the grounding and centering process.

When you are fully grounded and centered, open your eyes.

Take the time you need to write the details of your experience in your journal.

There is an additional piece of information that needs to be addressed: Most responses have come, as one would expect, during the journey itself and while in your power spot in the air. This is not always the case. On occasion, we have been informed by various participants in our classes that a clear and informative response has come "out of the blue" hours or even days later. Once during a weekend retreat, we received a phone call the following morning after this exercise. "The darndest thing happened yesterday . . ." Susan lived in a different state, had never taken this class, and had no idea of what we were doing. The synchronistic, and for her life altering, planetary healing information she had spontaneously received and could not ignore started with "Call Nicki Scully," and was directly related to our plea for help.

USES FOR THE BEACON

The Beacon is a place from which you can do many things. Following are some of the possibilities that we have experimented with in our Planetary Healing classes. Practice these and explore other avenues as they come up:

1. **Access other intelligent consciousness:** You will recognize that the Beacon puts you "between the worlds" at that intersection between the bands of time, or the realm of the Gods. From here, direct your call outward to connect with other seekers and travelers. It is possible to be aware of others from various traditions who are working on the same wavelength; this awareness will grow as you practice. As you beam your light and put out your call, you gain a direct understanding of love as the true motivating and bonding force. As your call radiates outward, notice where you are drawn. You will find that you can work with the intelligence and tools that are given to you in response to your call.

2. **Focus and spin the Beacon:** You must have a specific purpose for this exercise. To accomplish Earth healing with your Beacon, try asking for a deity or totem, one who is a guardian of Earth, or one who has the appropriate gift or skill, to take hold of your light and direct it as a tool. The spirit ally that responds

will help you generate more energy and will aid in directing it. Such allies apply their own gifts and intelligence to the situation while enabling you to make the most of yours. You can put out a request for the most efficient use of your light, offering it for a spirit guide or other appropriate intelligence to use as needed. You will also receive a teaching from this process.

During the disastrous oil spill of 2010 in the Gulf of Mexico, and before it was capped, I was conducting a teleconference to send healing to the region. Because this was in conjunction with a Planetary Healing class, we included a Beacon journey. As we generated our Beacons, I saw that the light from mine was picked up by a pod of dolphins who directed it into the darkness under the oil slick so that the creatures disoriented by the gloom could see their way out of the toxic spill and into clear waters.

3. **Use the Beacon for healing:** Set your intention first. Send out your beam in all directions and listen for the response. This exercise is not specific to humans, and can attract plants, animals, trees—any life-form having intelligence and the need of light to sustain its existence. Your rays of radiance move out like vibratory waves. As you feel yourself connect to the agony of a being or a situation, you have only to open yourself to that pain and receive it into your own center. As you open to that darkness (the disease or suffering or whatever you perceive as the problem), continue to radiate light while the Beacon consumes it. The darkness disappears because there is no end to your light. It is undiminished. It never depletes. The more you send it out, the brighter you become. You may see, feel, or in some way experience the emotional side of that darkness before it is absorbed and transformed by the light of your beacon. Do not fear this: open to the empathy, the direct, momentary knowing of someone else's pain. When you are in your light form, disconnected from a body, no understanding of the emptiness or darkness is required. This is not about "fixing it"—just sur-

render to the process to let the light receive the shadow. Your job is mostly to witness as the neutral observer. This exercise offers you a simple and profound way of converting dark or disturbing energy into light, or negative into positive.

7
Creating an Air Force

In the spirit of building an Air Force of like-minded, intrepid inter-dimensional travelers, we who are the pioneers of inner space travel can band together outside of space and time as we know it and work together to create change. The numbers in this force are growing. Whether you fly with a group or fly solo, we all share the same concerns and can work together to improve the quality of life for one and for all. Many of the processes in this book provide maps that this Air Force can use toward finding solutions to Earth's most challenging problems.

Early in the development of this work, Mark and I were given a journey to take with the specific intention of finding out how to live beyond duality, in a paradigm with no dissonance. We were shown a band of space dust spiraling toward Earth from somewhere out in the universe.

We were given the opportunity to explore a reality in this band where harmony exists in and of itself. As we moved closer to this grow-ing vortex of swirling stardust, we got a sense of the sustained ecstasy it was radiating. We could not penetrate very deeply into it, because it was too dense at its core. In order to find its source, we underwent a shift that was like a reversal in time; this caused the vortex to appear to shrink, allowing us ever closer to its center. Thus, we went back in time to when this force field was initially triggered; we were chasing the edge back to its conception. What we found was a state of pure joy, rapture, and ecstasy that caused our bodies to reverberate as though we were inside a loudspeaker of exquisite music, with sound and light components blending in absolute harmony.

Your first mission is to travel to this great spiraling vortex, approach it with respect and care, seek to enter and find its source, and return with a teaching that can help with our own planetary peacemaking. This spiraling band of love, which most resembles a spiral galaxy, cannot be entered directly. You must circle around it to find a way in that does not damage the delicate structure of energy. This is why we used a reversal of time to shrink the vortex for access. Once an opening has been located, and you have entered, you must spiral inward until you come to the center. This is the source where you will be given a teaching in answer to your question. In time, this growing force will envelope our planet and bestow its blessings upon us. The question now is how can we begin to enjoy the bliss sooner? What can we bring home from here that will expedite or install the process? Ask something about how we can sustain harmony—how it can exist in and of itself. Ask for peacemaking solutions to support our planet as we learn to live in harmony. Within the inner sanctum of rapture and ecstasy, receive the teaching you are given. This message may come in words, as a tool or symbol, or as an empowerment or initiation.

Having accomplished your mission, you will be given your own craft, intended specifically for you. It may be a plane, a spaceship, or even a dragon. As you come out of the swirling vortex, you will be piloting your own craft. You can land and park your plane at your Beacon altar. After you land, it is always important to wipe down, feed, or care for your craft as is needed. Think of it as if it were an extension of your own body, or a vehicle that you would care for as a fine car.

The idea of this Air Force is to find our numbers in the imaginal realm and work together to implement the solutions we are given in our journeys. Whether you take the following journey alone or with a circle or group, someone from the Air Force, maybe me, will assist in getting you to the place of ecstatic harmonics. Once you have received your craft, there are some specific journeys we will take together as you

Here is a sketch of my own personal craft, drawn for me by the iconic rock-and-roll artist Stanley Mouse,* after I described it to him back in the late eighties. As you can see, it is just big enough for me. Everyone gets a unique model that is perfectly suited to them. Once you are piloting, anything can happen. The crafts that come back through this journey have purpose, intent, and power.

become adept at traveling in these dimensions through space and time.

Remember, we are creating an Air Force here that gets stronger as it grows.

Although each person has his or her personal craft, you can join with others with whom you wish to share this work, or anyone you encounter while journeying. You can make agreements to flock for specific purposes, especially those aimed at creating healing for our planet.

JOURNEY
To the Center of Ecstasy

Place yourself in your power spot. . . . Move into your Beacon as described in the Beacon Journey. . . . As you enter your power place in the air, allow yourself to relax and float as a balloon. . . . Extend your call out through your radiating Beacon, requesting that someone

---

*See Mouse's gallery of classic and current work at www.mousestudios.com.

from the Air Force who has already completed this journey come to take you to the vortex. . . . Relax your concept of time; "when" someone hears your call and responds to it is of little importance to your here and now . . .

After a moment or two, you will become aware of a craft coming for you. If I am your guide, you will recognize my little plane. There will be a string or a number of strings dangling off its tail. Some of these may already be attached to other orbs of light that have been picked up along the way to follow this same mission. Whoever comes for you will have a tether to which your Beacon, which now looks more like a radiant balloon, can attach. Observe as you are connected to the craft that has come for you. . . .

If there are other first-timers joining this mission after you, the craft will gently circle the planet, picking up other balloons. Once all of them have been picked up, the craft and its orbs begin to circle upward in wide arcs. Anyone who happened to be searching the sky at this time would see quite an image: a peculiar craft with any number of shimmering orbs streaming behind like glowing balloons. . . . Look down and notice how everything becomes smaller and smaller as you rise higher; you can see the landscape shrinking below.

Continue arcing upward in wide, gentle circles. Ahead, you notice puffy white billowing clouds. They are truly majestic, at once fluffy and firm, and shining with light. . . . As you approach the clouds, you will see a square door with rounded edges where a part of the cloud hinges open. You have arrived at a threshold; all that is familiar will remain behind.

Look through the door. On the other side is a vision of outer space, dark black specked with starlight. As you pass through the threshold with the other orbs, you know you are entering a new reality, a new realm. As you drift through, heading into the vast beyond, you can immediately sense the mystical nature of this realm. . . . This is a magical place.

The pilot of the lead craft takes you on a tour to gain perspective in this new dimension. You can move at hyperspeed here: suddenly you accelerate with a "whoosh," zooming toward a new perspective of our solar system. When you slow down again, you are in a position to see several planets in orbit around the sun. The lead craft brings you closer to one of the planets. Can you recognize it? What do you notice from this perspective in space?

Continuing on toward your mission, the lead craft enters hyperspace again, so that just a moment later you find yourself approaching what appears to be a small planet, this time in a different solar system: this is a "fly by" to introduce you to the place of a future adventure. . . .

This planet is surrounded by thick clouds. The lead craft penetrates the substantial mass of cloud cover, where it is dark and smells acrid. There is even a weird taste. When you emerge from under the cloud, you find yourself facing a large volcano. Craft and orbs alike circle the volcano at a safe distance. You take in its awesome mass and its eruption of lava, ash, and steam that cast a red glow across the sky. As you come in closer, you can see the flickering, glowing rivers of lava. This volcano appears bigger than any existing on Earth at this time.

The lead craft locates a band of light, clear sky, and heads up between the clouds into the thinner atmosphere above. You all speed up and once again enter hyperdrive: whoosh, off you go with no effort. . . . The planet you have left is now a prick of light in the dark distance. Your leader now takes you toward the culmination of your journey, the swirling mass of stardust that you can now see before you. The lead craft moves in and pauses at the edge. Notice that you start at once to feel different—better, in some way you cannot yet define.

Look around to see if you can tell where you are in the universe. Do you recognize anything? Are there any celestial landmarks? The general direction of home can be sensed, but can you tell how long it will take for this positive energy, this exciting phenomenon to reach it?

Relax and notice the change occurring in your consciousness. You have entered a realm where the totally unexpected and new can happen. You can feel a pull toward the powerful force of harmony here; it seems to be expanding toward you and drawing you in at the same time.

This is an important moment: it is time to be released from your tether. Remember your mission. Call up your intention to find the impetus of this incredibly vast force field; be prepared to stay awhile, to be with something that cares for you and for all humankind. Remember there is a teaching there for you, and you will also be receiving your craft. . . . As you peel off from the lead craft, you must willingly travel alone, without guidance, to seek out the point in time before this swelling, spiraling force began. [*Long pause.*]

When you have accomplished your mission and received your craft, take a few moments to learn how to use your craft to move through space and between dimensions. . . . Fly back through the threshold in the clouds and return to your altar. Be sure the new craft is tended to before you ground and center, and open your eyes. . . .

If for whatever reason you do not complete your mission this time, the craft that led you will be waiting when you come out of the vortex and will return you safely to your altar.

Once you have received your craft, you will learn how to maneuver it as you practice the other exercises in this section. My craft was a bit tricky at first. I wanted to see the rings of Saturn up close, and as I whizzed around our solar system and approached Saturn, I had not learned to control it properly; my craft went "splat" right into the surface of the planet. Both my craft and I survived, and I was given training wheels, which I used until I was able to pilot my little plane safely. I can still see in my mind's eye the loops the tracks made in space as I figured it out. When you feel confident that you are ready, you can make yourself available to escort other travelers going in for the first time to receive their craft. From inside your Beacon, you will know when you receive the call from new orbs ready for this adventure.

BLANKET OVER KOSOVO

This next exercise became part of our Planetary Healing work during the conflict in Kosovo in 1998–1999. Our call to action at that time was overdue, prompting us to take a serious look at time, priorities, and distractions. Part of our commitment to Planetary Healing must mean integrating our intention for service into our lives. We must learn to walk in two worlds simultaneously in order to fit our Planetary Healing work into our busy lives and work schedules.

One night back then Mark and I went to Thoth to receive a mission for the Planetary Healing circle we were then guiding. The mission Thoth offered us that night involved a three-pronged approach for dealing with war and the consequences of the various forms of weaponry that are unleashed upon people of both sides, including civilians caught in the crossfire.

Although this action was originally designed for Kosovo, it can be applied to any of the myriad conflicts presently simmering or raging. As I prepare this manuscript, the entire Middle East is experiencing some level of upheaval following the revolutions in Tunisia and Egypt. Taliban, Afghani, and U.S. forces continue their conflict. And although Iraq is no longer front-page news, conflict and strife continue there. There are violent conflicts in many parts of Africa and in Mexico and what I think of as Gangland, USA, as bullets continue to fly and people continue to suffer. It will not be hard to find a conflict into which this attention and energy can be sent. Take your pick.

JOURNEY

The Three-Prong Mission

Prong 1

This is a good journey to do in a group or a circle. The more people you can engage in working with you, the more potent the result. But go ahead and practice alone if you do not have others to work with. This action also lends itself well to working with your craft.

Begin by preparing yourself with the Heart Breath. Visualize yourself at your altar where you ground and anchor yourself, and safely leave your body there via the Beacon Journey before boarding your craft. Use your craft to travel to your chosen area of conflict.

Once there, your craft begins to spread out over everything like a blanket. It is up to you, through your attention, to strengthen each fiber of the blanket as it takes shape. Your blanket connects to the blankets of others participating in this action. The blanket extends in every direction and covers the ground like a fog pouring in, following the terrain—thin on hilltops and thick in the valleys.

What we are doing here is constructing a blanket that makes the gunpowder dampen, the bullets slow down, and the overall impact of violence soften. We introduce a presence into the space. The mines do not go off quite as quickly; they are not triggered as readily. This blanket has an effect on the intensity of thought as well. It deadens the aggressiveness.

Pour yourself over this area, filling the space, becoming the blanket. In doing so, you become intrinsically bound with the molecular structure of the explosives. As the blanket, you connect to everything in the scene, from the burning gunpowder to the flying bullets, which slow down because of your intervention. Even a bomb or rocket drops into the mistlike covering of the blanket, so that its effect is localized.

The purpose for muffling the activity is to slow things down so that clarity and wisdom have a space in which to manifest. Think of how the power of the gentle is at work even during the fiercest thunderstorm. The lightning rends the sky, the thunder roars, but at the same moment the seeds are safely held in their cycle, preparing for the renewal of life.

Remember, it is not our personal energy that we are using. The raw materials for our blankets are all the prayers that have ever been sent or are currently coming into the area. Our contribution is to organize this energy and to strengthen the fibers of the blanket.

The next two parts are about getting to wisdom, which will ultimately lead to peace.

Prong 2

To satisfy your more logical, rational left-brain hemisphere, and to better understand the mechanisms at play in the situation you have chosen to tend, attempt to understand both sides of the conflict. It is not up to us to change anyone's mind, but we learn compassion more readily when we are informed and able to understand the opposing points of view. It is important not to enter the fray with preconceived judgments of who is right and who is wrong. Subjective opinions muddy the situation.

Between journeys, inform yourself. Talk to people who have lived in the place in question. Do your research to learn all you can on the subject, through the Internet and various other networks of information. Be discerning.

There are usually more than two sides in conflicts that result in war. Ask difficult questions. Work to understand the anger, always cognizant that the righteous wrath on both sides is also a part of you.

It is through this level of research that you may discover unique strategies for dismantling the conflict.

An exercise for Compassionate Listening/Becoming Your Enemy can be found in *Alchemical Healing*.* You will find this exercise to be quite enlightening with regard to cultivating a nonjudgmental view of both sides of a conflict.

Prong 3

What would our wise grandmothers advise? This third prong of the action is to consider the wisdom of the elders, especially wise women. Although gender generalizations do not always apply, most wars are designed, instigated, and fought mainly by men. In desperation, often after suffering incomprehensible loss and degradation, women will enter the fray in fierce defense of their families and communities, or in reaction to some horrific wrong. If your intuition is in tune with the feminine archetypes who are capable of embracing the entire conflict with love and compassion, you will be able to utilize a more right-brain, intuitive approach.

Ideological passion is sometimes difficult to appreciate when the issues are not your own. Such passion inherently fuels extreme viewpoints, none of which may be easy to understand. But opening to understanding creates space that allows resolution a way in. Do not get tripped up because these elders' perspectives are so different from your normal reality. This work will test us in terms of our judgments.

The third part of this action can be done through shamanic journeying and is facilitated through your personal connection with feminine archetypes.

---

*Nicki Scully, *Alchemical Healing* (Rochester, Vt.: Bear & Company, 2003), 306.

EXERCISE
OBSERVING WISE, COMPASSIONATE WOMEN

Start with the Heart Breath. When you have created a strong glow in and around you, shine that light upon your chosen situation with the intention of observing the women, specifically the wise elders. Allow yourself to bring a woman—a mother or grandmother—into focus. Use your inner sensitivities to perceive details that will help you to connect to her: What are her surroundings like? Is she indoors or outside? What type of clothing is she wearing? Can you see a pattern or patterns woven into her garment? Is there a fragrance that permeates this image?

This woman is a representative of the wise, compassionate women of the culture you are observing. As you feel her presence more and more clearly, allow yourself to absorb the wishes of the women. What do the mothers want for their families, now and in the generations to come? What are their dreams and ideals? What are their values? See them clearly: their faces, their clothing, their bustle in meal preparation. It is important to remain in observation. Do not pass judgment; stay open to receiving information. Feel the love and concern these women feel for their families.

Now give the same attention to the wise mothers and grandmothers on the other side of the conflict you have chosen. Once again see the details of their lives and feel the love and wishes they have for their families. This is a powerful force; combine the desires for their young to enjoy a long and rewarding life, as the elders from both sides desire the same thing. Now allow the elders' wishes to flow into and influence the heat of war. Imagine the calming effect as the warriors begin to think of home and yearn for a peaceful life with their families. . . .

Think of a long, happy, peaceful, life with your own family, and give thanks to the women who shared their perspective with you.

Ground and center. . . . Take some time to record the details of what you learned in your journal.

The perpetrators of violence are most often being led by their passions rather than the vision of the wise elder women, their grandmothers. How did they go astray? They may have been seduced by the taste of power as an outlet for their fear and frustrations. If we can begin by owning the anger we feel about the war or disturbance we can begin to dismantle it with compassion. If we can find the "angry warrior" within ourselves and heal that anger with our own love and compassion, we will be closer to what the iconic archetypal grandmothers wish for their families, and better prepared to share our beliefs with people at war.

8
Purification by Volcano
Setting a New Trajectory to Fulfill Your Life's Purpose

Now that you are part of the Air Force and have your new craft, you can begin the deeper work of traveling to specific places to receive pertinent teachings. Whether you perceive yourself to be on a shamanic road or in an alchemical process, or simply as undergoing personal transformation to become more spiritually aware, there are certain leitmotifs that you must experience or comprehend as you move toward greater enlightenment.

In shamanism, you will go through dismemberment; in Alchemical Healing, dissolution: these terms identify the essential experience of annihilation, or death, with a subsequent renewal or rebirth. Every mystical tradition includes some version of this process—some disintegration and reintegration that occurs beyond the literal level of the corporal body. It is in the space between the loss of identity, or death, and the renewal, or rebirth, where one is shamanically re-membered, reorganized, or put back together in a new and better way.

This alchemical Planetary Healing path provides a potent, scripted version of the dismemberment or dissolution process. It requires a level of trust in a process in which we intentionally enter a volcano. Why would we purposely allow ourselves to be blasted from the heart of a volcano, to be vaporized, actually? Most probably because it is kinder to the body to experience this death and rebirth as a conscious act of power than to suffer such a thing on the Earth plane. Through this rite of passage, you can be consciously involved with your own spiritual rebirth. It is an empowerment, an expression of your willingness to take responsibility for your physical and mental well-being.

Among other things, we learn directly that we are not just the sum total of our body parts. Through our willingness to completely release our corporal bounds, even for a few moments, we come to realize the true nature of immortality. This journey into the explosive heart of creation is an act of purification and trust, and must be undertaken with deep respect and clarity of intention; this allows us to be reconstructed with a new, or at least altered, blueprint and a more defined direction.

This initiation honors all of the five sacred elements: the earth that is the substance of this planet and the result of this ages-old and ongoing eruption; the water that is the sea surrounding it; the air through which you journeyed to be here; the fire that is the agent of transformation, the essence of creation itself; and Akasha, the element that informs you of the new possibilities awaiting you.

The intention that you carry with you into this journey will impact the result. As this is a one-time trip, it is important that your intention be clear and focused. Your purpose is threefold:

1. To express your dedication and commitment to the healing of the Earth
2. To find your soul's purpose and the unique expression that fulfills your personal commitment to serve in that healing
3. To receive healing with an opportunity to reconstruct your body.

To prepare yourself for the following exercise, in which you will learn a new way of developing and sending forth crystal thought-forms imbued with intention and power.

Although this volcano is located off this planet, when you enter into it and relate directly with the molten lava, you are relating, in effect, to the lifeblood of the Earth. The essence of this blood is the *chi,* which spouts forth as love and energy and life. Immersed in the blood as it expels you, you might be able to perceive your direction in the lava flows and perhaps gain new understanding of your life's purpose and how it can be fulfilled. Your purpose has been forged by the same power and energies at play in the creation of Earth itself.

You are a corpuscle in the lifeblood of the planet. This journey into the volcano helps you to become more conscious of your relationship to the systems of Earth. Earth is a complex, conscious being made up of bones of granite and blood of lava. As a result of this rite of passage, when you fearlessly enter her body with the consciousness of taking part in her healing, you will, at the very least, experience purification, renewal, and a new level of spiritual awareness.

As you enter into this process, it is as if you were going into the center of your own being, and your senses become less and less important. At the journey's end, when you burst out of the volcano, you will have the opportunity to expand into total awareness of your identity and of all aspects of your being. You will be connected to the very essence of your being, to your full potential, to all that you wish to explore and express in this life. In short, this journey into the volcano is a quest for the self that ignites transformation. You will become part of the amazing explosion at the center of the earth, feeling your own personal expansion in the process. By your willing and voluntary participation in this volatile journey, you secure your dedication not only to healing the Earth, but also to being everything you can be.

Before you take the journey, we want to give you a sense of what you can expect once you are inside the volcano. At a certain point, it will become so hot that you will feel yourself disintegrate. You will still be conscious and aware. Even as you shoot up the inside of the volcano, you will have a certain measure of control, despite the fact that you have left your body. Your cells will immediately start to gyrate back together, and into their new orientation. Although it happens very quickly, you may be able to observe this process of subtle reorganization while it is transpiring. You can either let it be, and your body will return to the way it was, or you can use your focused intention and discipline to heal and restructure the patterns of your physical form. You can even participate in the rewiring of your own brain. By the time you reach the top, before you are carried over the edge, you will be aware of an opportunity to discard, using the currents of the lava flows, those things that you wish to let go of before you commit to your renewed, regenerated self. Note that when you first saw this volcano from space as an Air Force traveler, it was erupting forcefully. Now, as part of the grace of this rite, the volcano is calmer. Lava is no longer spewing, but spilling over the lip of the caldera.

In the course of this journey, you will flow as the lava does, experiencing the initial force that pushes it up, rising swiftly as part of the column, then slowing at the top. There, the walls no longer constrict the flow, and you are part of the pulsing lava coming out of the top like blood from an artery. When you reach the apex, it is helpful to stay cognizant of the forces and aware of the center, although even if your mind wanders or blacks out, you will slide over the lip of the caldera and find yourself coming down the outside of the volcano. Then you can simply ride the current of lava flow all the way down to the sea.

By now your new body has taken on its initial appearance. If you have maintained a high comfort level, you can choose to ride an extra surge or two down the volcano, as if you were surfing. Why would you do this? There are two benefits: the sheer exhilaration, and the cleansing you will get from letting the lava flow over the surface of your newly created form. It is best to limit yourself to two surges. There is a fragility that you must respect at this moment.

As your new body takes its shape, notice and encourage the subtle and not so subtle improvements in your physical well-being, your clarity of thought, and the strengthening of your soul.

JOURNEY

Into the Volcano

As you prepare to take this journey, please remember that the Beacon and Air Force journeys are prerequisites to this purification by volcano.

To begin, breathe the Heart Breath to ground and center yourself. . . . In the light created by the Heart Breath, find your altar, and proceed to where your craft is tethered. You will use the craft you were given when you joined the Air Force. Spend whatever time it takes to reconnect with your altar and the importance this place holds for you. When you are ready, take one final Heart Breath, and then enter or mount your craft. Begin your ascent with a slow and growing spiral, always being attentive to others in the Air Force so that you can join with them as their numbers grow. . . .

Find the puffy white clouds and the door that marks the threshold into deep space. As you cross through, perceive the shift into consciousness beyond space and time as we know it. . . .

You are going to find the planet with the volcano that you were shown when you first entered this dimension. Enter hyperdrive with that intention, and you will be whisked to a perspective giving you access to that planet. As you get closer, slow down. You can see a thick covering of smoke, and as you circle the planet, you can see the volcano spewing out above the cloud cover. . . . There is an opening through which you can enter the atmosphere of this planet. The thick smoke surrounds you as you drop through. You can smell and taste the now-familiar acridness. Your craft has intelligence; it brings you down to where the water meets the side of the volcano. You can see the rugged slopes, with rivulets of lava pouring down, dividing into smaller and smaller streams that pour into the sea, releasing steam when the molten lava touches water. Undeterred by water, your craft dives right in, down to a landing strip at the bottom of the ocean.

Notice that although you are underwater, you have no trouble breathing, and there are no bubbles. You and any others who may have joined you park their crafts next to the landing area.

When you get out, you see a cave-like entrance that looks like the open end of a large, crusty garden hose, an empty tube with lava hardened on the outside. It is big enough for three people to step into together and walk along side by side. The walls are quite thick. From your vantage point, you can follow the winding path with your eyes, deep into the volcano until it disappears into the earth. You cannot see the top from here, even with your enhanced vision. The tube was created before the cone above the water took form, while the entire volcano was still underwater. Over the millennia, the gentle currents of the ocean have eroded and removed the softer material from inside the hardened walls.

Pause at the mouth of the cave and ponder your personal intention and your dedication to healing the Earth. . . .

Going up the lava tube feels similar to swimming like a fish, and the water gets warmer the further you go. . . . Soon you reach the surface of the water, which gets shallower as you continue walking up the tube, eventually leaving the water behind. The tube flattens out and gets wider. Its walls begin to glow red, and you can see that they are even brighter up ahead. Each footstep gives off a hiss until all the water dries off your body. The air is hot; its like being in an oven. . . .

As you continue deeper into the volcano, your body begins to realize the fragility of the inner structures holding it together in the face of the increasing heat. It is quite possible that the molecules in all your systems will suddenly scatter in all directions. As you focus your attention inward, your molecules begin to tingle. It is important to maintain clear awareness of your intention, dedication to the Earth, and the aspects of your own reconstruction that you will be co-creating during the brief opportunity before your new body comes back together and gels with the new program or blueprint for your life. . . .

As the lava tube gets hotter, you have to keep to the center to avoid touching the glowing red walls. Further ahead, where the tube begins to curve upward, the walls are changing from red to white hot. It is easier to float in the air rather than walk, now that your assembled molecules act more like an air current than the dense and consolidated body. Avoid contact with the walls of the tube as it bends more sharply upward. It is fully in the white-hot stage now and you find it harder and harder to maintain form. You sense yourself moving into a vibration that verges on total annihilation, until you are being held together by force of will alone. . . .

For the first time since entering the tube, you can no longer ignore the roaring, hissing sound. Before, you were able to tune it out as a distraction in the background, but this roar has grown so loud and overpowering that it is become a major force, furthering the dissolution of what is left of the fibers of your being.

The tube that you have followed enters a cavernous inferno, huge and intimidating and loud. The force expelling the magma comes from underneath. Five different columns of magma converge above your head. They are being expelled with such force that they rise above you, blasting up through the top, at least a mile high. Here, there is no rhythmic pulsing, but a constant torrent of the converging fountains. The flow is so strong that it is creating currents in the air that are pulling on you in all directions.

Focus on your intention. The force is immense. Because of the five columns, there are five directions for the equal dispersal of your molecules. The last thing you will be aware of as you lose your form is a blast of sound, as when a trigger releases everything at the same moment. Now let go: release yourself into the raging furnace. You have exploded through and through, as your molecules are pulled into the flow. . . .

You are being spewed upward at almost the speed of sound,

although you start to lose momentum as you near the surface. . . . New molecules begin to form in the lava during the ride. They begin to find their place as a new body begins to take shape. . . . Before you go over the top, time distorts. Though you are racing to completion, you have all the time you need to organize yourself and your thoughts. . . . This is the moment when your desire and intention about your reconstruction are introduced into the new reality. Stay centered and focused. Let go of what no longer serves you as you reconstruct into a new being. . . .

Once you reach the apex, you find yourself drawn to a particular channel that will determine which side of the mountain you will descend. Notice that you have your form as soon as you come out, although it still needs to solidify. As the details of your image and refinement come into existance, how does it feel? Continue directing your reformation as the final molecules find their places.

For some, the urge to combine re-creation with recreation is strong; or maybe you feel a need to add to or alter some small detail that you missed. For whatever reason, you have an opportunity to loop back, leaving the stream before the process is complete and diving back into the eruption. You now have knowledge within each cell and you will know what can and cannot be done. . . .

Everything has changed. Even the cells that were not changed consciously are replicas of their former selves. You have begun your final ride down the side of the mountain, and both you and the lava carrying you have begun to cool as you slide down along the rivulet. The work is complete for now, and you can relax as you move effortlessly down the massive mountain toward the water's edge. Enjoy the ride. . . .

You hit the water with a huge splash, as though from a water slide, amid a towering spurt of hissing steam. You can begin to feel your new body and skin cooling and congealing in the water. Although the water has been infused with the heat of the lava, the plunge feels cool to you. . . .

Swim back to shore where the new earth and lava meet. As you rest on the shore, during these last moments in your transformation, recommit your dedication to the healing of our Mother Earth. At this moment, as you express your promise, listen for and imagine a way of life that fulfills your sacred purpose ... When you feel well established in your new body, look around to see where you have landed. If there were others in the volcano with you, you may see them at the heads of other nearby streams. There are many lava streams emanating from the volcano.

Be careful as you climb up onto the recently cooled crust at the edge of the lava flow so that you do not cut your new, tender flesh on the sharp lava rock. Notice how healthy you look and feel. The cooling from the dip in the ocean seems to have given you more of a flesh-and-blood feel. Take a moment to scan your renewed body and feel its vibrancy.

Call your vehicle to come and retrieve you; it is very responsive to your wishes and commands. Fly back through the cloud door to your altar.... Tend to and give thanks to your craft....

Take the time you need to ground and center, using the Earth Breath as needed to enter fully into your physical body....

It is time to take a break and journal your experience.

MAKING CRYSTAL SPHERES

When you are ready to return to the volcano and continue your work there, you will have the opportunity to create crystalline thought forms that will be imbued with clarified intentions. Let me remind you that your purification and transformation by volcano can help you to recognize the fullness of who you are and the possibilities of what you can and will contribute in service to our planet.

Thought precedes form. The more you can focus on a clear intention, the more potent the transformation will be as thought takes form. In this section, we will show you how to create crystal spheres for individuals, situations, places, or environments. You can build complex programs that will deliver multiple instructions into the field where they are sent, or you can build simple forms with one single direction.

Pay close attention to the process as you build these crystalline spheres. You will also want to watch for how they interact with and influence the people or places after they have been sent.

As you create the spheres, the processes of attraction and coagulation become clear as the vacuum of the exploded thoughtform draws into itself whatever minerals and intelligence it requires to fulfill its reason for being. This is similar to the purification process you just went through. When you were in the volcano, your old programs were vaporized. In that natural impulse to fill the vacuum created by your own annihilation, your clearly held intentions attracted the design patterns that were then crystallized in your newly reconstructed body, in your newly remembered blueprint, or information base.

Start with a simple thoughtform that involves a single instruction. For example, think of a friend, coworker, or family member who is going through a difficult time and needs to develop some specific attribute: courage, strength, or endurance. Choose one quality to focus on and, as you follow the directions below, pour your intention for that quality into the growing thoughtform that will be created and empowered in the space between your hands.

If you wish to create more complex thoughtforms, you will have to be able to maintain your concentration and hold your intention for a longer period of time.

JOURNEY
Empowering Crystal Thoughtforms

Practice your Heart Breath and in its glow, return to the altar and prepare your craft. . . . Fly back to the planet where the volcano is, following the initial path through the portal in the billowing clouds.

Once you are circling the planet, take note of the power and vitality of the volcano. It is as if it calmed a bit for the work you did, and
now it has returned to the full force it was displaying when you first
saw it. Follow the base of the cone where the many rivulettes and
streams of lava pour into the sea until you find a beach with a flow of
lava that you can stand alongside.

Stand with your hands out in front of you, palms facing each
other. The growing nucleus of a thoughtform begins to develop
between your hands. Allow energy to flow out from your palms, filling
the space between your hands and enlarging the thoughtform. As the
energetic ball between your hands grows, begin to think about how
you wish to program this thoughtform. Infuse your intention into the
growing ball of light.

When the thoughtform begins to solidify and seems to be the
right size (you will know what feels manageable), toss it into the lava
stream. As your thoughtform contacts the lava, it explodes. It vapor-
izes instantly and transforms into a bubble of concentrated intention
within the lava. The crystal sphere will develop inside this bubble as
it follows the flow of lava to the sea. . . .Your ability to hold your focus
during the time it takes for the bubble to reach the water will determine the power of the crystal sphere you are creating.

Your intention attracts the minerals required to imbue the
thoughtform with the matter it needs to fulfill this intention in the
physical world. This occurs during the crucial time when the lava
is cooling and the ingredients are solidifying. Within the molten

magma, the minerals that create these crystalline forms leach into the void within the bubble. Your intention catalyzes and strengthens this process.

When the thoughtform bubble hits the water, a crust that has been forming along the way shatters, revealing the crystal sphere that bobs up to the surface of the water. . . . Go out and pick it up. As you hold it in your hands, once again focus your intention on what you want this crystalline thought form to accomplish. Then direct it to where you want it to go simply by tossing it there: your intention will carry it. . . .

It is not necessary to follow the course of the sphere as it flies to its intended target; you will, however, be able to see where it arrives. If you send it to someone in need, notice where it enters that person's field. If you toss it to a place currently in strife—somewhere rocked by war or cataclysm—notice where it lands and what effect it creates.

Once again, the farther upstream you are, next to the flowing lava, the longer you are required to hold your concentration. If you are closer to the water, you can make many simple spheres in quick succession.

Practice creating these crystal spheres, allowing yourself to work with intentions that are more and more complex. When you feel complete with this process for now, call for your craft, board, and return to your altar. . . .

Tend to your craft, then ground and center at the altar before opening your eyes. . . .

You can always return to this volcanic island to make more crystal spheres. You are welcome to land on the beach next to any flow and work with this process. You can pick a small, intimate flow, and play. . . .

This is a powerful tool for Planetary Healing that can be offered up most anytime for a wide variety of issues. To understand how it works, visualize the intersection of a slum in a city, the seawater, the beach, and the lava flow: all of these meet energetically where a junction of streets occurs in the physical world. Even though the people on the streets are not aware of it, the person building the spheres is taking care of business, and as a result, the street is upgraded, the quality of life improves in some small way: maybe the lights shine brighter, or perhaps there is less dust. Somehow it is a little less miserable as a result of your efforts. Keep watching and contributing—this can be very rewarding work.

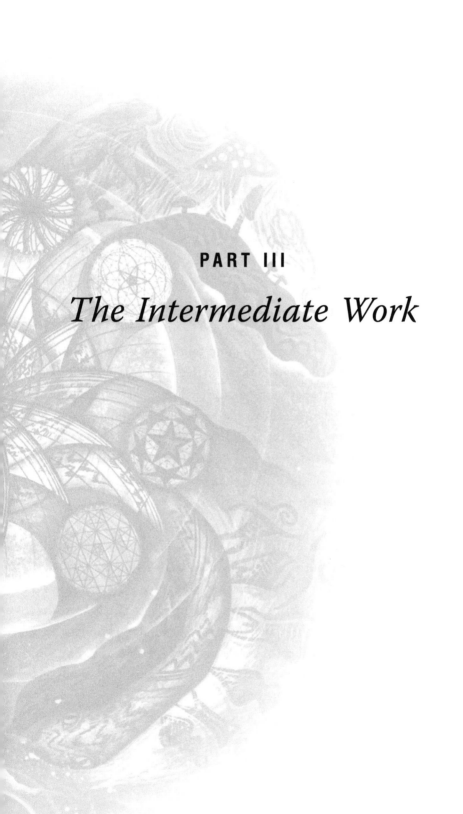

PART III

The Intermediate Work

9
Electromagnetic Current Empowerment

In our search for a deeper, more profound connection between ourselves and our planet, and between ourselves and the cosmos, we find symbolic replication throughout most of the traditional spiritual systems: certain religious and spiritual explanations employ very similar imagery or symbolism across cultures. The axis mundi is such a symbol, found all over the world in spiritual, religious, and secular contexts. The axis mundi represents the center of the planet, the center or our being, the center of the universe—it represents our relationship to everything around us, wherever we stand.

In the center of our bodies is our spinal column; this is the pillar that upholds and supports us. We can align our axis mundi to that of the earth by connecting with any of the symbols used throughout world religions and cultures to define that stabilizing aspect of nature: a tree, a mountain, a pillar. In the same way that energy moves through a tree, a volcano, or an umbilical cord, our vitality and life force, or kundalini energy, is channeled through the spine. This is the vital substance and animating force of creation itself.

The Sephiroth in the Kabbalah is an instantiation of the world tree, whose paths are the branches that represent the circuitry that gives it life. Yggdrasil is the world tree of the ancient Norse tradition, from which Odin hung in his quest for vision. He was rewarded with the runic system of divination still used throughout the world today.

The Earth is a dynamo. It creates electricity as it spins on its axis, its iron core spinning in its own magnetic field, and generating a hundred bolts of lightning per second at any given moment around the world. This field engulfs the Earth and protects it from the constant and deadly solar winds. When people consciously align with and connect to Earth's electromagnetic phenomena, their personal currents of electromagnetism are empowered, and they have more coherent energy to work with. This strengthens their protection and increases how much energy they can access.

With this empowerment, a channel within your internal energetic system is opened: you are now working directly with the dynamic attributes of the electromagnetic field. You can turn this connection on and off. When you turn it on, the energies flow through your body in tandem with the earth, moving from your left hand, up your arm, across your shoulder blades, down your right arm, and out your right hand. This sequence reinforces our natural tendency to receive into the left and generate from the right.

Once access to the universal life-force energy is established, as it was for you in the Communal Cauldron rite, you can use the awakened energy that flows from the palms and/or fingertips of your hands to "see" or receive information and generate energy. Usually, the left is most receptive, and the right is generative and used for transmitting the energy. When you practice healing, Alchemical Healing in particular, I advise working the energy with both hands to retain ambidexterity. What this empowerment adds is an amplification of the volume of energy you can access, and the ability to directly channel that energy to your point of focus. The energy either bypasses your physical body in an arc, or it passes instantly through the channel that is activated by this process.

One of the few rules in Alchemical Healing is that when you remove something from a person—undesirable energy, pain, or the spirit of a disease—you are responsible to conduct that energy safely into the

Earth, or some other appropriate destination, with a prayer so that it can be transformed into its highest potential. It is equally important to replenish and not leave any voids. Once the electromagnetic current and channel are activated, you can instantly pull out and conduct the energies of what you remove directly into the Earth, up to the sun, or wherever you are guided in the moment. The prayer for its transformation into its highest potential is always appropriate. It is important to always remember that if you take something out of a person, you must refill that space with the universal life-force energy before the healing is complete.

This activation can also be used as a centering device that focuses you and opens your channels, as though you were receiving an acupuncture treatment that aligns your meridians, or energy channels, with those of the planet. This has a stabilizing effect not only on your body and being, but on the planet itself.

FINDING THE CENTER WITHIN YOURSELF

The Center of the Universe is wherever you are, because your absolute presence is the center of your consciousness. Your awareness extends throughout the universe from the center point of your heart. When you align your center with the heart and center of the Earth, chaos is diminished and balance reigns. When we consciously align ourselves with other forces through spiritual practices or rites of passage, such as the individual empowerment below, the associated intelligent fields connect and respond to one another, thereby effecting change.

Individual Empowerment

There are two ways that I recommend accomplishing this rite on your own. It would be ideal if you have access to a strong, stable tree where you live or in some nearby park or wilderness. A planetary globe or even an Earth balloon will suffice as a representative of the Earth for our purposes. If you do not have a globe, you can use a crystal or any other ball to represent the Earth.

The idea is to bring yourself into alignment with the tree or globe. As the axis mundi, it represents the spinal column or central circuitry of the planet to which you are connecting. The tree in this work, is like an acupuncture needle whose roots pierce the Earth and touch the energetic meridian that ultimately connects with the Earth's central dynamic current. If we use a globe, the same alignment occurs. It is helpful to hold the globe so that your heart is level with it. The place you are is at the top of the globe, and the globe is aligned with the North-South axis of the Earth. Whether you are using a globe or a tree, it is important to align yourself with the magnetic flux lines, which means that you need to be facing south when you activate these energies for the first time. Note that the circuit is already there: it just has to be turned on.

After preparing yourself by smudging or burning incense if you have it, begin to breathe the Heart Breath, and stay with it until you feel yourself grounded, centered, and fully present. When you are aware that your light has become strong enough, invite your spirit guides and allies to witness and, by their presence, participate in this rite.

While continuing to breathe the Heart Breath, place your hands so that your palms are touching either side of the globe or the trunk of the tree at the level of your elbows, which are bent to 90 degrees. As you breathe the Heart Breath, redirect your out-breath so that rather than breathing out in every direction, you are offering your exhalation into the heart of the tree or the heart of the Earth in the globe or ball. Exhale not only the love that you continue to pour into your own heart flame, but the power and intelligence of Earth and Sky as they are alchemized with your love. Breathe with the additional intention of seeking harmony and alignment with the heart of the Earth. . . . Take several Heart Breaths that way.

As you stand there, connected and aligned to the Earth with the palms of your hands and through your heart and your breath, you feel a light touch, as though someone just came up behind you and lightly took hold of your elbows. Almost immediately, you will begin to feel a force of energy pulling your left hand away from the symbol of the

Earth (the tree or globe), though your hand will not actually move. Be with this force and *feel* it as it travels up your left arm. If it seems like the energy is getting stuck anywhere, take another deep conscious Heart Breath and relax, allowing your circuitry to open and receive this current. . . . After a short time, you will notice an opposite pull toward the Earth in front of you as the energy moves down your right arm and into the globe or tree. The pull may be strong enough that you feel your body beginning to twist, or it may be more subtle. What is important is that you stay present and observe the movement of the energy. If it gets stuck anywhere, breathe into that place to ensure that the channel stays open long enough to establish the electromagnetic current being activated for you.

Once the current is fully established and any erratic pulsing becomes stable and smooth, you can release your hold on the globe or tree, bring your hands together in the mudra of prayer, and offer gratitude to the intelligence that assisted you and to the allies that supported you with their presence.

Group Empowerment

As with many initiations, this one has additional power if done with numbers of people. It is ideal for one person who has already received this empowerment to stay to the side and give the instructions, checking to make sure everyone feels the energy as it moves through. If you are part of a group, circle, or gathering, follow these instructions:

Start in a circle and breathe the Heart Breath together, feeding your heart flames with love and feeling the connection as your flames unite. Continue to pour love on your flame and breathe the power and intelligence of Earth and Sky, directing the love to the center.

As your heart flames unite, and your collective glow becomes brighter, invoke Thoth into the center of your circle using your out-breaths as offerings. When he comes into focus in the center, ask him to assist with this empowerment. . . .

Once you become aware of Thoth's presence, and he has agreed to assist, create a line of people facing south. The first person in line places his or her hands on the trunk of the tree (or holds the globe if that is what you are using) at elbow height. Each person then takes hold of the elbows of the person in front, as though you were creating a train. . . .

Thoth takes the last place in line. Once again, breathe the Heart Breath and reconnect with your unified heart flame. . . .

Everyone will begin to feel the pull on their left side, the energy moving into their hand and up their arm. It is as if someone flipped a switch and the circuit turned on. . . . As the current moves up everyone's left arm, there might be a noticeable pull to the left as the energy current is established, and then a surge as it moves around and back toward the tree (or globe) through the right arm and hand.

Although it happens instantly, it might take a minute or two before everyone connects to the current. In the unlikely event that someone has a blockage and cannot feel the energy passing through, the person officiating need only move his or her hands (without touching) up or down the arm that is blocked, and it will open.

To reiterate: The amount of energy that moves through a group is exponentially greater than that of an individual. Blockages in any one person in the group are, therefore, usually overwhelmed by the flow.

10
Sound

Sound is an important element in healing, because it has different wavelengths, each of which affects the cells and organs of the body differently. The following journey involves a purification through sound. It involves a general housecleaning effort, while it allows you to retune your internal flute—your *Sushumna* canal, which travels up the spinal column—purifying this sacred, central canal through sound.

Now that you have enough experience of this work to recognize its potential, the time has come to develop your vessel. Most of us can physically handle a much higher volume of energy than what typically moves through us, providing our vessel is prepared. This exercise is designed to create more space, a larger channel, through which a much stronger current of the universal life force can flow.

CLEANSING THE CHAKRAS WITH SOUND

Chakra is a Sanskrit word that refers to the energy centers, often depicted as spinning wheels or discs, that reside in the subtle body along the Sushumna canal from the base of the spine to the top of the head, and above it. The universal life force, whose many names include *kundalini, prana,* and *chi,* moves up through the three channels, the Sushumna, the *ida,* and the *pingala,* to carry energy throughout the system. In some schools of thought, the chakras are also seen as openings through which we connect to the energies of various elements and dimensions. Most traditions count seven of them in the body and may include one or two above, although some have more above and below, and some include chakras in the palms of the hands and the soles of the feet. When our chakras are clear and functioning in harmony, we have more and clearer energy moving through us than when our energy centers are blocked, for whatever reason.

For the purposes of this exercise, we are working only with the first five centers. Each chakra has a unique shape as well as a variety of tones that emanate from it as we do this work. Because of the correspondence between chakras and the elements, and because certain issues are associated with specific elements (see chapter 10 in *Alchemical Healing*: "The Elements") each chakra will also have its own types of blockages or disruptions that limit the flow of energy, based in the person's life experience. During this exercise, be sure to notice the colors that you perceive at each center, and watch for how the colors shift as the tones change.

Over time, and through the natural course of life, the Sushumna canal and chakra entry points develop buildup, much as our arteries do, or the plumbing in our homes. This buildup can appear as crustiness or sludge. In this exercise, the vibration transmitted though your silent or vocal toning will break up the accrued grime and disperse it. Both silent toning and toning with your vocal chords have their strengths and purposes. Notice how powerful and focused the internalized silent tone can be as you seek out that perfect timbre that resonates exactly with the spot you are working with. Also notice how the tone can be held and amplified, even modulated, regardless of your breath. When you purse your lips and tone out loud, notice how your surroundings affect and, in some cases, empower certain tones (we all sound better in the shower). It is quite satisfying when the perfect tone is found and held, and you can actually feel the part you are working on vibrate. It also may be too intense to begin the cleansing with auditory sound.

Start your search for the right tone for each chakra internally and let the flow get started before blasting it with the power of your pipes.

This is a vibratory cleaning, like ultrasound that shakes loose the debris and carries it away.

For various reasons, some of what you find might not lift off during the exercise, and some of what does leave might return. We advise you to return to this practice periodically until the entire chakra system is clear. After that, only occasional maintenance is required to keep it that way.

When you first engage in this exercise, the lower three chakras will convey considerable information about your history and help explain your responses to life. The first chakra center at the base of your spine is associated with the earth element. Residue you find in the root chakra is often related to issues of survival, fight-or-flight responses, the capacity to fulfill your basic needs, and the basic structures in which you conduct your life, including your physical body. The second chakra is associated with the element of water and the reproductive system. Emotional and sexual issues and all that relates to reproduction and children often register in this center. The third chakra is associated with fire, along with identity and personal power. As you move through these lower centers, cleansing and clearing any residual debris, you might notice memories coming up about the specific incidents that caused the energy blockage at hand.

The heart center, the fourth chakra, relates to issues around love and your most intimate and family relationships. You will probably spend more time at this center than in the others, clearing in accordance with your heart's desire those no-longer-required furnishings that have lodged here. The higher in the structure you go, the more identifiable the blockages become. Although you may recall the specific incidents to which they relate, you need not dwell on them. Often there is more work here than can be done in one sitting. Just focus on releasing and return often until there is nothing left to release.

As you will see, everything changes at the fifth chakra center, for this, the throat chakra, is the shamanic doorway where we move from a state of individuated consciousness to the higher centers where we join with the collective. This exercise does not apply to the chakras above the fifth.

Kundalini is a Sanskrit word for the natural reserve of energy coiled at the base of the spine like the serpent that is most often used to represent it. There are many practices designed to develop the ability to utilize this energy as a resource. But when kundalini rises unbidden, in a person unaccustomed to such power, it can be a frightening—or at least startling—experience. Be forewarned that once you have cleared your chakras in this sound initiation, the likelihood of spontaneous awakening of kundalini is increased. In any case, a higher volume of energy will become your norm after this cleansing, and you will be able to handle unexpected increases.*

Once you have opened the flow of energy through your spine, the Sushumna canal itself dilates. The ideal is to practice until you have dilated the entire length of the canal, so that the flow of energy is consistant between your lower and upper chakras.

By expanding the column and keeping it functioning at its full potential, you further yourself along this path of awareness. As you become more comfortable with this practice, you will connect easily with the specific resonance of each chamber. The energy you liberate will not go in just one direction, as when you play a flute, but will resonate with everything around it. Your whole chakra system will reverberate with the limitless potential of electric energy.

Your maintenance program will be unique to you. The logistics are variable for each person—you will know what and how much you need. Think of each return trip as an opportunity to go back and clean up whatever is still left from the past, opening the way for a brighter, more powerful future.

---

*If the concept of *kundalini* is new to you, I highly recommend that you connect with cobra through my earlier book, *Power Animal Meditations*. In it there is a journey to awaken kundalini, which also appears in the journey CD *Awakening the Cobra*. In *Alchemical Healing*, one of the most important rites of passage is the Caduceus initiation, which gives more advanced techniques for working with the kundalini, and which takes your relationship with cobra to a deeper level. Although cobra as a totem ally is very powerful medicine, it is certainly not required for the work of Planetary Healing. However, the development of your capacity to work with and manage your kundalini energy will significantly impact not just this work, but also your life.

JOURNEY

Cleanse and Tune the Chakras with Sound

Take time to ground and center yourself using the Heart Breath in order to be in balanced connectivity with Spirit. . . .

As the radiant glow from your Heart Breath illuminates your inner landscape, picture a structure, tall and narrow, like a free-standing elevator shaft that disappears into a haze about three stories up. There are large round openings at each level that face each of the four directions; it looks vaguely like a traffic light. Each level is one of your chakras. The one you are walking to at the bottom of the column is your first chakra center . . .

Walk or squeeze in through one of the portals. The ease with which you can enter is determined by how much buildup has occurred in your life. Take a moment to relax and take it all in . . . This is your first chakra and the root of the entire chakra system . . . Look up and you will see a fifth portal that leads to your second chakra, above you.

The solid structure can be hidden by various substances of different textures, thicknesses, densities, and degrees of dampness. You might experience a growing urge to clean the place out, to make it shine . . . Now start toning and see what happens . . .

Begin experimenting with tones, silently. The chamber is so resonant that as you slide through the scale in your mind with intent, you will find a tone that resonates with the chamber. Maintain respect as you go through the spectrum of sound. Pay attention. Start with the shape of the lower notes and, with reverence, approach the right tone. Notice how physical alterations to your mouth, throat, and nasal cavities can influence your silent tone. You might feel emotional surges. When you hit the right tone and achieve resonance, notice how the walls and portals quiver and how the build-up loosens and is carried away with the sound. Notice how subtle changes in the delivery of your tone—breezier or sharper or louder—work on the different materials of which the buildup is comprised. Some of the stuff dissolves into a mist that flies out the four portals while another type of accumulated mass breaks up into chunks that need a little extra push. . . .

If you wish to incorporate audible toning, now is a good time to begin. Start with low tones and move up slowly and, again, with reverence. . . . As before, explore the effects of subtle changes to the quality of your tones. You are a complex musical instrument; the shape of your mouth, the location of your jaw, the depth of breath and how you release it are just some of the ways you can find the tone that works best for that chakra and the substance you wish to expel.

[*Long pause.*]

Step back and admire your work: the clean shimmering walls, any changes in color, the light, the unobstructed openings of the portals. If there is more work to do at this first center, relax and know you can always return.

Step outside your first chakra. See how bright it is now compared to the second. You can barely see the third chakra in the gloom above. Levitate to a second chakra portal and enter. Again, find the inner tone that resonates with this chamber. Again, practice with various tones and with altering the shape of your mouth as you emit the tones, noticing the variety of effects that result. The buildups in this chamber are usually quite different from those in the first chakra. As they are dissolved, memories and emotions may surface. . . . [*Long pause.*]

Experiment with moving through the large floating portals between the chakras. First, try the passage between the second and first chakras and clear it of any remaining blockages, using what you have learned with the silent sounds. . . . Then return to the second chakra. There are qualities to the materials you are cleaning out that are chakra specific. The densest and heaviest were at the foundation of this structure, for that is the nature of the first chakra and the issues from your life that are found there.

From the already-cleared second chakra, you might be able to move straight up into the third, clearing any blockages by toning as you go. Float through the glowing portal.

This exercise is much like spring-cleaning, especially the first time you do it. Unless you have practiced chakra-clearing methods from other disciplines, there may be quite a lot of buildup. Allow yourself to cherish the last moments these blockages are in place. Acknowledge that these are fantastic structures you created. They were perfect, maybe even essential at one time in your life, but they no longer serve you, and it is time to let them go. If you find yourself feeling a little protective of some area, honor that feeling, especially for those places that take on identity; you will know why some of these things are here.... [*Long pause.*]

As you complete your work in the third chakra, notice how much more room and light there is in the chamber. Take a final tour noticing how bright and wonderful it is when it is clean....

You are now ready to move on to the fourth chamber. Because this is the heart center, you will spend more time there and take great care. As you begin rising toward the fourth chakra, take a moment and look back through the canal to see how bright and clean your first three chakras are. Then, it is time to move on to the heart center. Remember to clear the transitional space of the portal as you pass through it.... Pay attention to your feelings as you enter the realm of your heart. Notice how comfortably cluttered the room in your fourth chakra may appear. It is time to honor and release the poignant memories that you are ready to let go of. Take your time finding just the right tone, for this is the most sacred center; it contains the altar that holds your eternal heart flame. Be still with this tone once you find it.... [*Long pause.*]

When you have completed your work and cleared the heart

center, continue to use your tones as you pass upward into your throat chakra, and the canal will respond and make way.... [*Long pause.*]

The fifth chakra is quite different. Each portal here has a membrane stretched over it like a drum skin. Sometimes there are openings, as if the faces of these membranes had been torn or scarred.

As you enter the fifth chakra center, you become aware of light pouring into your throat from the four directions. Listen carefully, for there is a tone that is being projected from the spirit world. When the tone intersects with the light, you feel a vibration in your throat, and the throat chakra opens. To find and contribute to this tone is as easy as matching or harmonizing with it, and the results are immediate; all the gunk that has collected is transmuted instantly. All tears, scars, and slits on the faces of the membrane are healed. The reverberation created by the intersection of the sound and the light is strong, like an inner storm that resonates throughout your being. The vibration resonates around the entire throat structure, as the light shines in from all four directions. The moment the tone is past the point of harmony, the process is complete.

Because of the harmonic of the tone and light, the four membranes in the portals of this chakra have transformed into crystalline lenses. A beacon of light now fills the entire chamber and shines beyond it. If you choose to pass through the upper portal and venture to the inner skull where your individual energy joins with the collective, the light within your fifth chakra is bright enough that you can always use it to find your way back.

It is a good idea to take some silent alone time after you do this work. You may want to journal about the experience while it is fresh.

After the Exercise

The fifth chakra is itself a portal to move from your individual perspective to the perspective where you recognize your connection with all. This chakra is the universal entry into universal oneness.

If you think of your chakra system as a musical instrument, you will realize the importance of maintenance. The cleanliness of the entire mechanism, including the channels between the charkas, affects the quality of the harmony of the instrument as a whole. Each time you practice this meditation, you will enlarge and strengthen your capacity for energy, light, and sound. As the structure is cleansed and cleared and comes alive with sound, it glows so brightly that you can hardly see it anymore. The force that you generate makes all the chambers glow brightest when you have completed the sequential toning at each chakra and are generating the light and sound through the entire structure simultaneously. You will notice that the light in the first four chakras is more diffuse, while the fifth beams brightly. When you maintain your chakra system through this practice, the quality of energy that you can offer in your other practices is obviously improved in volume and clarity. Being at your clearest and brightest, you will have so much more to offer.

11
Bat

There is a cave on the big island of Hawaii that is a power place for me. It was there, around Thanksgiving of 1980, that I went to determine the next direction in the course of my life. It was a solitary, sacramental journey, at a time when I knew that my current longtime relationship was coming to an end. Rock and I had been vacationing with our children on the big island when it became evident that our time together was over. He went home to Marin County, and the children followed a few days later, giving me some days alone to grieve and clear my head.

I set out with the help of my good friend Robert to find guidance for what was next for my two daughters and me. He took me to Waipi'o Valley, which back then was quite sparsely inhabited—I believe only seven families lived there at the time. This place will always be very difficult to get to, requiring four-wheel drive to navigate the incredibly steep road down to the valley floor. Robert's friends welcomed me there and made themselves available to provide support for me and hold space while I went on my adventure. They directed me as to where to walk to find the King's Trail and how to follow it to the beach. Many waterfalls tumbled from the sheer cliffs that surrounded the valley. It was beside a small, exquisite pool at the base of one of these falls that I set my intentions, honored the ancestors of the valley, and offered my prayers. I then walked in a leisurely way, following the lush pathway to the sea, through the most sumptuous tropical landscape I had ever seen.

The tide was low enough for me to round the bend in the cliff and find the cave. I had no idea as I entered that I would spend several hours in the company of bats, as I grieved for my lost relationship and came to grips with the fact that I was about to become a single mom, with no job and no prospects.

Once I entered the cave, I focused inward to deal with my new reality. It was a deep and emotional experience. Bat became the witness to my transformation. The creatures stirred when I entered the cave; they listened to my lament; perhaps they even assisted as I came to resolution. In time, my direction became clear: I was to move with my daughters to Eugene, Oregon, and there I would receive the guidance I needed to find my means of support. I knew that I would find a teacher to help me understand what it would be to become a healer. I could feel the bats' attention as I walked, shoulders square, head held high, out of the cave and into the sunlight.

After I worked through my personal needs, I was ready to rejoin Robert and his son and our host family, who had brought their kids and horses down to the beach. This was a lengthy, slightly curved stretch of sand, flanked at each end by the sheer cliffs and broken by a river pouring into the sea about halfway across. The entire length of beach was empty except for our friends and their horses. Despite my sorrow, I could not miss the spectacular beauty and ever-present magic that permeated the rest of this enchanted day. I was able to enjoy a rare treat: riding bareback, naked in the surf, on a horse that loved the ocean. We returned to the Kona coast to spend Thanksgiving with other friends before I returned to Marin County. I had moved to Eugene by the end of January.

When I was preparing to present a journey as part of the World Peace Prayer at the EarthDance festival in 2009, I was directed to go to the bat cave once again. Our schedule did not allow for a trip to Hawaii that summer, so Mark and I created a ceremony in our garden, dedicated to a trip to the cave in spirit. It was a beautiful moonless night. The plants in the garden shimmered under the starlight, vibrant and alive. We drank in the heady fragrance of nicotiana and brugmansia—staggeringly sweet and delicious, and nearly overwhelming.

We were lying on a bed that Mark had made down by the pond, snuggled in a soft duvet with down pillows so that we could gaze upward at the stars. When bats flew by overhead, we knew that we were there, and soon felt the familiar cave closing in around us. The journey that follows was extrapolated from my best recollection of what happened that night, although my possession by the bats was an experience unto itself that is difficult to describe.

Bat has many attributes, however for our purposes here, think of bat as an ally that has come forward to help us create peace on the planet. When I led this journey at EarthDance, I was struck by the fact we were using the energy of thousands of people; therefore, when the bats swarmed out, they connected us with all the other festivals associated with EarthDance—about three hundred simultaneous events that year.

Even if you take this journey alone, you will feel the connection because you will become awash with the energy from the bats in your cave, and this pulls you into a larger cohesive force. As you continue to explore the vibration and get to know yourself from this perspective, you may discover many subterranean routes that exist among caves all over the planet. This can be useful in moving around the planet in a powerful yet hidden way. It is in experiencing yourself as a bat that you truly come to know the power of these phenomenal creatures. This is a medicine that you will carry from this point forward.

Just as bats hold space for the dream that we are living while they hang upside down during the day, you can experience yourself holding space for the dream of the new world we are becoming. Doing so will show you how your soul journey fits into the greater journey of our transforming world. There is also the possibility of receiving your bat name during this journey.

If you do not have a group of people or circle to work with directly, take advantage of the relative modern ease in connecting with others through technology. Try getting at least ten people together through phone or Skype and practice this journey as a vehicle for Planetary Healing. You can work together for personal healing as well. When we join forces with others, we exercise our potential to expand and accelerate our power. In making music, a higher vibrational resonance is achieved when one string interacts with another. The more strings you play together, the higher the vibration and resonance, and the greater the musical effect.

This is a rite of renewal and rebirth for the soul. It brings healing, resonance, and coherence, for the individual, the group, and the planet alike. We believe that even a small circle of people practicing this journey can have a massive effect.

Bat naturally follows the chakra cleansing and sound initiation so that, fresh from the clearing of your Sushumna canal, you have the opportunity to work with the new volume of energy now accessible to you. Once you have experienced directing this greater energy through your work with bat, you have entered a higher level in your Planetary Healing work.

It is very important to remember, during the bat journey, to be conscious of your thoughts and motivations, because your focus amplifies your personal impact in the universe. In the greater scheme of things, your thoughts and actions affect one another and you are ultimately responsible for both.

Bats are highly social and live in large communities. They spend their days in the darkness of caves or under the bark of trees waiting for dusk, when they come out to eat and socialize. They are the only mammals that have the gift of true flight. But unlike the other species, it is the bat's mastery of sound and echolocation that brings order out of chaos. Whether it is for working together during a hunt or for storming out of a cave at dusk, bats are continuously aware of each other. As each bat contributes to the cacophony, location and landscape become clearer for all.

In the shamanic world, bats are associated with the Shaman's Death. This is not the death of the physical body, but rather the death of old fears, of the ego's control, of outdated belief systems. As they function primarily in the dark, bats are able to navigate through the unseen worlds with ease, thus being excellent guides to help us move through the unknown or unseen. Probably because of this, they do elicit fear and superstition in some cultures and belief systems.

JOURNEY

Bat

Begin by grounding and centering. . . . Practice the Heart Breath. . . . As you continue to breathe in this way, feel the radiance extend from your heart flame. Connect to that familiar feeling of universal love and feel yourself align with it. Within the glow of your eternal heart flame, you begin to see a landscape with an opening to a cave nearby. You enter this place and approach the cave. Familiarize yourself with the lay of the land and look for clues that would explain the shape and formation of this cave. Scuff the floor with your foot; make clicking sounds with your tongue. The sounds you make as you enter the darkness will tell you important things about this cave: for example, a small, intimate cave will sound different from a large, cavernous one.

As your hearing becomes more acute, you become aware of something else sharing this space. Your eyes take time to acclimate before they become useful in the gloom; use them to follow the sound up to the ceiling of the cave, which is crowded with bats. They are mostly at rest, although some are fidgeting. One in particular captures your attention. . . . You might feel a jolt as you connect with this one bat, and suddenly details of the cave, large and small, are very obvious to you. Along with the jolt, all the bats take flight and the cave is filled with their leathery wings, high energy, and the high-pitched sound that the bats are emitting. Every sound adds to your ability to "see": the sound itself seems visible. . . .

Your throat chakra, the shamanic portal into the collective mind, begins to activate in the melee. You can feel it grow and open while something inside it tries to find the resonating pitch. The moment your inner tone and your voice blend and contribute to the song of the bats, your senses become altered and you are no longer just in this cave. Your awareness includes all caves, and the passages that connect them. These underground openings permeate the crust of the Earth. The connections between the underworld caverns become clear and obvious, though some are as small as the gap under a door. As the mapping of Earth's underworld becomes complete, your ever-expanding frequency fills the voids within the Earth. Allow your compassion and deep reverence for the Earth and for all beings and creatures of the Earth to come to the fore of your consciousness. Bat awakens these powerful frequencies within you. As you feel the energy increase, follow it: it will lead you to all the places on the planet where others are gathered in celebration or wherever two or more people are gathered in prayer for peace on Earth. . . .

Notice how the frequency now emanates from you—from your hands and from all over your skin, from your throat and from the top of your head. It is secreted from your glands and radiates from your chakras. You are experiencing another cleansing and purification, at a deep level. You feel a rush of energy throughout your body. As the bat, you lift your arms and feel the energy move through you, up your arms and out your hands. Focus that energy to reach out and touch at least two people who are with you or to whom you would like to pass this energy long-distance. . . .

There is so much energy moving through you at this time, you can direct it through your hands to any place or situation on the planet in need of renewal or healing. [*Long pause.*]

When you feel complete with the empowerment and the healing you have accomplished for this moment in time, return to the cave where you started your journey. . . . Thank the bats for the activation and teachings you were given. . . .

As you leave the cave, you will recognize where you are, and easily find your way back into your physical body. . . . Use the Earth Breath to assist in your grounding . . . When you feel fully grounded and centered, write in your journal and capture the details of this experience.

12
Air Pollution and Adaptation

When I was dealing with breast cancer back in 1992, it occurred to me that we humans are in a "mutate or die" situation. We have created so much toxicity on our planet that it is literally poisoning us, and we do not have time for the slow process of evolution to create systems within our bodies to deal with the pollution we have created. This toxicity is surfacing in diseases such as cancer, lupus, and any number of autoimmune disorders, allergies, and lung problems, including asthma and emphysema. We need to adapt to what we have created in order to buy the time we need to reclaim our position as responsible stewards of this Garden of Eden, planet Earth.

Once I got to the other side of cancer, I wished I were able to have more children so that I could pass on the mutation. As I pondered this, I came to realize that there are many ways to influence our capacity for faster, even spontaneous, evolution (see "Bruce Lipton, Ph.D., and Epigenetics" in chapter 18). The arts, when infused with intelligence and emotion—whether as visual art, music, theater, or storytelling, to name a few—have tremendous power to inform the body. Healing modalities such as Alchemical Healing and hypnotherapy can also effect deep change and transformation.

Our subconscious mind does not distinguish reality from a lucid dream, a vision, imagination, or guided visualization. The more inner senses we bring to such experiences the more the subconscious mind receives it and informs the physical body accordingly, and the physical body responds by making the corresponding changes. This is how many of the techniques in Alchemical Healing work, especially those that deal with power animal, plant, or spirit allies: the more vivid your experience, the stronger the impact on your energetic and physical being, and the greater the possibility that lasting transformation will occur.

Our human bodies have approximately fifty trillion cells, all working together to function according to our needs and desires. Each cell comprises a universe in itself, surrounded by a membrane that allows or disallows exchange. The Earth is like a cell in the vast universe, with its own surrounding membrane.

SCARAB SHIELD

In this next piece of work, we connect with the Earth's surrounding membrane by taking on the form of the scarab beetle known as Khepera in the Egyptian pantheon.

In Egypt, the god Khepera* is associated with the morning sun that brings warmth and light following the dark, mysterious night. He appears as a scarab beetle, rolling his larvae in a dung ball in front of him. In the illustrations of him in *Shamanic Mysteries of Egypt* and *The Anubis Oracle* deck, while Khepera seems to be holding the Earth, he is actually wrapped around it, much as the atmosphere or ozone layer surrounds and protects us. He has the role of planetary guardian.

As you work with Khepera and absorb his perspective, you may start to perceive the orbits of planets, or certain cosmic, planetary, or individual cycles. You may access knowledge to forecast world

---

*See *Shamanic Mysteries of Egypt* by Nicki Scully and Linda Star Wolf (Rochester, Vt.: Bear & Company, 2007), 92–99.

events or your own internal events. You may also glimpse the way he interfaces with various forms of evolved intelligence that surround and watch over our planet, such as angels and seraphim; the way he monitors the heavenly bodies and what approaches the Earth from the far reaches of the universe; and the way he mitigates the relationships and alignments among planets and stars, and how they impact the Earth.

Khepera also helps us to filter the toxins, pollutants, and radiation bombarding us. Not only does he function as a planetary shield, but also his intercession aids individuals and supports our healing at a deep level. In turn, we carry that healing out into the world. The scarab journey allows us to take on Khepera's protective shield, and has many functions in healing the planet, ourselves, and others. As with the Air Force work, we suggest that you share this process as much and as fast as possible, for it is greatly needed.

The following journey and gift of the shield came to us in two parts. The first part came as we were preparing for a Planetary Healing phone bridge, not long after *Shamanic Mysteries of Egypt* was published. Through Mark, Khepera offered a journey to help us become more intelligent about what we allow into our bodies and what we choose to filter out.

Years later, in August of 2010, as I was preparing to present at the twenty-third annual New England Women's Herbal Conference, I asked Mark what I should be offering the students at my intensive. Khepera appeared to Mark at once revealing images of me working on people with asthma, allergies, and environmental sensitivities, mostly sourced from air pollution and related toxicity. I had a hard time fitting this possibility into the program I had conceived that involved blending Alchemical Healing with the Egyptian Mysteries; after some thought, I decided to ignore Mark's suggestion. On the day of the class, I brought my Anubis Oracle cards to the classroom with the intention of using them to see what wanted to come forth. I laid them face down in a circle and invited each woman present to pick the one that called to her. I was immediately attracted to a particular card, and watched with interest to see who would pick it. When the last woman had retrieved her card, there were only five left, including the one that was calling me. I turned it over and—you guessed it—it was Khepera. Mark had been right! This was confirmed very quickly as our initial introductions revealed that the group was loaded with health challenges that would respond well to Khepera's filter. I obviously needed to bring in a journey to help us all heal from pollution.

As our immune systems strengthen from working with Khepera, we can adapt so that we do not get sick from other hazards, including Earth-based pollutants and toxins such as heavy metals and chemical by-products. All metals originate from stardust, along with all that came into existence since the big bang. Khepera's shield works in both directions, mitigating the energies from above and below: radiation, other toxic particles coming in from beyond our atmosphere, any pollution within the atmosphere, and that which emanates up from the Earth.

Regulation of our exposure to these elements and certain of the radiations can buy us time while we are in the process of transmutation and the slower process of evolution. Meanwhile, by carefully allowing absorption of some elements and radiations (while remembering that there are many kinds of radiation, and some of them are deadly), we can hasten the process of evolution while protecting and strengthening individuals and entire populations.

During our work with Khepera some of the students reported that the filter he provides helped mitigate negative energy they were dealing with and also had a positive effect on their emotional stability.

A strong component of this shield is its function as a macrocosmic permeable membrane, which invites or prevents an exchange of energies and information. You will find your work to be more effective as you learn how to retrieve the information the shield lets in.

You may also notice that whereas the Beacon journey called your attention to your power place in the Air, this journey creates an altar, or power place within the Earth.

JOURNEY

Scarab Shield

Begin with the Heart Breath, taking the time to breathe deeply of the intelligence and power of Earth and Sky . . . As you draw in the energies from the Earth and Sky, look for the evidence of a protective shield that has always been in place, sheltering us from some of the more extreme, overwhelming energies. . . . It takes the shape of Khepera within the glow of your heart flame, as the colors of the dawn appear and he rises, his gossamer wings surrounding and enfolding the Earth . . .

Everyone has a power place with fond memories on this Earth, a place they went to often when they were young or the site of some unique and memorable event. Go to this place now . . .

Lie down and feel yourself absorbed into the Earth, into whatever that spot holds—grasses or mosses or sand, or even rock. There, for a moment, the surface takes your shape, and then settles back down to its prior form . . .

Feel yourself spreading into the Earth, spreading throughout the entirety of this Earth. Feel the heat of the core, the tug of gravity, the distinction between the side facing the sun's warmth and the cooler side facing away from the sun. Feel the pull of the moon. You are the Earth. You feel the sloshing of the oceans, the sands of Egypt, and the rivers that flow over your body . . .

Now turn your attention outward to notice the emanations that reach Earth from other heavenly bodies, especially those in our solar system . . . Feel these energies penetrate your atmosphere. There is a magnetic field radiating out from your core that reaches into space, gently parting the hard radiation carried by the solar winds, guiding it safely past you. Your atmosphere, wrapped in a thin layer of ozone, also shields you from most of the sun's other emanations, as well as from the cosmic rays and most of the rocks from space that have found their way to this corner of the universe. Become the atmosphere that surrounds the Earth . . . Feel yourself gradually take the shape of a scarab whose unfurled wings envelop the whole of the Earth and are what the atmosphere is made of . . . As you become the scarab, wrapped around the planet, notice how the incoming emissions are filtered through your body on their way to Earth. As Khepera, you allow only enough radiation to pass through to feed the plants and warm the surface and air . . .

Find joy in this experience. Feel yourself basking in the sun while cradling the spinning Earth. . . . [*Long pause.*]

As you commune with Khepera in this way, become aware that each individual in the mass of humanity is being uniquely affected by our heavenly compatriots—planets, stars, angels, seraphim, and other celestial beings and bodies that are constantly influencing us all. In your scarab form, as Khepera, feel yourself organizing and filtering these energies. Each person's relationship with the heavenly bodies integrates into your nervous system. Feel in your own being the complex web of humanity that encompasses the Earth herself. [*Long pause.*]

Extend your attention from the inhabitants of this Earth out to the more etheric citizens, the angels and seraphim and other intelligence throughout the firmament. Notice how they direct energy to and interact with the people of the Earth in accordance with the cycles we are moving through and the requirements of the moment. . . . [*Pause.*]

Come back to the unique blend of energies and influences allowed through for each person and follow the current that is yours alone . . . Follow the flow back to your personal self and wrap your luminous wings around yourself . . .

As you reenter yourself, feel the embrace of Khepera and the gifts you retain from your journey. The gossamer atmosphere folds under the scarab shell that becomes your robe and the beetle's antennae become your headpiece. You are now dressed in the scarab cloak of

Khepera, which surrounds and crystallizes around you, like a semipermeable membrane. All the openings shut down momentarily while you take pause, go within, and determine which parts you want to open and close . . . It is like wearing etheric chain mail that is very protective even though you can see through it. Your wings are like the wings of a dragonfly, made of a transparent fabric, strong yet flexible, with intricate webbing that enfolds and filters. Feel the protection of the scarab shield, the cloak that surrounds you. Notice its active filtering process. . . .

As you come to realize the cloak's attributes, it begins to integrate into your body . . . into your skin . . . into your field . . . becoming an extension of your nervous system. [*Long pause.*]

Listen now for a message from Khepera—perhaps he will give you instructions as to how and when you can use this shield, and for what other purposes. . . .

When you fully realize the cloak as part of you, you can expand your awareness once again to include all the living beings on the Earth. The fibers of the cloak continue to inform you; there are as many fibers as there are people on Earth. Allow yourself to perceive the emanations coming to us from above as well, and see the relationships among those above and those on Earth. . . .

The sun has now fully risen. It is a warm, lovely day. Thank Kephera for the shield and the new relationships that are available to you.

As you become comfortable with your new attributes and feel complete with this journey for now, focus on the Heart Breath, adding a few extra Earth Breaths as needed to help materialize your new sensory devices and to help you ground and return fully to your physical body.

Be sure to take some time to write in your journal. This will be very useful later on as you work more with Kephera.

Working with Khepera and his cloak offers us a unique opportunity to respond proactively to modern pollutants and natural phenomena. Next time you hear of a strong solar storm, shape-shift into Khepera and encompass the Earth with your cloak so that you can help filter the incoming ultraviolet rays. Among other things, this will help mitigate against skin cancer, which has been on the rise as the ozone thins.

The cloak is now part of you. Familiarize yourself with its functions; listen for information and let it teach you. When you choose to allow it to unfurl, to spread across land and sea and feel all of the heavenly influences . . . Let it teach you. . . .

It is important to unfurl it completely, occasionally, to embrace the entire Earth and allow the fibers to keep up with the new information that is continually changing. Your best teacher about the cloak will be the cloak itself.

13
Tackling Environmental Diseases

Environmental illness and various autoimmune diseases have reached a pandemic level in the world right now. The number of people suffering from environmental sensitivities is staggering.

My brother had serious asthma as a child, and his allergies have plagued him throughout his life, limiting the options of where he can live and travel. I often wonder about the connection between my parents' heavy smoking and my brother's asthma and allergies. According to the World Health Organization (WHO) website, "The causes of asthma are not completely understood. However, risk factors for developing asthma include inhaling asthma "triggers," such as allergens, tobacco smoke, and chemical irritants."

Smoking and secondhand smoke are two small ways that individuals pollute the air. Our exhaust systems, our aerosol spray cans, our decomposing synthetics and other toxic garbage—all contribute to the further poisoning of our atmosphere. Industrial waste compounds the problems; even if we were to establish effective worldwide regulations immediately, we could not instantly halt the impact of prior pollution on our bodies.

So much damage has been done to our immune systems that we are susceptible as never before to an ever-widening array of diseases. Many health issues that have recently shown up or radically increased—such as autism, Epstein-Barr, fibromyalgia, and a growing number of cancers—as yet have no identified causes. Could the new diseases be related to new pollutants, or to new levels of accrued toxins?

Some of the issues we are currently dealing with are the ramifications of altering our environment. Farming and mining practices send pollutants directly into our food chain and water supplies. Our bodies are habitually exposed to building materials and exotic pollutants from industrial and chemical wastes. Aboveground nuclear testing began at the end of World War II and continued until 1980. Certain radioactive isotopes are still floating around in the atmosphere and have lodged in the dust, rocks, and seawater. Radioactive material has always existed but used to be confined to its natural form. Now the demon that has been released will continue to wreak havoc for generations yet to come.

MUSHROOMS FOR HEAVY METALS AND ENVIRONMENTAL TOXINS

Mushrooms are Khepera's organic symbiotic partner. Whereas Khepera represents that which is above, outside, and surrounding our planet, mushrooms exist within the Earth. As above, so below.

Although I had heard of mycologist Paul Stamets's* work with the intelligence of fungi, I knew little about it until I heard him electrify an audience at the Oregon Country Fair with stories of his research. It was especially fascinating to hear how oyster mushrooms can literally transform a waste dump into useable organic matter. I was inspired to explore further, with an eye toward finding some ally that could help with the sort of environmental illness that I had been hearing more

---

*See www.fungi.com, and *Mycelium Running: How Mushrooms Can Help Save the World.*

and more about, such as chronic fatigue syndrome and other debilitating autoimmune disorders that kept people homebound. Some of my clients at the time were complaining that they could not use telephones or computers and seemed to have allergic reactions to plastics and even the walls in their own homes.

When I first received a call from Lawrie in December of 2006, she was undergoing allopathic as well as alternative treatments for non-Hodgkin's lymphoma. As a first responder in disaster recovery, she had been exposed to all manner of chemical soups. During our Alchemical Healing telephone session, I found myself calling on mushrooms to help detoxify her.

A species of mushrooms that grows in meadows responded to my call for that particular healing. I was subsequently never able to identify it. What I have found as I have continued to work with fungi is that the one with the right properties shows up. In this case, a particularly large one that was representative of the species offered its services. When it first appeared, Lawrie was able to perceive it clearly. This allowed her to make a connection with the intelligence of the mushroom from her heart. In response to her request for help dealing with the heavy metals in her system, they marched into her body—there were hundreds of them—carrying mops and buckets to aid them as they cleansed her liver and moved on to every part of her body. They seemed to have a great deal of endurance while continually absorbing the toxins from all her systems until they turned black and keeled over.

I was then guided to call on a Chinese twig that looked like the straw on a witch's raggedy old broom. Once in the body, the twigs gently expanded in every direction as they softened, like shredded wheat soaking in milk. They became bloated and spongy as they soaked up the by now liquified mushrooms. At this point, I had Lawrie stand under a warm waterfall, which rinsed the twigs and any remaining fungi and toxins out of her body and deep into the Earth.

Looking within her body, Lawrie could see that her liver had noticeably changed in its consistency and had returned to a healthy pink. As she thanked the mushrooms for their work, they reappeared, marching out of her liver and back up to her heart. They seemed to return from all parts of her body and exit through her heart, after which a door seemed to close there. They each left behind a small portion of mycelium, the threadlike network in the mushroom's submerged stem that enables the absorption of nutrients.

Right after this, we asked the spirit of the mushroom for another round. Those that appeared this time were much smaller than before. They went after tiny remaining shards of toxins, running up and down Lawrie's entire body to penetrate her cells.

To complete the session, we did a final cleansing with the Heart Breath, first directing the breath outward, and then focusing it on any place in the body that still felt heavy.

In a follow-up call with her recently, she was still in remission from her disease. She vividly remembered our work with mushrooms, as it had been quite profound for her at the time. She believed that it contributed to her healing, although no one can say for sure what factor or combination of factors was responsible.

JOURNEY
Mushroom

Fairy rings are natural occurrences of mushrooms growing in a circle in the forest, and sometimes in grass or rangelands. European folklore suggests that these circles attract fairies and can be used as portals or doorways. In the soil beneath each ring can be found a net of mycelium, the intelligent webwork that creates the outward manifestation of the circle. Mark and I were given an image of a fairy ring in a forest when this journey was gifted to us. Fairy rings are species-specific, but the image in our vision seemed to offer entrance to the entire fungi nation.

Start with feeding your heart flame and breathing the Heart

Breath, giving extra attention this time to the Earth aspect of the breathing exercise. . . .

Take a moment to tune in to and scan your physical body. Be sensitive to its state. . . . Breathe the Earth Breath and exhale with the intention of offering the power, love, and intelligence of your breath to the appropriate fungus that is willing to absorb the toxic wastes, heavy metals, or chemical poisons in your body.

In the light of your expanded heart flame, you will find yourself in a forest within a circle of huge old-growth trees—maybe cedars or redwood. . . .

Sit with your back against one of the trees. Ground and again breathe the Heart Breath, this time to add vitality to your inner landscape. Look around on the forest floor. At some point you will see, poking up from beneath the pine needles and other forest detritus, a single mushroom. . . . Connect with the mushroom and ask for its help.

This one mushroom represents the entire family of the species that has responded to your call. Share your breath with this mushroom; this will instigate the sharing of information as well. With every in-breath, you learn more—starting with something as simple and basic as the mushroom's smell and progressing to more complex thoughts and understanding as you draw in spores that convey information. The mushroom seems to bask in your exhalations. It visibly perks up with each warm, moist breath, while you, conversely, become more and more dreamy. Still basking in your breath, the mushroom gains knowledge from and about the toxins in your body and the effects they are having on you.

This exchange of information continues and refines until there is a shift: you wake with a start in the presence of the entire fungi nation. Fully conscious, you understand that there is an established hierarchy within the fungi nation and that they are conducting a meeting with the various parts of you and the toxins. With your awakening to this level of exchange comes a higher level of attention. You are wholly present; your subconscious mind and your High Self are equally aligned with this moment.

Listen carefully for the important information your various selves are sharing with the council. Gratefully receive any offers from different families of fungi who can tackle specific toxins or help you heal from them. Acknowledge the elders in the council. Your understanding and recognition of the various species and their unique gifts and intelligence will grow with time and practice.

Give your fullest attention to this communication for a little while. . . . At some point, one representative of a certain spectrum within the fungi nation returns your attention. The one-on-one bond grows. There is an understanding developing, with the promise of more to come. Look for how this bonding registers in your senses: Is there an actual taste associated with it? Can you identify a feeling in a particular organ? You might find that instructions come in the form of subtle desires—perhaps you will feel thirsty for fresh water, or you might feel an urge to take a nap on the earth under a pile of leaves. Pay close attention so that you can receive the directions that will invite more intimate communication with your new mushroom ally; this is the beginning of a long-term relationship and is an important key for your healing. Note that your relationship with this mushroom and the family it represents will be reciprocal. You will gain knowledge of the growth, reproduction, health, and various needs of this species. The mutual benefits of this alliance will reveal themselves further as you develop the relationship. You can always participate on a spiritual level with time and attention, but stay open: you may also find something you can contribute in the physical realm. . . .

Offer your gratitude to all those who helped you and gave you information. . . .

Commit to returning on occasion and being with this council.

Your sense of family now includes this ally and its family.

Ground and center yourself, using the Earth Breath to help you bring your focus back to your physical body and fully return....

Take the time you need to write details from your experience in your journal. They will provide important information as you further develop your relationship with the fungi nation.

14
The Consciousness of Water

One of my teachers, the late Nadia Eagles, used to speak with reverence of the unique intelligence of water. I had a difficult time understanding what she meant, yet always carried a sense of water as consciousness. Dr. Masaru Emoto's recent work, *Messages from Water,* indicates that water has memory as well. The patterns created by water molecules visually express the harmony or discord that the water has been subjected to. For example, tiny crystalline structures form in naturally occurring water (as opposed to purified municipality water) when words like love and gratitude are spoken to it. Conversely, crystals will not form in the presence of angry words.

So much of the planet is made up of water, and so much of our bodies are comprised of water, that an overview of its basic nature reveals considerable insight into our own nature. Water is fluid, reflective, cleansing. The element water governs the realm of emotions. Some of the human characteristics associated with it are sensitivity, reflectivity, receptivity, and nurturance. Even the basic nature of water is changeable; it can transform from solid to liquid to vapor. Although there are times when it appears to be still, the atoms of its molecules are in a constant state of motion.

Water is sensitive to outside stimulation, including temperature fluctuations, movement, or other exterior forces, like the pebble thrown in the pond. The relationship of each molecule to its neighbors follows a strict code of directives. There is nothing random about how water molecules respond to one another. The ever-changing patterns and waves give image to the forces moving through it.

The purpose of the water journey is to play with this sense of shared consciousness: being one, separating, and coming together again as one. The following meditation is meant to shift your vantage point. Think of it as a portal into another possible way of being. To experience it fully, you will need to relax your sense of self a bit. The idea is to melt into the oneness of the universe while at the same time maintaining a modicum of that driving individual force that has carried you your entire life. In other words, relinquish the role of observer and enter the stream as a full participant and co-creator.

JOURNEY

Water Initiation

Begin with the Heart Breath, giving considerable attention to connecting with the intelligence and power of Earth and Sky, and contributing love to your heart flame throughout. Reconnecting to the feeling of Universal Love also helps to prepare you for this journey . . .

In the radiance and glow of your Heart Flame, see yourself as water, as a number of collected water molecules. You are complex enough to embody feelings and memories, and yet small enough that all of your molecules can go through transitions together, moving as one when such moments arrive . . .

This finite number of water molecules also has the capacity to hold memories that span the eons that have witnessed the transitions of this planet. For great periods of time, you were in the form of ice. You may have been in an ice field creeping across continents, floating on the ocean, or lying on the surface of a lake. There were times when you were in the clouds, floating or racing above land and water. You know the thrill of precipitation, falling from the skies as rain or snow or hail. . . .

You are at peace with your current situation, floating near the surface of the ocean in a warm climate, just as you are at peace with your vague memories of every other moment in existence. Everything is and has been perfect. There is no emotional charge. Everything just is, including your memories. Rest with this knowing as you gently move with the lazy swells, up and down. . . . [*Pause.*]

Suddenly something jars your entire system. A great earthquake hundreds of miles away has sent a shock wave through the seas. You are instantly alert to certain sensations: The radiant sun has warmed the area you are in and the light is bright. You are now at the surface, as you have experienced so many times before, but this time there is an intensified awareness, an alertness to the events impacting you. . . .

You are now a thin layer on the surface of this area of the ocean, the warmth you stretch into excites your molecules; you feel the beginning of the transition from liquid to vapor. You, the collection of molecules that comprises your piece of water, is expanding and lifting into the air. While your chemical composition is still H_2O, you are now becoming one with the atmosphere you are rising into. Those molecules of water that you identified with now cover a much greater volume as you merge invisibly into the air. You can feel the air currents as you are slowly drawn upward, away from the sea. . . .

For a period of time, you take in the patterns of the swells beneath you. You have gained enough altitude to be able to see big events ensuing from that shock wave that awoke you. Water races out to sea and surges back, far into the land mass. . . . As you drift higher watching things settle down below, you start to take on a wispiness. You are becoming visible again as you enter the cooler climes of higher air. Take a moment to marvel at your new structure—that of a white, wispy cloud.... Others sharing this space join you as they, too, emerge from invisibility, and a large cloud begins to form ...

By now you have drifted far from the ocean. Events along the coast are behind you. You are high enough to see the textures and colors of the forest, fields, and mountains, but not the individual trees and plants and rocks of which they are made. But you know these trees, plants, and rocks intimately, for over the eons you have washed over the rocks, you have risen through plant stems, you have seeped through the soils and into the roots of the trees. Now, though, you float majestically overhead....

As you feel yourself slip back into that eternal rest, where everything that happens is perfect and holds no surprise, you have a moment to organize a wish—a wish for something beyond what nature would hand you. You are in a unique position right now, fully aware of your connection to every molecule of water that exists on this planet and elsewhere. Just as you are aware of them at this moment, they, too, are aware of you. Think about the wish you will make to send out to all the waters, mustering all your strength and focus. This chance is momentary and will soon fade away....

As your focus on this wish increases, agitated water molecules race past one another through the clouds. The friction builds an electric charge, causing an imbalance between the positive and negative.... Hold your focus on your wish as the cloud becomes more electric.... The growing charge suddenly explodes as a bolt of lightning and a clap of thunder, the shock wave coalesces your molecules into separate water droplets, and you find yourself raining from the sky. You have been here before, many times before....

The fall from the sky does not take long—it never does. This time you land in a body of fresh water....

Now begin to come back to yourself and imagine drinking this water, the molecules of water that were you; take them into your body. Feel yourself swallowing, and notice how this refreshes and nurtures you. Feel your body. Notice the miracle of your breath and your heartbeat. Keep coming back into your body and become aware of your surroundings. . . .

Offer your gratitude to all the elements, and especially the sacred water, without which there would be no body, and no life. . . .

Become fully grounded and centered, breathing the earth breath to help you connect more deeply with the material world once again before you open your eyes.

Be sure to write about your experience in your journal before the details slip away. . . .

15
Water Altars

We know the importance of water, and that life is absolutely dependent upon it. Yet does it occur to us, as we take our hot showers, turn on our dishwashers and washing machines, and water our lush lawns, that in many places in the world, access to water is limited? This scarcity comes not only from drought and the workings of nature, but also from events and situations that are human created. I believe that healing the waters is essential. By bringing purity and harmony into the waters of the world, we can make fundamental changes, perhaps even in the way the collective thinks and lives.

During the drive to my godson's wedding shortly following the harrowing events of September 11, I was very open and receptive to any process that would engender healing and sanity. We stopped on the way to visit my friend Kathryn Ravenwood, who lived in Seattle at the time. In her home, Kathryn had a room devoted to a water altar, which she tended every day. She shared with me her way of honoring water, and I will pass it on to you. I tweaked her system to make it my own and hope you will do the same.

If you take on this water altar, you are committing to honoring it and caring for it. I have done it for ten years so far.

To start your water altar, you can use any water that is available; however, I recommend that you make the gathering of that water as sacred and ceremonial as possible. You can create ritual at a nearby waterway, pond, or lake, or even consciously draw tap water with the intention of sanctifying it through your prayers. I recommend that you choose a special bowl, the vessel that will grace the altar.

As soon as I committed to keeping this altar, I knew the bowl that I would be using. It was a wedding gift, a clay vessel glazed on the inside and formed in the shape of a conch shell, with a capacity of about 1½ quarts. I keep it covered with an embroidered cloth on top to protect the water and to minimize evaporation. On top of the cloth I placed a starfish that I found on Orcas Island just before creating the altar. This altar sits on a high piece of furniture, thus allowing me to stand before it and offer energy to it through my hands when I make my prayers. My water altar is completely separate from my main altar, but they share the same room.

On the wall behind the water altar is a *thangka,* a sacred Tibetan painted tapestry with the image of Medicine Buddha, the guardian of the altar, who holds a vessel in one hand and a plant in the other. This

My water altar

Buddha has a mantra that I repeat each time I open my water altar, in order to invoke his presence. You can choose any guardian you like for your water altar, or none at all. I also have a painting, an illustration from *Power Animal Meditations,* hanging to the side that depicts the White Buffalo along with the Egyptian goddess Hathor holding the sacred Cauldron; this offers further guardianship and blessings to this altar.

Once, when I was in meditation and praying at this altar, I was given a song. Since then, I sing it to the altar whenever I am praying there, and when I offer the water back into the pond, the river, or wherever I go to change and renew it. The lyrics that came to me were: "I honor the sacred Altar. I honor the sacred Water. May it flow throughout the land. May it flow throughout the hearts of Man."

When you sit with your water altar and offer your prayers, you might receive a song of your own. You can ask for one.

Whenever I stand at my water altar, I breathe the Heart Breath and invoke Medicine Buddha, give thanks to him and to the White Buffalo and Hathor, and pray for the waters of the world. I breathe my prayers: that the waters flow clean and pure, and that all people and all plants and creatures have enough pure, clean water to drink. I pray for those places that are in drought, and those places that are in floods. I pray for the places where the waters have been fouled, and wherever there is pollution or danger of pollution. I send love and positive energy to the waters of the world, and I offer my breath and prayers with an open heart, in humility and gratitude for the waters of life, without which there would be no life. When I finish praying, I use a long crystal wand to stir the prayers into the water on my altar, which symbolizes all the Earth's waters. I ask that the prayers be multiplied ten thousand times.

Each month on the full moon or as near to it as possible, I exchange the water, offering the water in the altar to a lake, moving stream, river, pond with an outlet, or ocean. I sing and pray to it as I pour it in. I refill the water; usually from the place I pour the old water. If that is not appropriate, I draw the next month's water from the tap, knowing that my prayers and the sacredness of my care of this water will cleanse and transform any toxins.

When I travel, I often fill small bottles with water, and exchange it throughout my trip from any water sources available. I have had the privilege of collecting waters from many sacred places and waterways throughout the world, including the Nile, Ganges, Aare, and Amazon rivers, the Red Sea, and Lake Titicaca. If I know I will be visiting someone who keeps a water altar, I take along some of my water to share, and bring back some of theirs.

Often, when I am doing healing sessions by phone, I stand at my water altar and connect with the spirits of water and those that surround and uphold my altar, and utilize their energies in the healing work. There are times when I am distraught or upset, and I go to the water altar for solace and pray to the spirits of water for help. Water is a very strong conductor for the energies that we generate with and transmit from our hands. When I am working with the water altar, I almost always have my hands placed around the altar vessel, and I turn on the energy and let it run through my hands. Breathing the Heart Breath allows me to increase the frequencies transmitted and to deepen my connection with the water. You will also find that you receive wisdom and guidance while in the presence of your water altar.

There are a number of practices in this book that will further open your hands for transmitting energy. If your palms do not turn on and tingle when you put them on your water altar bowl, take several deep and conscious Heart Breaths; then place your attention on your hands as you inhale, and exhale through your hands and into the water altar. That will get the energy flowing. It will flow freely into your altar from then on. If at anytime it does not feel strong enough, repeat the process.

At the time Raven introduced me to the practice of keeping a water altar, she suggested I work with and empower my altar for a full year before passing the teachings on to others. As you take this into consideration while working with your own altar, we now believe that as soon as you are comfortable with your water altar and feel you understand how it works, you can share the process freely and often with other people. You can always refer people to this chapter in order to help them get started. You can use some of your water to seed their altar.

The waters of the Earth need our prayers. Please offer them liberally.

16
Tribal Alchemy's Journey for Peace

I was asked to help commemorate the bombings of Hiroshima and Nagasaki at a fifty-year anniversary event that was happening in Eugene. The following journey for peace was written specifically for that ceremony, and later edited to bring it more up to date for what was happening at the time I recorded the CD *Tribal Alchemy** in 1998. It was our intention to inspire listeners to vision solutions for the suffering caused by hatred and war. Unfortunately, although some of the stages have changed, the words still apply. According to Ploughshares' Armed Conflict Reports 2010 Summary, "our planet hosted a total of 92 wars during the last 23 years." There were 28 armed conflicts being tracked in 2009 alone; no doubt there are many more at this writing, especially given the massive uprisings currently occurring in the Middle East and Africa as this book enters its final editing phase.

Please be alerted that the instructions in this journey describe graphic images of the horrors of war.

---

*Tribal Alchemy contains three journeys, visioned by Mark and written and narrated by me and produced with music created by Roland Barker and the Tribal Alchemy band.

JOURNEY

For Peace

Ground and center. Focus on your heart and find the flame that dwells within. Feed your heart flame with love. Breathe the Heart Breath, invoke the power, love, and intelligence of Earth and Sky, and notice how your heart flame brightens and intensifies. The light cast by this fire illuminates your inner landscape. . . .

You see a well-worn pathway and begin to follow it. Sweet flowers grow along the edges and a soft, warm breeze touches your skin. As you walk further down to explore the pathway, you come to a fork and veer off into a tunnel of bushes and trees that gets darker as you enter.

The world you just left feels very far behind you. You come to the entrance of a cave in the rock and crouch down to enter. Inside, it is rough hewn with a strange, musty odor. Soon, you can stand upright, but you must feel your way onward through the darkness. Your bare feet feel dampness on the floor of the cave. Your sense of direction is lost, and it is difficult to discern up from down. . . .

Something inside you shifts and you see a small pinhole of light. You are drawn to the light and you look through the small opening.

You are transported to a scene of abysmal suffering somewhere in the world. . . .

You see a beleaguered city or village where no family is untouched by the suffering of war, and the cries of children pull at your heart. . . .

There is a trail of refugees driven by fear and desperation, walking to a camp where thousands huddle in squalor, many bearing the vivid scars of man's inhumanity to man; many with nothing but their indomitable spirit between themselves and famine, disease, and death. . . .

You come to a place where the pressures of poverty, overpopulation, and indignities drive people to throw themselves at even the smallest hope for rescue. . . .

Everywhere you focus comes yet another act of violence and degradation, terror and pain. The pain of these people becomes your pain, and the stench of death pervades even the safety of your cave....

Now comes a wind. You feel it enter the cave, this wind of time and change, which blows you back through the cave and onto the main path.... Shake off the dust and continue along your journey, feeling the heavy ache of sorrow turn to compassion as you lament how humanity inflicts suffering. (It is through the experience of suffering that we learn compassion.) Each step brings you to a sense of determination to see that we create peace and harmony for our world. Examine inside yourself what you can do, what you can contribute to peace: peace within yourself . . . within your community . . . for the children .... and for the future....

As you continue your journey, reflect on the knowledge that peace will not come to the world until each person finds peace within his/her self.

You arrive at a sanctuary where, upon the altar, is your heart flame. Feed the flame with your Heart Breath and your compassion for all the suffering that has ever been and is still occurring on our planet because of hatred and fear. As the flame grows and brightens before you, your compassion also grows, until it reaches a place from which you can begin to forgive. You can forgive your enemies.... You can forgive those who believe differently from you and look different from you.... You can forgive the perpetrators of violence.... And you can forgive yourself....

Focus on what you can do to create peace. Bring it into form as a commitment, a vow to action. See, hear, and feel from the depths of your being, from the marrow of your bones, what you can do to create peace. Now place your commitment onto the fire of your heart.

It flares into a bright blaze. In the radiant light of your heart flame, you now perceive a vision of a future where all beings live in cooperation, in harmony, in a world of natural abundance and prosperity, a world where people are at peace with themselves, and with one another....

It is this vision of beauty and peace that you bring back with you as you ground and return to your ordinary consciousness....

When you have fully grounded and centered yourself, you can open your eyes, knowing that you will share your vision with all who will listen. Together, we can make it happen.

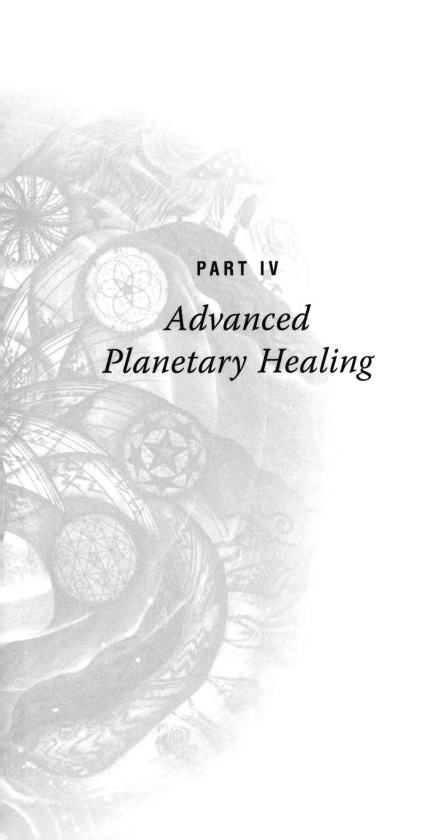

PART IV

*Advanced
Planetary Healing*

17
Introduction— Self-Realization

Some years ago, I had the honor of opening for Ram Dass at an event in San Francisco. This was during the time when I toured with Tribal Alchemy, a band that came together to make music for my journeys (and still does on occasion). These were my rock-star moments, and I had some of the most exciting times in my career playing at festivals and working with the energies of both the crowd and the band while empowering the people through visualizations.

I first met Ram Dass in the Haight-Ashbury section of San Francisco in 1967 where he was advising the Straight Theater people, with whom I was associated. It was one of the original Straight Theater producers who invited me to present at this event nearly forty years later. Although I never knew him well, Ram Dass and I moved in parallel circles and were well aware of each other. I was delighted these many years later that he was interested in what I was doing and chose to pay extra close attention to my performance. I was eager for his feedback. He was quite supportive of my work, letting me know that he appreciated what I was doing and liked the images I was presenting. Then he asked me if I was conscious of having suggested to the audience, in my introduction, that they could recreate themselves however they wanted when they came out of the void in the journey. He pointed out that, in fact, I had used the word *want* several times. In very clear terms, he let me know that he found that direction inappropriate.

After receiving this feedback from Ram Dass, I was extremely careful to make sure that the directions in my journeys pointed people into alignment with divine will, rather than their own. Later, when some of the work that came through required a greater level of ownership for our actions and creations, I became a bit conflicted. Some of the exercises and processes I was directing required participants (myself included!) to step up to the plate from a place of inner authority and responsible creativity.

As I became more comfortable with the realization that we are children of the gods or of some greater intelligence, and that we are learning to accept and step more fully into recognition of our own divinity, I found myself on the brink of a shift in my own deeply held beliefs about co-creation and its implications on our personal responsibilities and capabilities.

If we are truly to participate in creating spirit medicine for global transformation, it requires us to live our truth, to act in accordance with the wisdom we gain from our day-to-day experience—in both the physical and inner worlds. It commits us to being exemplars of the Golden Rule, and to be upright in our relationships and our dealings. It forces us to be accountable for our thoughts, our words, and our deeds. Sometimes it catalyzes movement into new territory, where we become available to forge new ideas and new solutions. The most exciting— albeit the most difficult stretch for me to make—has been the realization that we are good enough, smart enough, and responsible enough to take action on our own. I have come to believe that we contribute to the creation by using our divine right to influence life and the future from a place of heart-centered presence with our own High Self, the place of our purest inner authority and power. In order to fully realize our potential as human beings on planet Earth, and to prepare for whatever new challenges the future may bring, we not only take responsibility for our actions, we stretch ourselves to participate fully in the co-creative conscious evolutionary processes that will carry us forward.

18
Intelligent Evolution

Science has made great strides in both the understanding of DNA and its manipulation, yet there is ongoing controversy regarding the ethics of tinkering with this basic structure of creation. Already, many of our staple food items, such as soy and corn, are being routinely modified in order to streamline cultivation practices and create disease-resistant strains. Although science is limited by its requirement of empirical, measurable data, there is another approach to this field of study that has been practiced by shamans and healers throughout history and has begun to enter the radar screens of some mainstream physicists and bioengineers. Alchemical Healing contains many correlations with shamanic principles as they have been practiced over time, and some interesting questions have been raised: What happens when you manipulate DNA in or from another dimension? Can we effect healing and strengthen our immune systems through inserting, deleting, or changing information encoded in the human genome? Can a genetic manipulation or mutation in one person affect the collective genome? Where is the line that determines whether an act of conscious mutation is ethically viable?

Before we can begin grappling with such questions, let's take a look at the basic mechanics of DNA.

WHAT IS DNA?

The letters DNA stand for *deoxyribonucleic acid*. Heredity units called *chromosomes* are found throughout the body in all cells, except red blood cells. Each human cell nucleus is the repository for forty-six chromosomes, twenty-three contributed by each parent. Chromosomes are complexes comprised of coils of an extremely long DNA molecule wrapped around protein "spools." DNA molecules are molecular blueprints used in creating the body's protein molecules, the basic building block of cells, tissues, and organs. Proteins provide for the physical structure of the cell and are responsible for the organism's metabolism and behavior. Simply, protein molecules determine an organism's traits. Since DNA codes the protein's structure, DNA is recognized as the primary factor controlling an organism's characteristics.

In 1953, James Watson and Francis Crick revealed how the double helix DNA molecule encodes the structure of proteins. At the atomic level, DNA is a long, string-like molecule that resembles a chain. The links of the DNA "chain" are represented by four molecules referred to as *bases*. Specifically, these four bases are: adenine (A), thymine (T), guanine (G), and cytosine (C). The specific sequences of these bases along the length of the DNA molecule represent a four-letter alphabet (A, T, G, and C) that encodes the structure of each of the cell's 150,000+ different proteins. The A, T, G, and C bases collectively constitute the *genetic code*. A *gene* represents the length of a DNA molecule that contains the bases that encode a single protein's structure. When the A, T, G, and C base sequences of a gene are altered, by adding, eliminating, or substituting bases, the change in the DNA code produces an altered protein structure. Geneticists emphasize that *mutations,* which result from DNA-base alterations, are responsible for producing modified proteins and are the primary cause of evolution.

The Human Genome Project, completed in 2001, was designed to catalogue the total number of genes found in a human cell. The results reveal that a human being is created from about 25,000 different genes. Each of the body's differentiated cell types, such as muscle, skin, bone, and nerve, uses a specific and unique combination of genes to create their specialized functions.

In addition to mapping the human genome, scientists have now catalogued the genomes of a wide variety of microorganisms, plants, and animals. One of the biggest surprises offered by their work is that the human genome is surprisingly similar to the genomes of most other higher animals. In fact, through the study of DNA in various life forms, it has been determined that we share a common ancestry with all life forms on Earth.

For many years, scientists believed that genes were *self-actualizing* in that they were able to "turn themselves on" and "turn themselves off" in regulating the development and function of the cells. The notion that genes were self-regulatory led to the belief that genes "control" life and our fate. Consequently, the concept of *genetic control* led us to believe we had little control over the unfoldment of our lives. Genetic control invokes the notion that we are "victims" of heredity, since we cannot control the expression of disease genes passed through our family lineage. While science has since found this belief to be faulty, the mass media and elementary biology texts continue to mislead the public by emphasizing that genes "control" our traits and diseases. This disempowering belief leads people to think they have no control over their lives and must resort to "rescuers," such as the pharmaceutical companies, to maintain their health.

BRUCE LIPTON, PH.D., AND EPIGENETICS

Pioneering cell biologist Bruce Lipton, Ph.D., was cloning stem cells in tissue culture in 1967 when he made an astonishing discovery: gene activity in the cultured cells was controlled by environmental signals. Over the last forty-four years, massive scientific research efforts have expanded on this notion and have led to a "new" biology, which posits that environmental influences are more important in controlling an organism's characteristics than its inherited genes. The new science of heredity is referred to as *epigenetics,* in which the prefix *epi-* means "above." In contrast to *genetic control,* which literally mean "control by genes," the new science of epigenetic control reads: "control *above* the genes." Simply, the new science means that genes are controlled by the environment, and more importantly, by an organism's *perception* of the environment.

Lipton emphasizes that a human body is misperceived as a single entity, although in truth, it is a community comprised of about fifty trillion cells. The cells are the living entities; a body by definition is a "community" of cells. Epigenetics reveals that the fate of this cell community responds to our thoughts, and is influenced by and reacts to what is going on in the environment that surrounds the body. More importantly, our perceptions of the world cause the brain to release chemistry into the blood, which subsequently controls the genetics and fate of our cellular community. If we change our beliefs or perceptions, we change that chemistry, which in turn, changes our biology.

In the human body, stem cells are a population of cells that are kept in an embryonic state throughout life. These multipotential cells are available to replace the billions of aging and damaged cells that die in our body everyday. The fate of these "embryonic" stem cells is predicated by the needs of the body. Based upon the stimuli from the nervous system, a stem cell can contribute to the body's growth and maintenance, or it can participate in supporting a protective response. For example, a cell that might have been slated for bone growth could be redirected if an emergency arises—such as an inflammation—where you suddenly need a massive army of immune cells to fight a raging infection.

Knowledge is power. When we comprehend the nature of how we function, we can then apply our imagination coupled with our intelligence to change things. The same applies to what we believe. According to Lipton,* if we change our beliefs, we can profoundly change our lives.

---

*See Bruce H. Lipton, Ph.D., *The Biology of Belief: Unleashing the Power of Consciousness, Matter and Miracles* (Carlsbad, Calif.: Hay House, Inc., 2005); Bruce H. Lipton and Steve Bhaerman, *Spontaneous Evolution: Our Positive Future (and a Way to Get There from Here)*(Carlsbad, Calif.: Hay House, Inc., 2009); www.brucelipton.com.

An individual's beliefs are programmed through early life experiences in development. From halfway through fetal growth to the age of six, we are deeply influenced by whatever goes on in the world around us. As children, through the age of six, we download all information coming at us, for our brains are operating at the EEG frequency of *theta,* which is the hypnogogic state. Simply, a child's brain is in a state of hypnosis and is unconsciously recording all life experiences into the subconscious mind. These early developmental influences program the subconscious with certain beliefs about ourselves, what reality means, and what is possible in a human life. We automatically defer to the programmed unconscious beliefs *until* we make a conscious decision to override them. This undoing or reprogramming of learned perceptions becomes more and more difficult as we age.

The new science of cell biology underscores our ability to change our minds, and as a consequence, our destinies. One of the most important insights about epigenetics, is that through our perceptions, we can modify the readout of our gene blueprints. In fact, epigenetic modifications can alter a gene's reading to provide up to 30,000 different protein variations from the same DNA blueprint. Through epigenetics, we can cause a normal gene to produce a mutant protein *or* a mutant gene to produce a normal protein! Health and disease are not primarily encoded in our genes, for these states are primarily influenced by our perceptions and beliefs and their influence on our epigenetic mechanisms. The new science reveals our ability to change the readout of our DNA code in order to facilitate our adaptation to the needs of our time.

We are at the birth of a new life-changing discipline, one that may be the salvation of our species. To manage our thoughts, beliefs, and environments consciously and with intent brings the realm of indigenous belief systems into the mainstream with the blessings of many respected scientists. It is time to acknowledge the impact of our growing population and consequent Earth changes around us without fear, and to focus on those specific challenges we can embrace and influence. When we fully accept our power as individuals, and when enough of us are in alignment with that power, we will be ready to make the next quantum leap in conscious evolution.

Lipton teaches that we have genetic mechanisms to hypermutate our DNA to change how we function, a genetic mechanism that will allow us to survive and clean up the mess we have created. Bacteria use a similar hypermutation mechanism in learning how to block the deadly effects of penicillin. Yet, bacteria have taken the mutation process a step further, for some bacteria continue to mutate their genes until they are able to digest the penicillin so they can incorporate it into their diet. Nothing short of ingenious! This bacterial example illustrates what we are seeking to do with regard to our own DNA in this shamanistic and alchemical approach to conscious evolution: when we learn to utilize our minds and apply our attention to adapt to our new reality, the ever-growing challenges and degradation will become valuable resources.

It gets even better. According to epigenetics, not only can we create these mutations, we can pass them on from one generation to the next. We shape the future of our civilization through example, and we can heighten our exemplary behavior through art, articulation, and behavior, as well as procreation. We are all products of our environment, and we are all interconnected and affecting one another all the time. If we share with one another how to manage our lives, we will accrue the knowledge needed for civilization to survive. For example, if I can beat cancer, others will learn that they can beat it, too.

As we forge ahead as individuals and as a species, struggling to survive in an environment that is swiftly changing, how do we relate to our new world? How do we respond to pervasive pollution and toxins, so that what was once poisonous becomes neutral, or even nurturing? How can we change our response systems so that when we absorb the aroma of a new carpet or a new computer, we are bolstered instead of harmed? Our current design, as informed by the sum total of our evolutionary process, seems as yet unable to keep pace with the rapid changes in the environment and the attendant onslaught of diseases.

Intelligence has always played an important part in evolution; Darwin's idea that many things are tried in the fullness of time and only the strongest survives cannot explain some of the more intricate symbiotic relationships. For instance, there is a type of acacia tree that develops a series of tunnels and chambers that support the needs for a thriving colony of ants. It also provides food pellets for the ants on the tips of its leaves. The ants that live in these acacia trees are a fierce, biting type that protects their perfect home and host from being devoured by grazers. Someone put a lot of thought into this: maybe the ants, maybe the trees, maybe Spirit, or perhaps some combination of the above. Although we do not know how this symbiotic relationship developed, we can guess that a certain level of communication and intelligence was part of the equation. We will need to work with—and at the level of—spiritual intelligence. There are limitless opportunities to change—and we can. Humans are self-aware, intelligent beings who bear the responsibility to make the conscious choices that will allow us to evolve in a way that benefits our species, and the planet.

In developing the processes for Planetary Healing for this book, Mark and I were actively questing for a journey that would enable us to modify DNA as a means of attaining conscious evolution. Somewhere along the way, quite apart from this quest, Mark found himself drawn to the concepts of wavelengths and harmonics. He noted that entire fields of expertise and product lines have been developed around various electromagnetic wavelengths: AM, FM, and shortwave radios; walkie-talkies; microwaves; X-rays, which are used in medical fields and astronomy. For our purposes, he began to investigate some very specific combinations of wavelengths, noting that different combinations address different types of healing.

It was when he was examining the spectrum of ultraviolet (UV) waves that he remembered our desire to learn how to mutate in order to survive this increasingly hostile environment. It occurred to him that a potential direction we could take was in utilizing the known properties of ultraviolet light. We have all experienced sunburn from overexposure to ultraviolet rays, and the general populace is well aware of the risk of skin cancer. It struck Mark that cancer itself is the result of cell mutations. As we strive for conscious evolution, our aim is to direct the mutations ourselves in order to create positive changes that give us strength and nourishment, as opposed to negative consequences such as cancer.

The journey below was given to us in response to a direct question we had posed for guidance: "Can you give us a journey to alter or repair DNA in order to help us accomplish our goal for speedier, conscious evolution, and to help us adapt while we are dealing with the changes in our environment?"

In a vision, Mark was shown a cell, as if under a microscope. He could see a relaxing of the DNA coil inside the cell. As the coil was relaxing and expanding, the cell itself did not grow. Rather, there was a blurring of the DNA information as the unwinding coil stretched beyond the parameters of the cell walls. At this point, Mark could no longer see what was happening: it was as if the coil had moved not only beyond the cell walls but outside of the spectrum of visibility. Perhaps the coil had moved into another dimension to be altered. He understood that when the energy holding the coil together was relaxed and expanded, certain undesirable attributes fell out, and new beneficial codes replaced them. After this, the coil shrank back into the containment of the cell wall, reconsolidating into something slightly changed from its original form.

Once the spiral recoiled and tightened again, and everything was back in place, the reconfiguration was complete. No further alterations could take place.

In order to translate these images into the empowerment exercise that follows, Mark was given a metaphor that is revealed at the end of the journey. This allowed us to recreate his experience into a process you can follow to change your physical body at the cellular level.

It is important that you be in a state of communion with love when you take this journey, for love ensures that our direction for change is toward healing, surviving, and ultimately thriving.

JOURNEY

DNA Empowerment

Kindle your heart flame. . . . Practice the Heart Breath. . . . In the light of your heart flame, you will see Thoth's Magic Diamond (first given to you in chapter 3). Bring it into focus, and ask to be shown the facet that will take you into your DNA.

Once you are given the window, look through it and bring the image into focus. . . . You will see a warehouse full of identical round baskets, stacked to the ceiling and filling every available space. The baskets look like those of a snake charmer. They all have lids on them, and you cannot see inside them.

Change the focus of the diamond so that your vision penetrates the baskets. Now, you can see that each one contains a tightly coiled cobra, which almost completely fills the space inside. Your vision shifts again so that you cannot see through the baskets, but you can hear that the snakes have begun to move. There is a growing sound, like that of a breeze blowing through dry autumn leaves, as the snakes relax and uncoil, slither and stretch. Then, for a moment, all becomes still. . . .

In this quiet stillness, you can imagine changes that would cause your health to improve and your body to thrive. These changes can happen only at the cellular level. . . . [*Pause.*]

Hold this vision as the cobras begin to stir and slowly return to the tight coil. For a moment, you can again see within the baskets just as the cobras complete the tightening of their coils; you can see that there is no room to spare. Notice that something about the pattern on the cobras' hoods looks slightly different from before. . . .

Once again, all is peaceful and quiet in the warehouse. Step back to take in the whole of the building. You need to step back farther.... You are suddenly blown back, like a leaf in the wind, farther and farther, until your perspective changes. You now can see that it is not a warehouse at all—it is you, lying naked in a field in the sunlight. You understand that your DNA has been altered in a way that empowers it.

Spend a moment admiring yourself and the awesome magic of the complex and yet simple components of your DNA. Thank Cobra for this teaching and for the empowerment for your DNA.

Refocus on Thoth's Magic Diamond and you will be in the presence of Thoth. Ask if he has any further message or teaching for you at this time.

Ground and center back into your physical body.... Breathe the Earth Breath, and feel the love that surrounds and enfolds you as you return fully into heart-centered presence.

Write your experience in your journal.

19
Evolution through Shamanism and Alchemy

Shamanism, a field that has been until recently relegated to indigenous and tribal people, is an age-old methodology that is found on every continent. Although the word *shaman* comes from a Tungus language of Siberia, where it referred to the medicine men and women of a specific sect in that region, its meaning has spread. Now it refers to medicine people and healers anywhere on the planet who, among many other spiritual responsibilities, travel into the spirit world to bring back information, power, and healing for the benefit of their communities. Shamanism is a way of experience, rather than a religion. There are no rules or doctrines with any form of shamanism, however there are many similarities between tribes and from continent to continent that defy explanation.

Shamans undergo rigorous training to develop heightened intuitive sensitivities, oracular skills, and methods for healing, usually after responding to visions or a calling that is also recognized by their tribe or community. In some Native American tribes, they are sometimes recognized after vision quests that require lengthy fasts without food or water or other initiatory rites of passage. Often they are "wounded healers" who receive their visions through traumatic injury or illness, delirium, or, as with the shamans from Siberia, what we might consider madness.

Shamans enter a state of altered consciousness in order to pass through the veil between dimensions. Many shamanic traditions employ the use of sacred, divine plants for medicinal or ritual purposes, or as ways to commune directly with Spirit. To name only a few: the sacrament of the Native American Church is peyote, the Bwiti people of Africa use ibogaine, South American Andean mountain people eat San Pedro (Wachuma), and indigenous cultures around the world where psychedelic mushrooms are ingested consider them the "flesh of the Gods." All are valued for their direct connection to a greater intelligence that often communicates through vivid hallucinogenic visions of great depth and complexity.

One example of a plant teacher that is reaching into the mainstream and affecting the collective consciousness, much as LSD did in the '60s, is ayahuasca, a brew made from a combination of plants that grow in the vast Amazon jungle that reaches into Brazil, Ecuador, and Peru. Initially, and for millennia, the plants were used by various indigenous tribes for ritual, for medicine, and as a teacher. The concoctions shared one essential ingredient, a particular vine that contains the psychoactive alkaloid harmaline. It is only in the past several decades that this vision vine has sent its tendrils out and around the world, sharing its wise counsel in brilliant colored visions to circles gathering on every continent, except perhaps Antarctica. This powerful plant ally, like others mentioned above, requires the guidance of an experienced shaman who has the skill and integrity to be responsible for those who participate in their ceremonies.

Experiencing psychoactive substances or divine plant medicines does not make a person a shaman, nor are they recommended for our purposes here.

Despite the fact that Western mainstream culture has mostly dismissed shamanism, the techniques of shamanic methodology are being more widely explored for their effectiveness in healing, and as a path toward spiritual awakening. Many people are currently using shamanic tools—including guided journeys and rituals—that do not require the use of mind-altering substances. These techniques, such as many of the practices in this book, catalyze shamanic experiences, even for the untrained. In this chapter, we will explore the possibility that shamanic tools can help us understand and perhaps even speed evolution. Hopefully this discussion will inspire you to find a powerful new path in that direction.

How do we tweak the future from the present? How do we access the greatest wisdom to help with our endeavors? Whether we are consciously involving ourselves or not, we are involved, because we are part of the collective mind.

As with most of this Planetary Healing work, the shamanic process in this chapter requires getting out of intellect mode and going into the inner, intuitive world. It asks us, in many cases, to leave our egos aside, expand our consciousness, and enter a more collective stream of intelligence. Sometimes it feels as though we have become one with the universe, or with God.

By whatever means, we are seeking a quantum leap in consciousness, perhaps a mutation, rather than the slow business-as-usual evolution. Of course, evidence shows that the occasional leap during our evolutionary history just may be business as usual; it could be that what we are feeling are the preliminary pangs of a growth spurt.

We take our free will seriously, and well we should. At the same time, there is a popular school of thought that suggests there are no accidents, and that everything is going according to plan. If that is the case, we are let off the hook, but is it true? And if we do have free choice, we must face the consequences of our choices. If we are unwilling to take responsibility for our thoughts, ideas, and actions, we are betraying our freedom—accepting the rights that our choice gives us while forgoing the responsibilities.

Many people and cultures have drifted away from sharing our consciousness with the Creator. Because we have millions of people expressing the more base human desires, our contribution to evolution has been tainted by hedonistic, self-serving urges. Are enough of us ready to introduce loftier, far-reaching goals into the stream? Enlightened people have always walked among us, encouraging us to look at the greater picture and consider the good of all. Those of us at work on Planetary Healing are evidence of their influence. Now is the time to join them en masse and turn this ship of fools around. Evolution happens—only its outcome is in question.

Shamanism works because it operates from an inherent respect for the power of our thoughts; it allows us to witness and feel the changes we are participating in; and it focuses on what is beneficial to the greater community. For this reason, shamans and practitioners make great partners to help during our evolutionary process.

There is an insidious, yet powerful force of sleepy complacency that seems to have overtaken the majority in our culture. If you are reading this book, you are most likely not representative of the mainstream. Yet it is important that we acknowledge the power of a shared conscious intention: those of us coming together intentionally for Planetary Healing can unleash more potency than the deadened majority.

We are both visionaries and pragmatists, looking for long-term solutions that manifest as concrete, positive change in our physical world. Envisioning the potential outcome of this work and how it will manifest in our lives is just the beginning. We still have to go through the steps to bring these changes into fruition. We can start by envisioning a world in which we live more in touch with our intuitive side and our connection with a higher wisdom that resides within—the High Self. It would also be a great gift to the coming generations if we were to reawaken a deep connection with the true source of magic.

In *The Botany of Desire,* Michael Pollan speaks of the evolution or adaptation of plants, which involves a high degree of intelligence at work. There are plants that seem to have figured out what we like about them, and they have improved those attributes to get us to cultivate and nurture them. It took a long time, but they have got us working for them. It also took a long time for the magnitude of the plants' endeavors to be recognized—plants have intelligence and can intuit a mutually beneficial partnership, or rather they grasped the potential and then worked with the magic and caused their wishes and desires to come into reality (or fruition, as it were . . .). There is a certain chauvinism that we, the people, have been guilty of for some time. There is so much more going on all around us than what we perceive and interpret. Wouldn't it be marvelous if we opened our eyes to the magic, living in awe of and respect for the mystery and magic around us? Then future generations could build on that connection and delve much more deeply into the potential for magic that we have only glimpsed.

This work is about how to access that potential magic, and how to use it for the community—to move beyond doing it for individual advancement. We are at a threshold. How do we invite that potential without continuing to throw roadblocks in front of ourselves?

Although it is difficult to fathom these mysteries with our ordinary consciousness, perhaps we can raise ourselves to touch or conjoin with, even for the flash of a moment, the intelligence and wisdom responsible for the creation of the stars, all of life, and everything else. The following journey ambitiously seeks to do just that.

JOURNEY

Process for Evolutionary Understanding

We recommend that you set aside a quiet time and prepare for this journey with grounding meditations that are familiar to you. A recording of something with a consistent cadence would be helpful—for example, drumming with a simple rhythm or chanting.

Start with going in and finding your heart flame. Sit with it, acknowledge it, and begin to slowly feed and nourish it. . . .

Notice how your breath affects the flame. . . . Feel the essence of love that resides in you. . . . Allow your love to grow with the fire. . . . There is a growing energy that radiates from you.

. . . Know that all of this radiance has an infinite source that fuels the intensifying of this flame and this love. . . .

Notice a deep pulse, a slow, strong beat that grows with your attention until its power begins to tug and pull on the core of your being. This pulse is powering your radiant love. Be with it and feel its growing strength and coherence. [*Pause.*]

Now, imagine the influence these radiating energies are having on people, regardless of how far they are from you. Look for resonance, and notice how some people naturally increase their radiance in the presence of yours. . . .

Sit with the growing love you feel for yourself, others, and everything. . . .

Now be in your body in all of its glory. Acknowledge and thank the senses you have been gifted with, that have served you your entire life.

Think about your abilities of sight and hearing; think about the nerve receptors on your skin. Remember your senses of smell and taste. Acknowledge them and recognize what they are sensing for you at this moment. . . .

Imagine that all of this information is being channeled to one part of your brain that is actively processing it. Imagine that part, for the moment, is separate from any other part of your brain. Acknowledge, honor, and thank it for the service it has always rendered to you. Admire its intelligence: it already knows that you are about to process more information of a different sort than it is used to receiving, or that it has ever received before. . . .

Notice the observer part of your brain, which is the core of your identity, the witness. It is the gate to divine mysteries that come to us in dreams and visions. This is the part of the brain that witnesses the reception of information from your other senses and interprets that information. Memories are sorted and stored here.

You are about to transmit a desire for more information, which you will then receive. Emit the following wish into the universe: "With all respect, I wish to know what direction we the people, the entire human community, can take on the evolutionary path. What are the mechanics of how evolution works? What are the options that we can work for consciously and with compassion? How do we accomplish this?"

Transmit and receive . . .

Practice propelling the wish, strengthening the call, and articulating your desires without words. Feel it like a hunger. Look for and recognize any attempt from the universe to address that hunger. [*Long pause.*]

Take as long as you need. Sometimes this question requires a gestation period, and you may need to come back again to retrieve your answer, or to better understand your vision and the particular form it took. Be open to whatever path by which the information may come; it may even come at the cellular level or as a tone. The strength of your appeal will begin to abate when it is time to come back.

Ground and center yourself in your physical body and ordinary consciousness. Take the time you need, and use the Earth Breath to assist in your grounding. Take plenty of time to feel your body, and wriggle your fingers and toes. Even once you have fully come back to yourself, do not rush your reentry: allow any hypersensitivity you may feel to recede before you attempt to interact with the world.

Journal while you are grounding. Memories created in the right hemisphere of your brain can fade away like dreams.

You can repeat this process with other questions once you are comfortable with the way it works.

When we reach full communion with the universe, all our desires seem petty—even those for the future of all humankind. Even the desire for guidance may seem small in the larger scheme of things. We can allow ourselves to drift beyond guidance and join all of creation in that broader realm where, as long as the stars are burning and the planets are revolving, everything seems perfect.

The hallmark of the mysteries is how unfathomable they are, especially by the left brain. If we focus on our right brain, we may be able to sense the answers more clearly. By practicing these processes, we come closer and closer to connecting the two sides of the brain, but there is always more work to do. The deeper we go, the deeper we get. The power of shamanism is in getting beyond our basic senses and habitual interpretations, giving up control, and allowing the magic to sustain us. It is hard to do that from the same part of the brain that makes a business plan!

20
The Pandemic of Cancer
A Shamanistic Approach

The pandemic of cancer that is raging throughout our planet touches all of us, either directly or indirectly. Almost everyone knows someone with cancer. While there have been many advances in cancer research and treatment in the past twenty years, many new cancers have also emerged.

In December of 1992, I was diagnosed with breast cancer. Since then, I have watched with dismay as more and more women are forced to make decisions about how they will deal with this horrendous disease. Some young women are now choosing prophylactic removal of their breasts rather than live with the fear of contracting the disease that took out their mother, sister, and/or aunt. Although the statistics rise and fall, there is still a one-in-eight chance that a woman in the United States will contract breast cancer in her lifetime, and in some communities it is as many as one out of two or three. Why is this happening, and what can we do about it? I spent considerable time thinking about what it means to have cancer when I was dealing with it. When I first contracted the disease, I wondered, as most people do, "Why me?" I looked at my life and my exposures to toxins and radiation, and I looked to available research. It appeared to me that the prevalence of cancer, and specifically breast cancer, is a direct result of our lack of respect and care for our environment and the poisoning of the food chain with pesticides and other toxins. It is a phenomenon from which no one is immune, occurring on a planetary scale. The cancer pandemic is related to runaway technology, yet technology alone is unreliable at best in dealing with the problem.

When I faced the dilemmas of dealing personally with this potentially fatal disease and examined my options, I discovered that the medical world saw it as a numbers game. It was all about odds. When all the pathology reports were in after the lumpectomy and re-excision, my numbers did not look so good—about a two-in-ten chance of long-term survival.

In the United States at that time, and even more so now at the time of this publication, many people's resources were only as good as their insurance policy. I was lucky to have a policy that included chemotherapy and radiation. Alternative therapies, usually extremely expensive, were not covered. It continues to be very expensive, almost impossible, to get alternative coverage in the United States. Most experimental clinics are in Mexico or Europe, so that travel and lodging costs come into play as well. Although I was barraged with suggestions and written material about all manner of cures as soon as I was diagnosed, I could not try every alternative therapy that appealed to me: my resources were limited.

Cancer had never been part of my personal reality. I had no fear of it, nor any reason to consider myself at risk. Yet there it was, an olive-sized malignant lump appearing out of nowhere, altering my every waking moment with the sheer knowledge of its existence in my body. I realized I would have to face it squarely, or die. As an Alchemical Healer, I was in quite a dilemma. I knew in my heart of hearts, with additional strong input from my guides, that I could not work my own healing alone.

Each woman faced with this disease must decide for herself how she will deal with it; whether she chooses conventional or alternative methods; whether she opts for relentlessly aggressive methods or lets go and lets the chips fall where they may. Perhaps more important than what protocol they choose is how committed they are to following their chosen path. When I was given a 20 percent chance of survival, I asked my oncologist what distinguishing factors he thought determined on which side of the statistics his patients were likely to fall. He gave considerable weight to attitude. Confidence and trust in the process are fundamental to good results.

I determined that I would have an easier time than most in my situation because of the skills I carried from my healing and shamanic work. I made a twofold decision: I would offer myself to modern allopathic medicine, following the rigorous protocol of surgery, chemotherapy, and radiation; and I would set about to find the most efficient way to infuse my shamanic experience into the allopathic protocol. My doctor's encouragement of my warrior style served to bolster my confidence, especially when the side effects kicked in and things got really difficult.

I found it extremely important to supplement the allopathic program with many adjunctive therapies. They were crucial to alleviate the trauma caused by caustic and invasive procedures. I used acupuncture, massage therapy—including lymphatic drainage massage—castor-oil packs, herbs, and nutrition. (More recently I have learned that certain herbs neutralize certain chemotherapy protocols, so if you are dealing with cancer, check with your oncologist before ingesting herbs during allopathic treatments.) I created my own blend from what I knew and the many options I was shown. For me, holistic meant the whole of what was available. The flood of information became overwhelming, and, at a certain point I had to tell well-meaning people that I was no longer receiving suggestions and advice. One piece of advice I would like to offer to those who have to make hard decisions regarding treatment choices: give yourself to whatever you choose 100 percent, and make it a requirement of your support team that they do the same.

The bringing together of the allopathic and shamanic roads to healing required confidence in both. The final combination had to be something I could get behind, something I could embrace with all of my heart. The entire journey was bracketed on either end with tours to my beloved Egypt, during which the Egyptian Mysteries left their magical marks. The journey itself was a long, intense, complicated dance that included many allies. Some worked in the hospital and cancer clinic, some cooked us dinner, and some were etheric and worked from the spirit realms. It was a powerful dance and, in the end, my cancer was completely cured.

COUNTING COUP ON CANCER
Shamanism and Metaphysics Meet
Chemotherapy and Radiation

Upon learning of my diagnosis in early 1992, my first inclination was to look at my calendar to determine how to fit cancer into my busy schedule. My first book, *The Golden Cauldron* (an early incarnation of what is now called *Power Animal Meditations*) had just been published, and I was gearing up for a promotional tour to follow my annual mystery school pilgrimage to Egypt. Nothing could alter my plans. My surgeon cooperated by arranging a lumpectomy for me on Christmas morning in Eureka, California, while I was en route to San Francisco to catch my flight for Egypt. Two nights later when the lab reports came in I learned that the tumor was malignant and growing. Although they had removed the lump, the margins were not clean. I carried on with my plans and left for Egypt the following day.

Needless to say, the work in Egypt had an unusual flavor this time; it was there that the healing began. My personal participation was deep and focused, and quite in sync with the vision quest that was unfolding for me as I guided a large group through the ancient mysteries and sacred sites. By the time I returned home, I had received clear guidance and felt secure with my chosen course of action. Back in San Francisco, I underwent breast conservation surgery in the form of a re-excision during which my surgeon attempted to achieve clean margins but was not able to do so. He also took a number of lymph nodes, about half of which were cancerous. I met with an oncologist to discuss an appropriate course of action to combat this extremely aggressive cancer that had already metastasized. He suggested an equally aggressive treatment protocol, one from a not-as-yet published study at Johns Hopkins, which included a surgically implanted catheter to deliver many of the five chemicals I would receive weekly for sixteen weeks. He warned me that it would be extremely difficult.

Mark and I journaled some of the shamanic visioning work we engaged in during the intensive chemotherapy protocol. I found this process to be a vital link to my own understanding of this challenging treatment. Mark's visioning also enabled me to work with the chemicals, aligning my spiritual energies with whatever was going on in the treatment at any given time.

On January 28, 1992, in the oncologist's office, I sat in a comfortable pink La-Z-Boy type chair. Next to me was a tall stand with a bag dripping clear fluid down a long tube into the catheter that had been surgically implanted above my heart. This enabled the fluid to enter directly into a large vein with enough flow to keep the chemicals from burning the veinal walls. On my lap was whatever portable typing device I had at the time; Mark was sitting next to me, eyes closed, speaking in a quiet monotone, describing his visions to me. Allopathy meet shamanism. . . . We were observing and recording the process of chemotherapy, while attempting to establish rapport with the potent chemicals—barbaric agents of death that would be fighting for me and my survival.

As Mark focused inward, he saw a staging area filling with abstract beings—a mighty force was gathering. They came out of shadows in the fog, alien beings with tendrils, horns, claws, and misshapen bodies. The first thing he saw was the horn of a being who looked similar to a Viking, although resemblance to humanity ends there, as from it protruded an uncoiling tendril. There was a short creature with brown hair and long claws that the others were backing away from. As Mark described them to me, the fog began to clear. It is difficult to do justice in writing to how inhuman these beings were. They were such base, chaotic creatures, of such low intelligence, it seemed they had no business being alive.

I realized that it would be up to me to control this force, to direct this horde when battle was engaged with the introduction of the chemo drugs into my body. My intention to be in charge immediately brought a semblance of order into the ranks, dividing them into platoons as a hierarchy developed.

A serpent-dog was coiled around my legs and feet like a boa, his body that of a dog from about waist level. It was he who, like a general, barked commands and delegated directions. I knew I must not take the edge off their fighting rage by taking a placating stance. I had to allow them to stay revved up for the fight. It was important that I, as commander-in-chief, remain a rallying point. My commands were to be passed down through the ranks.

At 1:45 p.m. antinausea drugs were being dripped into my catheter in preparation for the noxious chemicals that were soon to follow. I found it interesting that the consciousness of these powerful chemicals was already present and felt before they actually entered my bloodstream. Today I was scheduled to have Adriamycin, Vincristine, and Methotrexate; tomorrow, 5-FU would be introduced; and I would be taking Cytoxan by mouth every day.

With prompting from my inner guidance, I psychically reached into my rib cage and ripped my chest wide open to allow the beings to enter and begin the great battle for my life. We could clearly see their barbaric mentality as they crawled, hopped, and jumped in, entering through the opening in my chest, which extended from my Adam's apple to my sternum.

At 1:52 sterile water was dripped into the catheter. The serpent-dog stopped shepherding the troops a moment to check in with me, nuzzling my hand, then returned to the action. He observed all that was happening with keen, sharp eyes. We were aware of rippling earth and roiling seas. All the violent oceans poured into the opening in my chest, followed by a sandstorm. The staging area emptied, even as additional hordes poured in over the hills. Bodies, some still writhing, lay strewn across the field, early casualties from the over excitement. Someone blew a horn and the angelic host was awakened. Angels streamed in like wind-driven fog.

Now it was time for the actual chemicals: the storm began, the battle was engaged. . . .

As that first battle raged within me, we went home from the oncologist's office. That night as we looked within, we could see that the opened area of my chest had taken on the appearance of a cave in which an aged crone was laying a fire. She then set up housekeeping, building shelves, hanging herbs, and sweeping the floor. Throughout the entire four months of chemotherapy, in our mind's eye, I would look like a statue with my arms and hands extended, chest ripped open to form the cave. My staunch allies would be the ever-vigilant crone and the serpent-dog, who stayed wrapped around my feet and legs (years later I discovered that the serpent-dog was an aspect of the Egyptian god Anubis: what a pleasant surprise that was!). In front of me lay a stark, rocky plain, the staging area ringed with craggy volcanoes.

That first night, comforted by the crone's presence, we became aware of the thunder of distant drums. As we drifted off to sleep, we could see the glow over the horizon from the advancing army, marking the arrival of reinforcements, the new chemicals making their way toward the staging area.

The next morning I went for my second day of chemotherapy. As I prepared to receive the first dose of 5-FU by way of a computerized pump that I would wear on my body, we looked in and saw that the newly gathered force was on the move. This new army was more evolved than the last, their great drums provided a cadence that these bearded warriors would move to. Some of them rode doglike creatures and went about regulating things. Their campfires were made of the torches that had caused the glow across the horizon the previous night. They smeared themselves with ashes, emitting guttural sounds as they whipped themselves into a frenzy.

The dog-serpent and the crone looked very regal. The crone moved her stuff to the back of the cave, out of the way, but kept the fire burning. Then she went away, leaving me to tend the fire with my attention and my breath. I realized it was very important for me, too, to maintain an air of nobility right then and throughout the entire course of chemotherapy. I was in command of the chemicals, and I would keep them focused on the job at hand. It was not easy.

Within two weeks, my hair began to fall out. I had it cut short so that it would not be so messy. It did not take long before I was completely bald, and soon I had no eyebrows or eyelashes either. I continued to support my treatment through shamanic observation, acupuncture, massage, herbs, and Alchemical Healing. I could not take the pills prescribed to control nausea because they caused a strong reaction; I felt as though I was jumping out of my skin, and then I would throw them up. I found pot to be helpful, on occasion, both for controlling the nausea and as a spiritual ally, providing access to a level of consciousness where I could more easily make changes inside. I could not smoke, however, so my oncologist prescribed a prescription for government-issue THC, which had just become available.

On March 17, everything conspired to create a most unusual healing experience. Four close friends who had studied Alchemical Healing with me for many years were working on me, as they did every Monday and Tuesday evening throughout my chemo protocol. Mark had just done a lymph drainage massage and manually cleared my liver.

Music was an important vehicle for journeying during this ordeal, and on this night we played a new tape, *Voice of the Four Winds,* by Dik Darnell. While they worked on me, the music pushed me into a place of prayer. I called out to the spirits and gave thanks. When the music next shifted, I found myself traveling inward, spiraling through my body until I entered a level where I could observe what appeared to be the patterning of genes.

A couple of days prior, I had seen a TV news broadcast that mentioned the possibility of an anomalous gene (later identified as BRCA1) found in women with a proclivity for breast cancer. With the support of the music, I was able to connect to this gene. But what to do? I have never thought of violence as an appropriate means for making much of anything better. Yet here I was, my body a battlefield, filled with a nuclear arsenal of chemicals developed to deal cancer its deathblows without doing irrevocable damage to healthy organs and tissues. I had tried the Pac-Man approach, visualizing everything from the chemo to friendly alligator spirits gobbling up the cancer cells. I had attempted to connect at the molecular level and transform the cells, but always with some confusion as to whether I was killing them in that process. I had spent a lot of time simply dealing with the toxins to clear them out of my system. But this time, with the magic of the moment and the music, I was able to hold the gene and know it transformed and healed through love. This was very profound: some basic pattern in the blueprint of my body shifted from life-destroying to life-affirming.

When the music again shifted, I found myself desiring to strengthen and protect my organs, particularly my heart. It was as if all of the diverse traditions of my experience blended with the eclectic qualities in the music, the healing hands of my friends, and all events that had contributed to the current moment. I prayed for my heart to be opened. Layer upon layer of bright patterned veils opened to reveal yet deeper patterns until all barriers dissolved, and in that moment, the music passed through my whole unobstructed being in rushes. I felt the birth of hope and a bright future in place of a dark and shrinking universe. I knew myself in total unity with all of life and all of spirit.

There were many opportunities, even during the most miserable of times, for the magic to enter and nourish my healing process. My spirit guides and totem allies were always available. Sometimes, for many days at a time, I could do nothing more rigorous than go to the bathroom. I learned viscerally this truth: what cannot be taken from us is our intention, our attention, and our imagination, with which we can change our reality. These are true tools for transformation.

We have conscious choice from moment to moment in every thought and action. By our responses, we affirm or destroy, and our choices help to determine the quality of our lives. I chose to make use of this opportunity as a rite of passage. Not long after completing treatment, I was healthier than ever and had fully resumed an intense schedule of travel, offering seminars and leading groups to sacred sites all over the world. As we complete this book, I have been clear of cancer for nineteen years—plenty of time to reflect on the fact that the gifts from this experience far outweigh the suffering. I am grateful to tell the story here and feel the blessing in reaffirming my life and my healing.

Cancer can be a tremendous wake-up call. It forced me to recommit to life and to make choices about what is really important to me—often very different choices from those I had been making. It taught me to have compassion for those less fortunate and certainly for those of limited physical capabilities. I have learned to adhere to the limitations that my body imposes on me from a position of reverence and respect. Most important, it gave me the ability to help others facing similar choices, not because my actions would necessarily be right for them, but because I am still alive to share the experience.

Our illnesses can be our most powerful teachers. It is through our adversarial situations that we learn and grow.

Each of us who contracts and lives with this disease is in a sense taking a hit for all of humanity. Perhaps those of us who have found our way to long-term remission have in some way mutated, and that adaptation has entered the human morphogenetic field. At the very least, those of us who survive stand as examples for others, and we offer hope for the very real possibility that we are learning to somehow live with what we have created.

MIRACLE IN THAILAND
Acacia's Story

On December 26, 2004, my stepson Luke Scully was taken from us by the tsunami that swept across the beaches of southern Thailand and eleven other nations. On December 26, 2005, that same sea gave me back my daughter.

Two and a half years before that Acacia, also known by her given name, Spirit, first contracted non-Hodgkin's lymphoma. She had surgery to remove a large tumor in her neck and went on for chemotherapy treatment at Stanford Medical Center. A year and a half later, the cancer was back.

This time they recommended a stem cell transplant, which she refused. She suffered mightily through a second round of chemotherapy. As predicted, it returned a year later.

In November of 2005, I left a group I was leading in Peru a bit early to be with Acacia after she was hospitalized and subsequently diagnosed with recurrent lymphoma, now in her brain, central nervous system, liver, and left kidney. Allopathic options looked both harsh and limited, and it was clear that they would be unable to "fix" her. We decided to see what it would take to get her to Thailand for the memorial we were planning for Luke and his girlfriend, Angie Foust, on the first anniversary of the tsunami.

After pondering this, Acacia's doctor at Stanford offered her the first treatment of a rigorous chemotherapy protocol, one that would give her enough recovery time so that she could travel. As is often the case, the chemo wiped out her natural immunity and left her vulnerable to infections and abscesses. She was hospitalized during her recovery and almost did not make it.

It actually took a number of miracles and a couple of extra days just to get Acacia to where we were meeting in Thailand, but her strength and determination prevailed, and with the help of her equally persistent friend Maria (whom we now call St. Maria), she arrived at Krabi airport in a wheelchair. The shape she was in was frightening, with abscesses on one leg from her knee to her ankle, her skin red and inflamed and looking as though it would burst. We rushed her to the hospital, where they wanted to perform surgery immediately and keep her for at least a week. The doctors spelled out their predictions in grim detail.

Acacia listened as we explored our options and attempted to negotiate with the doctors for time with her family. We were especially concerned because there would be no medical support at Railay Bay, where we would be spending most of our time. A doctor took Mark and me aside and described, step by step, how Acacia's organs would shut down and what we could expect as death approached. He said it would take about four days.

Finally, quietly but firmly, Acacia declared, "I did not come to Thailand to spend my time in the hospital. Take me to Railay Bay." Despite the protestations of the doctors, we wheeled her back out to the van and continued our journey. Acacia said, "Okay, Mom, it is your turn. Gimme some of whatever you've got." She stuck her leg up and over the seat so that I could reach it. As I opened to allow the energy to pour through my hands and into her leg, the swelling began to deflate like a balloon right before our eyes. Perhaps she had only needed to elevate her leg sufficiently. . . .

Friends and family decided to charter a bus to take us to Khao Lak a few days before the anniversary. Thousands had perished there with Luke and Angie, and we didn't want to be part of the huge crowd predicted for the government's memorial. Acacia gamely joined us.

Back at Railay Bay, the family wanted to do something special to commemorate the moment that the tsunami had hit the year before. My other daughter, Sage, and Luke's other sisters, Ruby and Pearl, envisioned people holding hands in a chain stretching the length of the beach. They produced a flier, and the vision spread further by word of mouth. As we began to gather, our numbers did not look promising: there were perhaps thirty of us standing in a line near the shore. Then all at once, people started pouring out of the jungle, out of the hotels, out of the paths from neighboring beaches. It was amazing! Hundreds of strangers came together to share this moment. A bell was sounded, there was a moment of silence, and then, as one, we walked into the sea holding hands.

It was right after this ceremony that Acacia told me she wanted to take LSD, right then and there. I went through a gamut of emotions, unsure how I would handle such a journey under the circumstances, yet, given the circumstances, I could not deny her request. Maria and I chartered a long-tail boat to Chicken Island, where Acacia could swim in pure unpolluted seawater.

Under my guidance, we made our prayers and set our intentions.

The three of us began to feel the effects of the LSD as we crossed the channel to the island. With our amplified senses, we perceived the majestic splendor of our surroundings with crystal clarity. We all felt a deep appreciation for the abundance of beauty around us. We expressed this through our rapt attention as each gorgeous moment unfolded into the next. We stopped along the way to swim in a deep-water lagoon with steep cliffs towering above shallow caves, forming the head and neck of the chicken the island is named for. Thick schools of fish surrounded Acacia, nibbling at her while she swam, enticed by the bread we offered them. Acacia's huge smile in a storm of brightly colored fish is an image I hold with love and joy, one of my most precious memories.

We continued to the beach, a small spit of sand at the other end of the island. I feared that Acacia, her skin sensitized by the chemotherapy drugs, would get burnt to a crisp in the mighty Thai sun, so she snorkeled wearing a hat and a sarong draped over her back. It was hours before I could get her out of the water. When she finally climbed back onto the boat, we were amazed to see that her leg was less inflamed, and that fresh pink skin replaced many of the oozing sores. So much healing had occurred while she steeped in the gentle saline sea. Equally healing was our laughter. We laughed till we cried, then kept on laughing. . . . This was a day of love, expansion, clarity, and joy—a remarkable day that will live on in our memories. On this day, I believe I witnessed a miracle. I know the condition Acacia was in when we marked the moment of one year since the sea took our loved ones, and so many more. And I know how deep our feelings were running. I know the changes I witnessed when Acacia embraced that very sea and emoted love and joy; it was as if the sea then embraced her and she came out healed. I believe Acacia became so filled with love and lightness of being that there was no room left for cancer.

Acacia's courageous presence in Thailand added depth, richness, and poignancy to an already complex spiritual and emotional ride. Her determination to participate in life to the fullest inspired deep respect and love in all of us who were privileged to share this precious time with her.

Back home in Oakland, Acacia went through tests to determine the status of her cancer. The first CAT scan, which covered her body up to her neck, was clean: no signs of cancer in her liver or kidney. Subsequent CAT scans of her neck and brain and a spinal tap to check her central nervous system all revealed that she was cancer-free. Her doctor, after expressing surprise at this amazing turn, reminded Acacia that it is the nature of her particular form of lymphoma to return again and again (this was, in fact, the third recurrence). He urged her to continue with chemotherapy treatments. She took his advice initially but stopped a short time later. In her phone calls home, Acacia was very clear that she felt complete, especially since further tests showed her to be clear of cancer. At this writing, she has remained free of cancer for more than six years.

We cannot say how this miracle happened. Many factors came together in support of Acacia. I will name several, and leave it to you to ponder the possibilities: Throughout this time, I wrote a very public e-mail newsletter, keeping my readers informed throughout the ordeal of the tsunami, the loss of Luke and Angie, our search for them when they went missing, and our journey to Thailand with Acacia.*

Thousands of people were praying for Luke and Angie, and again for Acacia when her story became part of that saga.

No one can say for sure what it is that helped the most: the prayers or the chemotherapy; the LSD, or the ocean, or the beauty of the landscape; the love that Acacia experienced and with which she was held. The single treatment of chemotherapy before the trip to Thailand may have had some curative effect.

As someone intimately connected with her throughout the entire five years that she suffered with this disease, I can say that by the time she came to Thailand, things were really dire. What I saw on that magical day in the ocean was a fearless, courageous person facing death by fully embracing life and immersing herself in beauty and joy. She was completely held in the embrace of a gentle ocean that washed through her body, mind, and soul. I saw laughter at such a deep gut level that whatever the ocean might have missed may have simply been expelled in her throaty expressions of joy.

Back in the sixties, we used to joke about the safety of taking LSD. We figured we were so expanded that if a nuclear device hit nearby, the

---

*The link to archived letters from that time are at www.ShamanicJourneys.com/lukeandangie.php.

radiation would not affect us because it would just pass between our molecules. I sometimes think that Acacia was so expanded to such a degree that day, and had attained such oneness with Creator, that she was truly open to a miraculous healing.

Acacia is very clear about her experience. Although we did set an intention at the beginning of our journey, she asserts she had no meet-or-greet with God, and no shamanic journey into death, illumination, and rebirth. Nor did she spend any conscious energy on her trip trying to heal herself or even asking for help. She simply had the most gorgeous day of her life.

21
The Parabola
A New Vision for Healing Cancer

In Egypt, there is a healing god called Khonsu, a moon god related to Thoth. It has been said that when Khonsu is called in to perform a healing, the diseases come to attention. They know they will be feasted and honored—and then they will go away happy.

I learned about the healing prowess of Khonsu while researching for *Shamanic Mysteries of Egypt,* and I too came to attention: we had been using a similar modality for cancer for a few years by then.

This new response to cancer entered Planetary Healing during a healing session for a friend with metastasized breast cancer in 2004. Janice lay at the center of a circle of seventeen women in her home in Portland, Oregon, while I conducted a healing with Mark by way of speakerphone from our home in Eugene.

VISIONING THE PARABOLA

I directed everyone to begin with the Heart Breath in order to make sure that every person was heart centered and that we were connected through the expanded heart flame of the group. We used the breath like bellows to increase the glow from our heart flames until we had generated enough light for a cohesive connection among us. As soon as we made the energetic connection to Janice and her circle, Mark began pacing; something new was coming in, new and unexpected. This would be the blueprint for a very different way of dealing with cancer—the concept of enlisting the cancer cells to depart not only from the body, but from our planet as well.

Mark saw a parabolic structure that was shaped like the circle of women surrounding Janice. It emerged in his vision as a vessel, with Janice at its center. It was immediately clear why the vessel was a parabola: any support that entered it would reflect to Janice in its center, and anything transmitted from Janice in the center would be directed straight up into the sky.

I found myself invoking—and suggesting that others invoke—any spirit guides and totem allies, ancestors, and deities of all pantheons that were willing to help us with our healing work. Intuiting that the circle of women could be more effective if they were conducting the universal life force energy through their hands, I guided them to breathe open their hands from the inside, using the Heart Breath, so that the powers of Earth and Sky would enter the stream of energy passing through them, and through their hands. (Please note: healers who use their personal energies are in danger of depleting themselves. The universal life-force energy awakened in this way is infinite and always accessible once the conduit is opened.)

As the women directed energy to Janice, it became apparent that energy was being offered from every direction and dimension in the universe. At the focal point of the parabola, Janice was poised to receive it easily. She spoke her willingness to accept help and healing from all who were present. I suggested that she relax her body and open, much as she would during a lovemaking experience. Once it became apparent that Janice was filled to capacity, it was time for Janice to release her cancer and allow the energized flow to carry the cancer cells away and into the universe.

As the flow began to shift, Mark had a vision of the huge, expanding universe, hungry for new material and intelligence to nurture life on planets where the attributes of cancer cells would be welcome. Janice spoke her willingness to assist the cells in their departure with the help of the energy being transmitted from the parabola. She honored the disease and invited the cancer cells inhabiting her body to take this opportunity to leave. It was clear to all of us by then that we could use the parabola to conduct the cancer cells out in a way that was attractive not only to us, but to the cancer cells as well.

We then visualized the cancer cells as seeds carrying life to new places in the expanding universe.

As Janice transmitted the cancer cells from her place at the focal point in the center of the parabola, it seemed as though cells were flooding forth like a stream from a high pressure hose out into space, heading off on a new adventure.

We observed the transmission of the cancer cells peaking, then ebbing, until all the cells that relinquished themselves during this process had disappeared into space.

The amount of energy that passed through the healers in the circle was great, but they were not through yet. It was now time for Janice to be refilled. Although there are very few rules that govern Alchemical Healing, some are all-important: when we remove inappropriate energies from the body, we must offer them somewhere to go. We must be responsible for conducting such energies safely, with a prayer for their transformation into their highest potential. At the same time, whenever something is taken out, it must be replaced with something more appropriate, or filled with sufficient energy to make sure the healing holds. There can be no space allowed for something undesirable to enter. When this rule is followed, the entire being is strengthened rather than diminished.

The flow of energies for refilling Janice initially came from the group, but soon took on qualities and strength from a greater source— so great, in fact, that the whole circle was being replenished with love and compassion. Once Janice and her supporting circle were fully refilled, we all grounded and centered ourselves, and remained for some time in a state of awe.

Teleconference technology works well for this kind of ceremony. I began conducting cancer healing phone bridges soon after the session for Janice, and continued holding monthly group healing ceremonies via phone and web for six years. During these sessions we could sense the eagerness of the cancer cells to depart on their unique adventure, once they had been appropriately acknowledged and honored.

Participants on these bridges have cancer, know someone who is dealing with cancer, or join the circle to add their support. You can listen to a number of recordings of parabolic phone bridges at http://shamanicjourneys.com/cancerbridge-podcasts in order to follow my voice leading the following journey.

Janice was in remission for several years before her cancer returned. At this writing, she is still fighting the good fight. As you participate in the ceremony below, please include Janice into the center of the parabola when it is time.

RECIPE FOR PARABOLIC HEALING

Although this process is ideal for a group or circle, individuals can practice it too. Whether alone or with others, you will always be working with the original and ever-growing circle. You can enter into this ritual on your own behalf or that of other people suffering with cancer. You, or the others you wish to work on, will be placed into the center of the parabola once your connection to it is well established and the flow of energy is strong. If you do not have anyone specific in mind, you can focus on a particular hospital, send out a general call for anyone who has cancer anywhere in the world, or stand in support of others. The addition of your focused energy is always utilized and appreciated.

In the process we have developed, we neither judge nor banish the cancer cells and see nothing intrinsically evil about them. They leave of their own accord, and once they have left, their trajectory always takes them away from Earth, away from us. Many respondents to our phone bridge healings have spoken of feeling a sense of relief, even joy from the departing cells. Perhaps they are responding to a call or need elsewhere that is more appropriate for them, even useful. Perhaps, as some have described, our clear intention, coupled with the power of the parabolic form that carries it, encourages a wholesale exodus of the cancer. In any event, the ceremony provides an opportunity for us to engage in a moment of heart-centered, proactive co-creation and problem solving.

In no way do I suggest using this method for other virulent cell structures such as infections or other non-cancerous diseases. Cancer cells are unique in that they seem to have beaten the system, so to speak, and in doing so have revealed an intriguing intelligence. In the laboratory of the human body, there are complacent cells that act the way we expect them to, as they have for generations. These are subject to programmed cell death, or apoptosis, the mechanism that forces each cell to keep to the general cycles of cell life, dying when damaged or no longer needed. Cancer cells, on the other hand, are super cells that have overcome the limits imposed on normal cell life and reproduction.

Our parabolic vessel helps us to focus the cancer cells and send them out into the universe. The parabola is a mathematical curve that is often used in everyday life. Imagine a satellite dish as an example: this is not a random shape; it is a parabola in receiving mode. The dish gathers all of the incoming information from satellites and, regardless of where that information hits on the surface of the dish; it bounces that information to one focal point. Consider, too, a car headlight. The parabolic dish that surrounds the bulb is in sending mode, and serves to focus the light from the bulb into a beam that shines directly ahead where we need to see.

Here, we use this parabolic structure to help us direct cancer cells from Earth out into the universe. Each cell is on its own journey. They start out crowded together in a tightly focused beam that is constantly changing direction with the rotation of our planet. As the beam becomes diffuse, they drift farther apart until each is truly alone. Sooner or later, each cell will fall to the surface of some receptive planet. This planet, once too hot or too dry, will have sufficiently evolved (as new planets do) for life to take a foothold despite ongoing harsh conditions. Through eons of evolution, this life will continue to evolve from that little spark to a world full of complex and varied life forms. There are billions of galaxies, each containing billions of stars.

How many planets exist that are ready for life is unknowable, but the cancer cells seem willing to take the opportunity we offer. While some cells may end up voyaging for eternity and others may fall into a star or black hole, think of what it means to be the one cell that jump-starts a whole ecosystem.

The earth spins as it wanders through space. Consequently, every time the parabolic ritual is used, the dish is aimed at a different area of the universe than ever before. Even when it looks as if it is aimed at a place covered during a previous exercise, the angle will have changed, and new "targets" will be exposed.

In this visualization, we invite the cancer to leave the host they are harming and go to a place where each cell may be the spark of life that takes root on a planet that is ripe for life.

In Alchemy, we begin with identifying the "matter," the prime material that requires transformation. I think of the colloquial question "What is the matter?" Cancer is certainly a worthy "matter" to be transformed alchemically. Although this process can and will benefit individuals, it is ideal for use at the collective level, where group energies intentionally expressed create the strongest influence. This vessel is strengthened by each and every person who takes this journey.

JOURNEY

Parabola

Start by grounding and centering. If you are working with others, acknowledge the people in the circle. If you are alone, take a moment to honor your own willingness to do this work, and take your place in the original circle that continues to be strengthened every time this journey is taken.

Focus on your heart flame, and feed your flame with love. . . . Notice how your heart flame grows. Bring in the Heart Breath, starting with the Earth Breath and moving into breathing in through the crown the intelligence and beneficent energies from the cosmos. . . . When you exhale, send the energy out in every direction from the heart.

Take a moment to align yourself with the universal love that permeates the universe. . . .

Build a strong fire with this alchemy. . . . The radiant light that is emitted connects to the heart flames of others who are working with you as well as all of those who have done this work before. Feel your connection to the large and growing circle. . . .

As you connect, continue to practice your Heart Breath, feel your heart flame unite with the heart flames of the other people who are part of this circle. . . . Feel the geographical span of the greater circle. It is as though you are part of a great, glowing circle whose light gets stronger with each breath. . . .

Invite your spirit guides, ancestors, deities, animal totems, plant spirit allies, and any intelligence throughout the creation that is willing to help and support you and all participants in this process. . . .

Now shift the focus so that you are exhaling from your heart into the center of the circle. Notice how the circle creates the shape of a parabolic curve—the vessel you are surrounding is a parabola.

As you continue breathing the Heart Breath, allow the energy of compassion to flow from your heart, through your hands, and into the center of the circle.

As the current gets stronger, and when all present are fully engaged and connected, place yourself in the center if you are the one with cancer, or call into the focal point those you wish to work with who are dealing directly with the disease. As we invoke the energies of Earth and Sky through this parabola, the center of our circle becomes the antenna. If you are in the center, speak your willingness to receive and be strengthened by the energies that are flowing into you. . . . Relax, and open further to the energies pouring into the center from every direction—from the outer circle, from the Earth as directed through our Heart Breaths and our hands, and from the intelligence of the stars and the outer cosmic energies.

When the energies in the focal point feel full to you, they can be extended throughout the circle, until all present are full. . . .

Now it is time to redirect the flow of energy and send the cancer cells out, straight up from those in the center of the circle. Invite cancer to respond to your call, stating your intention and honoring out loud.

Salute the cancer cell. Thank it for the depth of its teachings. Honor its potential out in the universe where it will help instead of harm, and offer your prayers that it will achieve its highest potential. As you appeal to its intelligence, honor with confidence its ability to find its way.

Continue to hold your intention as the migration of cancer cells begins. . . .

In response to the invitation, the cancer cells start to leave, transmitted outward from the parabola. As the group continues to transmit the energies, the flow of existing cancer cells gets stronger. By virtue of the size and power of the collective circle, the transmission flows in such a strong current that it attracts many cancer cells from hosts who have not been specifically included in the process. [*Long pause.*]

Not all the cancer will evacuate at once, but we can hope that we are conducting a portion each time we do this. Keep up the transmission by simply paying attention as the process continues. . . .

Allow plenty of time for the process to complete itself. . . . This is a moment of power.

Now is the time for you to simply hold space for something unimaginable to occur; open to divine intervention. Take the time you need to observe and enjoy this part of the transformation process. [*Pause.*]

Eventually, you (and your group) will move into a sense of completion. This feeling of being spent reflects the void created by the new absence of cancer and the waning flow of energy.

When you feel complete for this round, it is time to refill.

Remember what it was like to be in the womb, connected to your mother through an umbilical cord. Each of us, and the entire parabolic vessel, is connected to the Great Mother. It is from this vast and infinite source that we are filled and renewed. Allow yourself to experience the vital energy from the Mother entering and pouring through your entire body, your consciousness, your soul, and your spirit. [*Pause.*]

When you and every other being holding space in the parabola are filled, offer your gratitude. It is important to honor and give thanks to all beings supporting this work: all the unseen spirits, your totems and guides, deities of various pantheons, the great mysteries, the plant spirits, the energies and powers of the earth and the cosmos. Remember to thank yourself and everyone who has taken time to strengthen the parabola to lessen the suffering on the planet. Take a moment for honoring and thankfulness.

Pause. . . .

Ground and center. . . .

As you slowly and gently return to your current place, know that the parabola continues to function. Also, the structure of the parabola that you have tuned into remains viable beyond the time when you are focusing on it. Remember that it is strengthened every time anyone does this work. You can return to the energy of healing with the parabola at any time.

You should drink a full glass of water after you complete this meditation.

Record your experience in your journal.

PART V

It's About Time

22

The Enigma of Time and Other Dimensions

Did you know that the sunlight falling on your arm took only eight minutes' travel time from the sun? Yet it took a hundred thousand years, more or less, for each photon to travel at the speed of light from its origin in the core of the sun to the sun's surface. How is this possible? It happens because time ticks by at a slower pace in the gravitational well of the sun's mass—that plus the fact each photon takes a crazy zigzag tour known as the drunkard's walk. In this chapter, we will focus on the distortion of time.

Time has been puzzling humans throughout history, and numerous theories attempt to explain it. As with most topics explored in this work, direct experience mines the deepest treasures. There are a few things that we can say about time, both from studying others' theories and from delving into it firsthand.

EXPLORING TIME

It appears that time is a construct. It did not exist before the big bang, and then during our evolution, its existence has been a constant influence. Human beings play with time on a regular basis and, in doing so, rearrange its order: we bring the past into the present and the present into the future; we suspend time, and, during our most profound experiences, feel complete and total presence in the absence of time.

Descriptions of the experience of time include being "in time," "out of time," and "on time"; we have "time out" and feel time "stand still"; we "waste time," "spend time," and on and on. While it is often said that time is an illusion, our experience of it is very real. We habitually see ourselves moving through it, and occasionally find ourselves outside of it. Time is also described as flowing like a river, or existing as a thread in the tapestry of reality. But what is time?

What we do know is that the measurement of time, historically, was divided into minutes and hours by a monk in Europe who was attempting to be efficient with the workload of the monastery. Prior to that, greater natural phenomena—the movement of the sun, phases of the moon, tides and stars, equinoxes and solstices—served to mark the passage of time and offered reliable rhythms for those whose attention to these events aided the survival of their communities and tribes.

Although traditional thought presents the flow of time as a steady and consistent pace, many feel that time is speeding up. We tend to take on that perspective as we age, or when we are having fun. Of course it is possible that time is speeding up as we approach the end of time, and our clocks and other ways to measure time are all speeding up, too. As soon as you place a measure on it, time becomes elusive. The very measuring of time is what limits us, what ultimately binds us in time.

Until the observer observes, all possibilities are still in play. There are as many possibilities for our future as there are renditions and memories of history. In one way, we do not have to guess about the future: we can view the possibilities, choose the one that excites or pleases us, and then draw it toward us or, more accurately, move into it. There is no predetermined future because we are creating it at every moment. Imagine a magic carpet that not only takes you to existing destinations, but also helps you make changes on your way there.

Part of the important work before us now is aligning with the future we want to be in. All the possibilities are laid out before us. . . .

TIME AS A DIMENSION

Time was not always viewed as a dimension. We were so thoroughly immersed in it; we could not find an objective way to look at it. Einstein shocked the scientific world when he proposed that time does not progress at the same rate everywhere. There is no master clock that everything adheres to. Einstein's position was, simply put: the speed of travel and gravity will each influence the rate at which time passes. While his insights filtered out from academia into the minds of the general public, the image of time continued to evolve. Soon, relatively speaking, the concept of time having been created during the big bang became acceptable. Suddenly the three spatial dimensions gained a fourth partner—time.

In the hundred plus years since Einstein's revolutionary insights, enough people have truly understood them to make casual conversations about them possible. Quantum physics and string theory were radical ideas, but they, too, have entered the mainstream. That there may be more than four dimensions was an idea that was once considered to be quite bizarre—now the question is "How many?"

What are the possibilities for traveling into other dimensions? Do we need to create new organs of perception? It appears that, currently, our ability to perceive is compromised by the limits of our body.

Astrophysicists have reported that our universe contains way too much gravity for the matter it contains. The answer to this conundrum could be that gravity leaks here from other dimensions and is evidence of their existence. How can we access other dimensions to learn more?

Our corporal bodies may simply not be adequate for a prolonged journey into other dimensions. Embracing any such exploration requires a confidence that the body is safe and that the connection to our mind and spirit remains intact. In entering new dimensions, we are taking a risk: how do we know we will be able to come back? We are not simply going to another place, as in taking a trip to Mars; we are extending our senses into an entirely new and different universe where something as basic as a molecule of water might be assembled differently. Perhaps we will not discover how to examine new realities and map new frontiers like technicians with special tools, or explorers with the right ships. Then again, maybe that is just what we will do. For our purposes right now, an extra bit of respect and care may be prudent when we attempt to escape from the known reality where the rules for survival are understood and understandable.

There is a schism created between the mind and the body when we experience interdimensional travel. Mark has one memorable experience during which his body recoiled in terror at how far he traveled on his journey. As a result of that fear, his body pumped the adrenaline needed to keep him alive. Conversely, his mind was fully at peace with the journey, moving through concepts of eternity, infinity, and an all-pervasive dimension where time did not exist at all. He saw the work of an omniscient intelligence that he knew himself to be part of. He witnessed the magnitude of Creation, looking back toward infinity before the big bang and looking forward to see that there is no end in sight. He came to the conclusion that our intelligence was created to witness the magnitude of this one perpetual event. Yet within that expansiveness, he realized that his tiny brain and limited intelligence could not comprehend the vastness of the multidimensional terrain of the All.

He also learned that the intelligence of his body, something closer to the animal being, could feel threatened when his High Self goes ajourneying. The occasional and random surges of adrenalin continued for days and the emotion they invoked was fear. That, unto itself, was a profound teaching, and has influenced our work with time and dimensions and how we have presented it to others ever since.

We have come to be intrigued by the idea that time is a dimension. This appeals to us because it infers the possibility that there are even more dimensions in addition to time. If we can even begin to understand time, then we may be capable of understanding some other seemingly unfathomable dimension. But which, if any, of our senses will we employ when we are navigating other dimensions? Our senses inform us; we can see the stars at night, for instance. And although current technology has expanded our sensory capabilities (now we can "see" planets orbiting stars, and "see" what the various stars are burning for fuel), technology will not be assisting us in our quest here; we will have to expand our sensory capabilities using other means.

Shamans and mystics have a long tradition of working their magic from other realms; for us to do the same will require a shift and growth in our abilities to perceive and work within these realms. The following exercises are offered as a way to do just that, and they come with our hope and prayer that personal epiphanies and new insights for planetary healing will occur as new paths of perception are opened.

BREAKING REALITY BARRIERS

The exercises in this section are designed to give you an experience outside your usual perceptions; perhaps even beyond the parameters of your own imagination. They also offer interesting ways to explore the dimension of time. Please read through them before you practice them, as they are not given as journeys, rather as instructions.

EXERCISE
Shrinking Consciousness

Instead of going to an abstract point outside of yourself, you are going to practice working from a point within yourself.

When you walk up to a tree, there are certain mathematical ratios between you and that tree that you have lived with your entire life. Wherever you are in relation to what you are focusing on (e.g. the tree) is your point of perception. This point provides you with a sense of identity defined in relative terms: it tells you where you fit into the scheme of things. When you begin the exercise of shrinking your point of perception, do not imagine your body getting smaller. Instead, the tree, or whatever you choose to relate with, starts to look larger; everything about it starts taking on gigantic proportions. As your point of perception shrinks, this phenomenon accelerates. You move from perceiving the tree to perceiving its bark, with its marvelous texture. Then the textures in the bark become cavernous. What used to be flakes on the edges of the bark are now boulders casting deep shadows. As the bark becomes a huge landscape, everything starts to speed up. Your point of perception gets so small that you cannot see the horizon anymore.

A fractal complexity nearly explodes as you race to become this infinitely small point, this ever-shrinking dot. You crash through a barrier beyond which the tree is no longer matter. Now you see the space between the molecules, a sky of many points.

As you continue shrinking, you start to question, *At what point do I become too small to exist? Is that possible?*

You can shrink your consciousness past the microscopic level, smaller than anything you have ever considered. You will have broken the reality barrier. No matter how small you get, you can get smaller. Smaller, that is, until there is no point in shrinking further. The mysteries are laid out before you; the shrinking has stopped.

There are two ways to return to the starting point, but first notice the sense of motionless floating that accompanies the cessation of shrinking. . . . It is during this pause that you may witness the building blocks of our universe, and how mysterious energies flicker into and out of our dimension of reality. The first way back feels like buoyancy in water when it begins to lift you, giving direction to the surface. In this exercise there is a force directing the growth of your sense of perspective—guiding your return to the norm.

The second way home is for you to discover on your own. . . . Wait for it; it will come for you. . . .

Now that you have an idea of how a shrinking journey proceeds, you can choose where to practice this exercise. Place yourself next to whatever you want to observe as you shrink. It can be a plant, a tree, or whatever stationary object you choose. From your Beacon, establish yourself next to the chosen object. If you remain in your power spot in the air, you will be able to perceive air molecules.

EXERCISE
Expanding Consciousness

Be sure to start with the Heart Breath. From wherever you choose to practice this exercise, expand your consciousness to include your entire altar and the area around it, then again to encompass a larger area, including the nearest town or city; keep expanding further to include the world, the solar system, and then the universe. Now go one step further and break the reality barrier. Do it again. You are beginning this exercise with a series of leaps that grow your sense of size, your point of perspective to and beyond the edge of the universe. Traditional and accepted knowledge has us in a finite universe and has allowed scientists to measure it, weigh it, and even count the molecules it contains. Our purpose here is to blow the walls of their box asunder and to fly past this reality barrier in all directions simultaneously. Or, as Buzz Light Year says, "To Infinity and Beyond!"

Notice your energy levels. Notice how with every leap, when the energy you put into the expansion was exhausted, you came back to your regular point of perception. To describe how to do this; to give clear instructions on returning, would be like instructing a child on a pogo stick how to return from the apogee of each hop.

EXERCISE
Slowing Down Consciousness

Notice what happens around you when your relationship to time increasingly slows down so that everything else moves ever more quickly, inversely proportional to your rate of slowing. As the molecules close to you move faster, you feel their heat. The more they speed up, the warmer they feel to you. The visible light starts advancing through the spectrum—as light speeds up in relationship to your pupils, the colors begin to shift. Now slow down by quantum leaps, until you can witness the life of a tree in a split second. The tree bursts out of the ground in an explosion of energy. You understand the tree as energy—its entire life is as brief as an exploding bomb. Each type of plant now burns at its own rate. The fields burn differently from the forests. Take in the soft fire of bushes and the glow on the ground, which is the shimmering of the grasses and the weeds. Slow down further. The Earth is burning like the sun now, spinning like a top. . . . Now slow down a million times more, and watch the universe speed up. The planets race around the sun, the stars race around the galaxies, the galaxies are spinning, dipping, spiraling, throwing sparks everywhere. Now slow down again. . . . What do you see? And again . . . Now come back, back to your traditional sense of time. . . .

Take your time. . . .

EXERCISE

Speeding Up Consciousness

Now speed yourself up in relation to time. As you speed up, life around you appears to slow down. Notice the temperature dropping as the molecules slow down. The air becomes thicker, the colors turn bluer. Notice that fire, the life of a match, now takes years. From your perspective, it is so cool and so dense that you can cut the flame into pieces. Speed yourself up even more and move to a really big flame. It is now so slow and cold that you can cut the flame and stack the pieces. You can see the energy as solid, and make forms out of the energy now, the molecules are moving so slowly. You can touch and manipulate them, or if you wish, you could build with them.

When you are ready to come back, relax, breathe deeply. Notice a gravity-like pull, a current that brings you back to traditional time.

These exercises on time can help illustrate the phrase, "everything is energy." The electrons that make up a table repel the electrons in your hand when you slap it. It feels like solid matter, but it is mostly space. Play with time and see what other insights reveal themselves. Maybe this time you will explore the sun, walking through its majestic landscapes.

The following journey takes place at the ancient enigmatic Sphinx in Egypt. It will take you backward in time—further, perhaps, than you have ever considered going before . . .

SPHINX JOURNEY
Time as an Oracle

Breathe the Heart Breath until you stand in the nexus point between the Earth and Sky. The light radiates from your heart center and surrounds you. It is within the glow of this light that you, in your balanced and centered and grounded state, can begin to perceive yourself standing in front of the great Sphinx in Egypt.

It is dawn. The sun has not yet risen, but the stars above are fading. . . . Feel yourself in the stillness of early morning, that tranquil place between night and day. . . . Raise your head slowly and gaze into the face of the great Sphinx. As you bring the Sphinx more clearly into focus, stand between the paws of the Sphinx. Look up at this magnificent being.

The dawn begins to emerge behind you.

Gather your intention at this time, as you prepare to request permission of the Sphinx, the guardian of the necropolis on the Giza plateau and known to some as the great Earth Altar, to explore the mysteries of time.

As you gaze up at the Sphinx, its calm, regal face is looking at some distant point behind you. The Sphinx, as it appears today, is draped with fine sculpted stone that hides the ancient, weatherworn surface within. Your perception shifts and you can see through these outer stones; as they fade away, details emerge to reveal earlier and earlier incarnations, indicating that the effects of time, wind, and water are fading too.

The paws of the Sphinx regain their definition; they look new and fresh. The face moves through its various alterations. Through all of these changes, the eyes remain constant, and focusing ahead on the same point. For a brief moment, the Sphinx loses its form altogether, and you glimpse the original rock outcropping, the natural stone as yet untouched by human hands—just a glimpse, and then the shaping of the sphinx begins anew.

You have arrived at that nexus, the space between the unshaped Sphinx and the carved and sculpted Sphinx. [*Pause.*]

Return your attention to your breath. When you inhale the Heart Breath now, focus on your breath, your love, and the energies of Earth and Sky; hold this breath for a moment to allow these ingredients to blend and alchemize within your heart. When you exhale, direct your breath from your heart, like a great beam of light, into the heart of the Sphinx, carrying your respect, your humility, and your request. . . . [*Pause.*]

As if in response to your request, the heart of the great Sphinx opens, and as the first ray of the rising sun touches you from behind, you enter the open heart of the Sphinx. For a moment, you are in total darkness; the light from the sun cannot follow you into the stone. . . .

Within the heart of the Sphinx, you have a sense of knowing the crystalline medium within the stone. It is within this matrix that the totality of information becomes accessible to you.

From this vantage point, the history of humans and our accumulation of knowledge are revealed as a tiny moment compared to the hugeness of the knowledge available throughout the universe. You feel yourself transfigured as you meld into the cold, old stone. . . .

You move back through time, sensing from within all the changes.

The very stone itself begins to heat and soften as it returns to the molten core under the mantle of earth.

Experience the forces of heat, pressure, and gravity, and move beyond that which will become the Earth's crust....

Drift back further and faster to a time of less gravity, less heat, back to and before the very formation of this planet....

You are floating in dust, floating in space, as you explore the nature of the universe before our solar system, before the creation of our galaxy. You take in the accumulation of dust and debris of older spent galaxies. Even the molecules are less complicated now. ... Notice how intelligence permeates the entire field of primordial space.... [Pause.]

Now, it is time to start your return, moving forward in time. Observe the assembly of the molecules, the aggregation that becomes our planet, the minute crystals that precipitate and become the stone that will become the Sphinx.... Notice the knowledge you gain and the deep profound understanding that is waking within you....

You are racing forward in time toward this moment in your life, aware of influences and momentums that shape the destiny of you and entire cultures....

As you come back closer to this current moment, you retain the awareness that the firmness of the stone, its absolute stillness, is an illusion....

Every moment in your life has led you to this point. Do not slow down. Let your momentum carry you forward, beyond this now. You are part of a great flow....

It is moving so fast and there is so much going on at once, yet within the vastness you glean a hint of where this will lead, a hint of what is to come in the rest of your life, and of all life....

As though on a bungee cord, you have gone far into the past, and then from there shot as far as you can into the future, with eyes wide open, and then back to this moment. As this moment comes back into focus, the all-pervasive intelligence remains the one constant throughout the ever-changing universe.... This is the last thing you notice before you start to feel squeezed and find you cannot stay within the stone of the Sphinx. You are being expelled.

You find yourself once again standing between the paws....

Back in the daylight, you greet the risen sun.

Your entire story, as well as the story of the universe, is impressed within the stone in the heart of the Sphinx. With this new avenue of information open for you, feel how deeply connected you are with the heart of the Sphinx. This abiding connection will ground you now and be available to you throughout your life. In the deepest recesses of your being, you know that this is your sacred connection to the oracular source in the stars. This understanding will grow over time. [*Pause.*]

Reconnect to the Heart Breath and offer your gratitude to the Sphinx, the majestic Earth Altar.

Begin to be aware of your physical body once again. Come back into your body at this time....

Breathe the Earth Breath, and then the full Heart Breath to ground and center yourself....

Record your experience with the Sphinx in your journal. Your perceptions of the future might reveal some surprises, and will certainly make interesting retrospective reading in the future.

23
The Cave of the Ancestors

Our ancestors provide a continuing source of wisdom and guidance, if only we can connect with them. Each of us has an ancestral lineage, not just for our bloodlines, but for our souls as well. We can follow our mitochondrial DNA all the way back to the mitochondrial Eve—placed, according to a Rice University study in 2010, at about 200,000 years ago. Our spiritual ancestry is harder to pinpoint.

Think of all human beings across time as being connected by threads. Through time, the threads are spun into ropes. Each of us living here and now, in the present, holds onto some rope, which extends back into the past and onward into the future. We are being supported by all the ancestors who have preceded us and by all the progeny that will follow us.

One problem we face in current time is that the rope between now and our ancestors has become a bit frayed. Actually, in some places, it has been cut, tattered, torn, and broken. Consequently, we are missing out on much of the wisdom of our past and the potential it holds to inform our current endeavors. We have compromised a structure meant to support humanity across time, and we do not even know how much has been lost.

When we look at our personal family lines, particularly in recent years, we find dysfunction in almost every thread. Many people have disconnected from family for safety and sanity, but in so doing we have also lost the importance and relevance of our ancestry. Many Americans whose lineage goes back to Europe had their lines cut during the Inquisition, when millions of women, healers, and heretics were burned at the stake. Add the Holocaust for Jews, the slave trade for Africans, and other historic genocides: many of us cannot trace our lineage or name our ancestors beyond our great-grandparents.

Reconnecting our ancestral lines brings us healing. Once healed, this connection enlivens, supports, and feeds us. Between the collective field of intelligence, which surrounds us, and the DNA within our cells, we have access to an uninterrupted recording of the entirety of our human, pre-human, and even pre-Earth existence—the memory of everything we have ever been. We have, accessible to each of us, a record of lessons learned by our ancestors, their struggles and accomplishments, and even a hint of their dreams and aspirations. The purpose of the quest in this chapter is to reconnect with the wisdom of our ancestors, and heal the broken lines to our ancient past.

In 2006, Linda Star Wolf and I had completed writing the first ten chapters of the manuscript for *Shamanic Mysteries of Egypt*. I was heading off to Egypt and planning to take my participants through the first rites of passage that Star Wolf and I had articulated in this writing. According to my guidance, I needed to enter a cave and submit to the pantheon of Egypt in order to receive the initiations myself before sharing them with others.

I spoke to an Egyptian friend, Marwan, who said, "I know the perfect cave for you. But you have to come early enough because it will take us three days and we have to get special permits." The cave, he told me, was in the White Desert. We dillydallied in our preparations, and by the time we got our passports to the government, we were too late: permission was denied for the time frame that we needed. Marwan was not worried. "We'll just go off-road. I'll find it."

Marwan knew of this cave and its whereabouts because he had visited an archaeological dig happening nearby in the late nineties. Tools found at the site, a prehistoric village on the edge of a dry lake bed, were dated to be approximately 6,500 years old. Just beyond the site of the ancient village, a limestone cliff juts out from the desert floor. At the top, there is a square-cut opening into a cave. Inside the cave are carvings of a lion's paws, antelope, and, on the far back wall, handprints of the ancestors who inhabited the region.

The White Desert is not like deserts in the States. Bare of almost all growth, it is extremely desolate, with relentless sun. At the same time, it offers an environmental niche, a unique ecology whose abundance of life becomes evident only with great patience (a small yellow bird, curious and quite unafraid, visited us and explored our camp and tents). An incredibly huge expanse of sand with astonishing and distinctive mineral formations jutting upward, the White Desert is exquisite with its strangeness and other-worldly play of light and clear, bejeweled night sky. We set off from Giza for our expedition—Marwan, his dog, and I—in a jeep outfitted for desert travel with all the comforts of life, including a solar-powered refrigerator that afforded us fresh food for the duration of our trip. We went as far as we could on the main road and then, to avoid checkpoints, went off-road in search of the cave. After many hours out in the vast desert, following a compass and a GPS device, we found the site just before sunset.

I knew as soon as I saw it, even from a distance, that I was headed for a profound vision-quest experience. We scrambled up the steep incline in time to check things out in the cave before darkness fell. When I entered the cave, I was filled with a sense of reverence and awe; this was surely the cave of the local shamans who had taken great pains to create the entrance. Judging by the size of the handprints on the back wall, the people were smaller than we are today. I imagine them standing on one another's shoulders to blow the minerals that left a stencil of their handprints, so clear that they could have been imprinted the day before. I snapped a very few photographs before I was overcome with the sense that flashbulbs were inappropriate here. But I am really glad I took the few I did so that you can see the hands they left for us. I made some sketches of the lion's paws and when it became too dark to see, I went down to where Marwan was setting up camp on the desert flats below. We ate well and slept well, and rested throughout the following day.

The cave

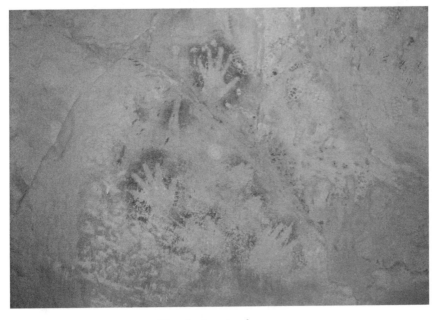

Handprints in the cave

The next afternoon we entered the cave just before sunset, and I set up my altar toward the back. Marwan and I offered a short ceremony of gratitude and intention to begin the vision quest that would lead to my initiation. Marwan and his dog went below to stand guard and explore the surrounding area.

Although many of the details of my experience are difficult to articulate, and it would be irreverent to speak of others, I did interact with ancestors throughout the night, and experienced many of the rites of passage in *Shamanic Mysteries of Egypt*. The presence of the lioness was strong. At times it was as though her eyes were everywhere, penetrating my every thought and action, and at the same time aware and watchful lest any intrusion approach.

I spent much of my time lying down toward the back of the cave in pitch darkness, yet the strength of the light entering the mouth of the cave would catch my attention every time I sat up. I finally had to investigate, wondering what could be causing the sunset to linger so long. It was the stars! The starlight radiating from the belly of the goddess Nut (pronounced Noot, Egyptian goddess of the night sky) was so bright I could have read by it. I stood in astonishment, nearly brought to my knees by the awesome vista of desert and sky. Humbled by the gift of Nut's blessing, I took it in with deep gratitude, and then returned to my altar to complete my journey. The deepest darkness just before dawn found me singing at the top of my lungs, chanting mantras that rang out over the desert as if from a sand-and-limestone-encrusted bell. "Love Will Prevail" still echoes in my mind when I remember the last hours of my quest.

The presence of the ancestors—my ancestors—was palpable; I felt somehow connected to rites that had been held here thousand of years ago, and was honored to continue what had been previously generated by the elders of this land. Although we cannot know how long this region had been inhabited before the village that was recently found and studied, the sense of continuity, of a living chain of life and wisdom, gave strength not only to the moments of my quest, but to the realization that our connection with our ancestry is a vital and potent means for healing ourselves, and our planet. Yet much of the healing that was to come from this journey came later, after I had returned to the States. Because of the profound nature of the vision quest experience, I found it difficult to speak about it to any but my most intimate friends and family, and even then I chose my words very carefully. I felt and still feel extremely protective of this cave and the shamans' spirits who continue to dwell there.

Before I went to Egypt, I had been invited to participate in the International Conference on Shamanism, which was to take place in Santa Fe, New Mexico, in January 2007. For my subject I had chosen "Becoming an Oracle," though when I named it, as often happens, I had no idea what exactly I would be presenting. This is a way of keeping the magic alive; I commit to a "Big Subject" and then wait and watch for how the universe will deliver. As the time drew near, still unsure of what I would be teaching, I consulted with my visionary friend Gloria Taylor Brown, who said, "Of course, you're taking them to the ancestor cave." My first response was a vehement, "That's impossible!" She explained what she was seeing and hearing: that the ancestors were offering to help. The need to heal our relationship with our ancestors cannot be ignored if we are truly interested in healing our planet and ourselves. The ancient shamans whose spirits still inhabit this cave told us that they would receive and help those we sent to them, provided they entered in a respectful way.

I ask that before you journey to the Cave of the Ancestors, you clarify your intention, purify yourself, and be prepared to humbly request their assistance. You may wish to choose a thoughtful gift to give them in spirit. Remember that when the cave was active and people were alive and inhabiting the nearby village, there were grasses upon what is now the stark desert, and antelope and lions roamed there. I recommend that you read the journey all the way through before you take it, so that you are prepared for the detailed instructions that you will receive along the way.

Initially, on your first journey to the cave, you will be invited to reach up and place a hand close to one of the hands on the wall. Reaching out in spirit, you will feel a very strong electrically charged connection when your hands meet. Once the connection is made, the transmission will begin and you will receive information directly from these ancestors or from others you may be directed to at that point. The purpose of the first journey is to heal the frayed and tattered lines between you and those who came before. Subsequent visits, once you have made relationships with the ancestors there, can be intended for healing or oracular advice, or perhaps to receive teachings and wisdom not yet considered.

You can always go back to the cave. Any place we take you to on these journeys are points of accessibility, with very specific opportunities attached to each. We can offer some guidelines, but it is up to you to discern what each place holds for you. In the cave, there are many possibilities. Some of you will recognize it as a portal. While you enter in the White Desert in Egypt, you can come out anywhere. It is an intersection point that connects to every sacred cave on the planet.

Whatever you choose to do here, drumming or some other musical support can be helpful. If you would prefer to take this journey as a guided meditation that has already been set to music, it is one of nineteen journeys in the program *Becoming an Oracle.**

JOURNEY
To Heal Our Ancestral Lines

Start by grounding, centering, and breathing the Heart Breath. . . . And so it is, within your glowing heart flame, that you find yourself in the White Desert of Egypt, a barren land of stark beauty. For millennia, harsh winds have carved the minerals into craggy cliffs and impossibly shaped formations jutting up from the vast sand sea. It is here, many thousands of years ago when the land was still green and the savannah supported antelope and lions, that Egyptian ancestors dwelt beside a lake bed, now long dried up. Not far from the lake bed that resembles an imaginary moonscape, there is a cave in a limestone cliff. Its opening was carved by ancestors who were the shamans of the time.

---

*Becoming an Oracle is a seven-CD audio program created and narrated by Nicki Scully and published by Sounds True, Louisville, Colo., 2009.

It is late afternoon when you approach the cliff; the entrance to the cave beckoning you. You head toward this cave of the ancestors, knowing that there you will reconnect to your frayed and broken ancestral lines. As you make your way up the rocky sand toward the opening of the cave, you can feel the gravity of what awaits you, and you realize this is more than you may have anticipated. Each step brings you to a deeper sense of the sacred. Take a moment to consider how very long ago it was when the ancestors dwelt here and used this cave. . . . At the opening of the cave, you pause, turn, and gaze out across the vast desert. Take a moment to center yourself. Contemplate what brought you here. Consider your intention as you prepare to enter the cave and meet the ancestors. [*Pause.*]

Now, close your left hand into a gentle fist and look at the fleshy hollow between your thumb and forefinger. Now lift your fist high and pause . . . You will feel something moist as a drop of liquid takes form upon it. How magical: it is the nectar of the gods. Give thanks for this opportunity. Go ahead, lick the drop. . . . Feel and taste the sweetness of the nectar as it enters and moves through you, as if you were being filled with liquid light. . . . Your internal frequency begins to shift. . . . You are in tune and in touch with those who carved the opening that leads into this cave. Any nervousness you may have felt vanishes. You become fully relaxed and confident. . . . Quite purposefully, you enter the cave.

It is cooler inside the cave. About four or five feet inside, on the wall opposite the opening, you see the lioness paws carved into the stone. Stop for a moment to give honor and respect to the great lions that once roamed this land, and especially the one who guards this cave.

Now turn to the left. You can see almost to the back of the cave. As you make your way farther inside, you notice on the walls an array of scratch marks left by the ancient ones. You can just make out the graceful horns of an antelope. Honor the antelope that fed these ancient people.

[*Pause.*]

Now climb up onto a platformlike formation in the floor. It is an easy climb: put your knee up first and then pull yourself up to the next level. As you near the back, on a wall off to the left, you see up high the hands of the ancestors. Take a moment just to feel the sacredness of this place and contemplate the age of the handprints. [*Pause.*]

Look for the handprint that seems to call to you. Reach toward it, but do not touch. The connection to the ancestor's hand comes with a jolt as the recognition of skin and calluses with the underlying structure of flesh and bone immediately fuses with your own hand. Although the fusion happens instantly, the transmission itself will take some time. Be with the ancestors. Once the connection feels established, drop your hand and know that it remains connected. Receive the wisdom and healing that are here for you now. [*Long pause.*]

Within the transmission received from the ancestor, you may see images, perhaps a history of the ceremonies and meditations that have taken place in this sacred place, or teachings of what they saw and how they saw them. You may even receive messages from other ancestors, from anywhere in the world. [*Long pause.*]

When the experience is complete, thank the ancestors for the teachings they have given you and know that you can come back whenever you feel the need or desire. . . . It is time to begin your return journey. Climb down off the platform and make your way carefully down to the lower level of the cave. Be careful with your footing on the rocks. As you move slowly back the way you came, acknowledge the antelope and, of course, the lioness, with deep gratitude. . . . Keep going all the way back to the opening. . . .

Step out of the cave and into the glaring sunlight. Yes, you have spent the entire night in communion with the ancestors. As you stand before the opening, your eyes adjusting to the light, you will begin to return to this physical form.

Ground and center yourself....

When you are ready to open your eyes, take the time to write about your experience with the ancestors in your journal.

This journey can provide a venue for various kinds of transformation. When you are ready to confront whatever those issues are that need to be transformed in you, the cave offers a good, safe place to enter with intention in order to create that alchemy.

The cave offers many other possibilities that you will only encounter as you pay your respects and spend additional time there. It can be used to commune with the ancestors and as a place of healing: sometimes the ancestors function as oracles. Also, remember the portal function of the cave allows you to visit other caves all over the planet and access information and guidance. You can also sit outside the cave entrance and look out over the veld, allowing yourself to be taken back to when people actually lived there.

24
Building a Wise Future

We have all heard tell of the Golden Age that awaits us at the end of our current travails here on planet Earth. While many stories speak of the glory time to come, few actually address how we go about achieving it. The alternative apocalypse does not bode well for enlightenment, because those left on Earth would be contending with survival issues that preclude the luxury of intellectual and spiritual pursuits. Perhaps the Golden Age could become manifest with grace and dignity—maybe it is closer than we think.

As we were going to sleep one night, I requested from Thoth, through Mark, a piece of work that would supply tools for bridging the time between our current challenges and the promised Golden Age. How are we going to get there? What are the steps we can take? Could we have some tools to help us get there faster?

Mark began describing the vivid experience that was being given to him. He became like a statue, a symbol for the human vessel that was sculpted with hammer and chisel—knocked into shape, hardened and fired, and otherwise forcibly fashioned with the crude, heavy hand of life (in the realm of hard knocks, as it were). As the images were being described, I drifted off. Once again, as if I were listening to a bedtime story, Morpheus* carried me away before my questions were answered.

---

*The Greek god of sleep.

I fell asleep somewhere between Mark's first image of Thoth standing next to a boulder, and his deeply felt experience of being rendered, in the end, into human flesh and bones.

Several days later, we were running errands in town when I suddenly came to, recalling our quest, I realized that I had missed an extraordinary opportunity for a new teaching. Mark remembered doing the work, but could not bring to mind any details. When he is visioning, he is operating so fully from the right brain that the next day, it is like trying to remember a dream—and about three days had passed. Our question felt so important that we decided to attempt to reconstruct the teaching. Thoth allowed us to retrieve it, but not without considerable work and painstaking attention. The result was well worth the effort, for it revealed a sophisticated practice that is not only unique in its artistic design, but also illustrative of our power to co-create in a hands-on, intentional way.

We began our reconstructed vision by imagining Mark inside the boulder, seated in the lotus position. Thoth first tapped on it with stone, and Mark could feel the reverberations within. That was his grounding. Amid the "clunk, clunk" sound, as Thoth continued, stone hitting stone, a chunk of the boulder chipped off, exposing a section of Mark's soft and fleshy shoulder. Next to that section he built a fire, and when the stone surrounding the fleshy area got red hot, Thoth threw water on him, so that it hardened around Mark's skin into a somewhat discolored shell. Thoth knocked again on the boulder. The big chunk that fell off this time exposed Mark's right ear, shoulder, right arm, and right leg. Again, Thoth could not continue chipping away until he had covered what was exposed with new shell. He tapped a few more times, put down the rock, and blew a whistle. Another chunk fell off, exposing Mark's back, which, under prodding, appeared to be soft.

Mark bravely held himself throughout this multisensory experience until we fully understood that we were being shown how an individual can be chiseled from the initial boulder, or first material, in a variety of ways, many of which were experienced in this process. Afterward he conveyed each detail as if from objective observation. The statue reconstructed from the original experience was burnt and pocked with hammer marks. Its color variations revealed exposure to high temperatures. There was rust in some places, and its soft parts looked sandblasted, with pit marks and miniature craters. There was nothing uniform about it, and different areas revealed the effects of exposure to extreme elemental forces. Still, in the end, a couple of soft areas remained.

When his work with the boulder was finished, Thoth reached into a window in a stone wall and pulled out a small opalescent statuette, careful not to bump it against the rock as he brought it out. He seemed to be looking for someone to hand it to. It looked sort of like an Oscar from the Academy Awards, only slightly bigger, and with a soft whitish glow. Unlike the statue he had just carved out of the boulder, it had a milky white surface with no impurities, and a uniformity of color and hardness.

Peering in, Mark could see through the window in the stone wall to many rows of similar statuettes, receding back as far as the eye could see. At a certain point, the tops of their heads began to look like a beehive formation. Thoth compared the old battered statue to the ivory-colored statuette in his hand and the lesson became clear: we can help, we can participate in the changes we want for the children coming into our world.

Thoth handled the new statuette carefully; it was clear he would not put it down in the dirt. It was also clear that this statuette, having been brought out, now had to be dealt with: it could not go back through the window and would dissolve if not empowered and given the opportunity to come into life.

Next Thoth gave us step-by-step instructions for our part of the co-creative process in infusing these perfect statuettes with all we want to bring into the future—the best of what we can imagine and with our most noble intentions. It took some time for the magnitude of this possibility to sink in: Thoth was offering us the opportunity to consciously help bring in new beings with the attributes and qualities that are needed on Earth for a brighter future.

It would be a great arrogance to want to clone ourselves or predetermine the character of a specific embryo in a specific womb—or to assume we could do any such thing. This work must be understood as more general, designed to assist us in co-creating the fully realized human being that we all have the potential to become. Hence, however and wherever the result appears in the world—it is the ideal offspring for that place, and we as co-creators will not be able to see or know the whereabouts or result of this co-creation—we do it because we know what is needed, and offer what we would hope for our loved ones and the future of humanity.

As in any co-creation process, it is of primary importance that we enter into this work from a place of clarity and purity of intention. If our minds stray or our intention becomes distorted, Thoth, the principle of the highest concept of mind, is the safeguard that disallows the completion of this piece. If you have not done it with absolute impeccability, it simply will not happen. If you practice this process and become adept at working with these statuettes, your time and attention will have a powerful effect.

THE STATUETTE

First we had to learn the process of creation, a craft that demands coordination and practice, skill and concentration. There are four steps to this art, outlined below. Each time you follow the instructions, you will go deeper and gain skill. The statuette, perfect in form, will become animated with the spirit that you impart as you sculpt the fire. Its nervous system will receive its contribution from the material created by focused sound. When you meld the two, the fire and sound, a new, coherent substance manifests that will add life to the statuette, and in turn convey the attributes and intentions from you and your High Self into a child that is about to be born. This contribution will influence a real birth somewhere in the world and one child will have been helped. It is important to note that nothing will go out into the world from you until you get the entire process right. It is through practice that you will become proficient enough with the first two steps to even begin invoking your High Self, and any attempt that does not complete all four steps will fade back into the prima material.

Step One

The first process involves molding a figurine out of fire to animate the statuette. The fire Thoth built near the stone wall is still lit. Breathe the Heart Breath, building up the energy and heart connection with which to connect to Thoth and the fire that is there for you. . . . It is reminiscent of a cheery bonfire, as on a camping trip, surrounded by river rocks that define the circle within which the fire burns. There are ample rocks, and you will find use for a couple of them during step two. Using your will and intention, take one flame from the bonfire. You are not grabbing a burning log—just the flame. When you reach into the fire you can mold the shape of the flame, but it has no consistency, and as soon as you take your hands away it vanishes. You can effect a change in how fire acts. Use the flame as if it were a tangible object with the capability of being molded. It is like working with cotton candy: you can barely feel the substance, but you can see tangible results of how the energy is molded.

Practice molding the flame. Each time you remove your hands, hold what you have created with your will and concentration. In a short time, whatever you have created will dissipate, but do not be concerned about what happens to it or where it goes.

Practice this until you become proficient at shaping and sustaining the energy of fire and until it can hold for some time once you let it go.

Step Two

Now, you are going to make sound with two stones, each about the size of a grapefruit, to create new matter. This matter will hold the characteristics of the new life you are bringing in. As you gain skill in this practice, you must also keep yourself clear and focused on your chosen intentions.

Pick up the two rocks, one in each hand, and knock them together. Hear the sound that results and attempt to hold it in place, again using your will and intention. You have just created the first bit of matter—it is hardly discernible and dissipates very quickly. Now start knocking the stones together in a continuous rhythm. The ensuing raps fortify the first one and the material you are creating gets denser, more tangible. With each impact, each time you knock the stones together with intent, you make more and more material. Move your hands around a little. As the source of the sound changes location, the resulting material will become even firmer and will last longer. When you have enough material to work with, it looks like a three-dimensional image with tiny, barely tangible lines going every-which-way, almost like a wad of crinkly cellophane.

Put down the stones while watching the material you just made, holding the energy with your gaze and your will. Now, reach up and mold the force that has gathered. Although it starts to leak back into the universe immediately, you have a brief opportunity to mold and shape it into a rough statuette. The speed at which your creation bleeds away will be influenced by your ability to hold focus, which will in turn be strengthened with practice. Alternate your practice. Shape and hold some flame, then make, shape, and hold some sound. As you become more proficient, material from each practice will linger longer as you begin working with the other.

Step Three

Next, it is time to start blending the two practices.

We live in, and on, all of the building blocks of life. What you are engaged in is the animation of life, sculpted from the eternal flame, surrounded by its energy and molded with the intention of its creator. Begin knocking the stones together again, holding the energy with your eyes. Each time you knock, the three-dimensional grid gets stronger. While you hold the ephemeral structure with your gaze, you can reach beyond it and mold the fire, sculpting what you want and then bringing it over to be wrapped in the sheet. A molecular bonding occurs as the sheet adheres to the form that you have sculpted with your hands.

Mastery of this step is imperative before you move on to the next and final one. As before, as when you practiced with the individual components, your creations will eventually fade away. The one big difference is the time it takes; the combined energies are more stable than each alone. It is paramount that you maintain clear and concentrated focus throughout in order for this ritual to come to fruition.

Start by sitting in front of the bonfire and choosing a strong-looking flame. Reach into the fire and pull the flame toward you, holding it with your will. Gently shape it into the size and form of Thoth's ivory-colored statuette. . . . Hold that new form in the air in front of you with your eyes while you reach down and pick up the two stones. Knock them together to create the material needed. When you have enough (you will know when that is), put the stones down and reach out to massage the new material around the flame statuette that you have held fast with your eyes and will.

Notice that once the two have been blended, a stronger consistency emerges. It does not melt away as fast as the flame or matter did on its own.

Practice this a few times until you become proficient in the practice. Each time you do it, the form will eventually melt away. Forms will not accrue as waste floating around.

Now is the time to put it all together. Before you can combine what you have learned and contribute to a real birth, you must learn to hold and infuse your intention and your prayers, and to conduct the qualities that you are invoking for this child—this part of you and the collective creation that will be coming into the future. It is important for us to be conscientious as we proceed so that we do not burden the new child with our personal issues or limitations. This part of the process requires careful consideration and forethought. When you are ready to put all the parts together, you need to develop your intent and purity of thought by invoking your High Self and your prayer before you begin.

We wish for this child to come in carrying wisdom and compassion, without needing to learn many of the lessons that have been so hard won for us. To do this, we must tap into our infinite experience and the wisdom of the collective intelligence in a way that allows the next generation to come into life with fewer limitations, fewer shackles, and a greater capacity for resilience. You might wish to write your prayer to help you remember what you are choosing to contribute, and add it to your Heart Breath, exhaling it into your creation as you mold and hold the combined material.

As you form and meld together the two components, fire and sound, hold the awareness that you are participating in a birth that will happen somewhere on this Earth. Again, please note that you will not be able to direct the statuette to a particular place or person, nor will you know where it is born.

Practice steps one and two with the addition of maintaining your clearest intention, after careful consideration of what you wish to contribute to the basic program of the new person.

When you feel ready, proceed to step four.

Step Four

This next step will be the culmination of all of your work. This is when co-creation can occur between the Divine Spirit and your High Self. Because of the time spent practicing the basic components of this process, your hands can deftly prepare for the statuette while you clear your mind and enter that deep meditative space that is the hallmark of one's High Self. Allow your ego to step aside and for something bigger to step in and guide your wishes for the children that are coming into our world.

The stage is set; all is in preparation for you. There is the fire, there are the stones, there is the opening in the stone wall where the ivory-like statuettes will be drawn from, and there stands Thoth, ready to assist.

Greet Thoth as you take your place and prepare. Thoth's presence is representative of both your High Self and Divine Spirit, as well as a gestalt of all of humanity's High Self. During this moment, while you and Thoth acknowledge each other, you will be given a brief glimpse of a fleshy, webbed tube that immediately whips back and out of sight. This is the universal birthing canal, the passageway between fetus and birth. The next time you see it, you will be presenting something to it.

Ground and center yourself. Breathe the Heart Breath. Pay particular attention to the love you are feeding to your heart flame, and the love and intelligence you are drawing from Earth and Sky. . . .

As you continue breathing the Heart Breath, take a moment to reflect upon what you are doing. . . . Review and focus on your intention as you align your love-fueled heart flame with the intelligent field of your High Self and they merge into the collective intelligent field of our universe. . . . Hold in your mind the love and the qualities that you wish to imbue into the statuette that Thoth will hand you when you are ready. Allow the wisdom of your blessing to come into focus.

As you continue breathing the Heart Breath, begin the first step of shaping the fire, and then hold what you have created with your eyes and your will while you use the stones to create the matter through sound. If you ever feel your fabrications are distorted in any way, simply release them and begin again. Do this as many times as you need to until you have one that meets your standards. It is okay to keep throwing away these sheets and fire sculptures. Through practice, you gain the ability to do each part of the process well and to bring them together successfully.

Notice the calmness that enters you: as you step into your divinity you become one with your High Self. Thoth nods and reaches into the window of stones, pulls forth a statuette, and presents it to you. Hold your focus and concentrate on each aspect of this process.

Once you take the offered statuette from Thoth with intention, wrap it with the etheric substance that you have created with fire and sound. There is an instant melding of your creation with the statuette. Even at this point, if you have any reservations, the statuette will simply fade away with all of your contributions, it will dissolve and return to the realm of pure spirit.

It appears as though hands are coming out of the webbed tube to receive the animated statuette from you. The statuette takes on a burning essence that you can perceive, and disappears at once into the tube. There it follows its own journey into life on planet Earth, coming forth into new awareness, new life. The statuette, now a newborn, finds its own path, because each entity, each creation, has its own path.

Thank Thoth for this opportunity to participate in the creation of our future.

You may choose to offer yourself to this creative process as much and as often as you feel called as long as you can hold impeccable attention and concentration.

Our evolution happens mostly through inertia and unconscious behavior. By stepping up to the plate of conscious creative sculpting in this way, we influence and co-create the future. When you do this work, you are also working on yourself. Concentrated focus on this practice develops your personal connection to life and brings you to a deeper experience and awareness of self. At this level, you become aware of yourself as creator. You take responsibility not only for your own body and its maintenance, but also for your own manifestations.

The goal of the noble art of alchemy is enlightenment, the spiritualization of matter. When we attempt to influence the future by doing the above exercise, we are consciously applying the sum total of the wisdom gained from this life journey toward the realization of enlightened future progeny. In practicing this work, you are involved in the alchemical rebirth of the whole of wisdom. You are literally sending the best of yourself into the future, your future—our future. Where it goes, you cannot know; it does have a life of its own.

25
The Wave

We think it is time for all of us who are seeking to heal ourselves and help the world to step into our full inner authority as adult children of God and take responsibility for our thoughts and actions. The wave presupposes that by the time you get this far into this book, you will be prepared to stretch the limits of your creative capacities with discernment and courage.

It was time for the annual Egyptian Mysteries retreat here in Oregon in 2002. I looked forward to it for two reasons: first, the work was always a new stretch; and, second, Normandi Ellis, my favorite author on matters mysterious regarding Egypt, would be joining us again. Normandi provided extraordinary knowledge, inspiration, depth, and humor, and was a joy to work with. These retreats repeated for about a dozen years, during which we covered a wide range of subjects.

We were always vague in our announcements because part of the mystery was that we were not let in on what we would be teaching until just before the event. The year 2002 was no exception; only a few days before Normandi was due to arrive did Mark and I begin to receive our instructions. As is often the case, we were on the road when they came in, on a short drive to visit friends up the McKenzie River.

As soon as we started following the river, Mark looked inward and saw a vivid though unfamiliar image of the Black Isis. She was squatting in the act of birthing, with a rapturous look on her face. As she came more into focus, he saw a continual breaking of water. Isis was holding the moment like a perpetually flowing fountain—eternal, gushing forth, in an ongoing act of giving birth.

The idea of ecstatic birthing is somewhat of a conundrum, although it is not foreign to me. The more novel phenomenon of freshly bursting water as a constant definitely added to the mystique.

In the explosive rush of discovery, Mark grasped the mood this image carried. Even in the throes of perpetual birthing, Isis does not get old and tired. Fully awake and alert, she exists on the constant edge of creation itself, continually giving birth to the universe.

The closest image Mark could find to describe living on the crest of creation was a wave. Every occurrence in the universe has its fleeting moment. The next occurrence is building up to its point, organizing for its brief cresting moment in reality and the subsequent dissipation of its energies. The wave metaphor is helpful to understand how anything that happens—every occurrence that will have its moment—comes to organize itself. Thus, the universe is created, then created again, and again. The momentum created by the rhythm of reality dictates how the entire universe—the slight repositioning of a planet, the aging of a piece of fruit, the movement of sound through the air—every large and small phenomenon is being recreated and determined each moment by everything that led up to that moment. There is really just one moment: every moment is the big bang. Isis is continuously giving birth to the entire universe.

It is a prerequisite, in order to fully explore the wave, that you be fully engaged with your High Self, fully present, and centered in your heart. If not, you simply will not achieve what you set out to do in your journey. Your High Self is not shackled to the density, bias, or judgments that cause bad decisions to be made. Your High Self is a wonderful bright star; part of the point of this exercise is for you to tap into it. This work catalyzes the kind of insights that engender new ideas and solutions. We see examples throughout history in which spontaneous revelations have instigated everything from religions to philosophies to new scientific discoveries.

When working from the High Self, the boundaries between "self" and the rest of the universe will blur. To be effective, the ego steps back so that resonance with all of creation will be amplified. All of creation includes an intelligence that permeates everything—always has and always will.

And when working from the High Self, each of us can become involved in creation, in the buildup that gathers as the wave crests. If we can tweak the energies a little bit during formation, the results will be different than what would have happened if we had not gotten involved. As the wave crests, there is a little frothing line that is our moment of material reality: and then it passes.

We have spoken earlier of how each of us influences reality through our more or less conscious thoughts, observances, and actions. The Wave exercise allows us not only to witness the creation process, but also to participate consciously in the moment.

There are many things that you can do with this process. What is your passion? Is it health matters or the quality of our air? What is the burning issue for you? Where do you most wish to serve?

What we found as we explored this process is that many things that we thought were important fell away. It was astonishing to me that none of my prior knowledge—including the knowledge that helped me decide what I was going to work on in the wave—prepared me for how I would look at that issue from my Higher Self. The closer you come to unification with the whole of creation, the more perfect it all appears. In this state, I recognized the perfection of some of the things that I so strongly felt needed to change to make life better. Part of the exercise actually involves holding to your initial intention by hanging on to a little bit of your personal will, because when you are totally in sync with the High Self, nothing needs to be changed! It is all beautiful and all perfect.

There is a brief pause, about a fifth of a second, between when something happens and when that event registers in our brain and reaches our senses. In the wave journeys in this chapter, we attempt to whittle down the lag time between what happens in reality, and the time it takes for our senses to process it, in order to get to the moment of creation. We will dive down into depths, ride the surge back up, and experience being catapulted into a more direct experience of creation, without the lag time between what our senses register and the actual experience itself.

We will be working with the metaphor of the wave with the support of a few principals from the ancient Egyptian pantheon. First, we must generate enough energy and light to attract Sekhmet, the Egyptian lion-headed goddess who is the feminine face of the sun, and whose name means "the power" or "the mighty one." She wears the cobra on her diadem, representing the power and energy of kundalini—the life force energy that she provides. Journeying into the wave, we are tasked to find Sekhmet and motivate her to tickle forth an extra surge of the raw material of creation from her consort, Ptah, that ineffable source deep beneath the wave.

Ptah is the creator god who speaks the material universe into being. He is usually pictured as a man wearing a blue skullcap that symbolizes the celestial waters, reflected in the terrestrial depths of our metaphoric wave. For our purposes here, Ptah represents the reservoir, the primordial ocean from which all creation is born, the amniotic fluid that nourishes the dream that has always been held by Ptah. Sekhmet represents the process of formulation of the universe, the action and flux, starting with an inkling that this prime material is going to be of substance. Her energy catalyzes the transformational process and brings forth the material world.

Isis is the crest of the wave itself, the eternal moment of creation, bursting forth in the ongoing ecstatic act of giving birth. She is in total rapture as creation gushes forth from her. In short, Isis, the great Mother Goddess who by her wisdom, power, and love re-members her murdered husband, represents the ongoing climactic moment of the finished product of the universe, which is all of creation that can be measured and perceived.

If we are to influence the creation of our moment-to-moment physical world, we must apply our will in concert with the creation of that which we wish to change—hence the co-creative process. For example, if someone you know has a growing tumor and you are tracking its progress, you know that if the tumor is left to run its course, it will grow, and the situation will get worse. If you enter the journey of the wave with intention, when you work with Sekhmet and the powerful energy of kundalini surging up into the cresting of the wave, you can influence the reality of the tumor. If it is your will and desire to change the course of that tumor, you begin by working through the wave with the moment-to-moment creation and recreation of that tumor, perhaps shrinking and dissolving it. You will understand how this works once you have been through the three dive exercises, and you will be able to apply this to anything you would like to influence on the planet.

This task requires self-examination regarding our motives, our ethics, and our integrity. This is a defining moment, and once again the question needs to be asked: Do we move forward to access and develop our full potential as adult children of the gods, and embrace our divinity and the responsibility that comes with it? Or do we shirk this responsibility and diminish ourselves in order to avoid it? The latter leaves us following the trajectory that we have already set for ourselves, asleep at the wheel.

THREE DIVES

Before beginning this process, be sure you have completed the chakra cleanse exercise found in chapter 10, "Sound." By now you will have practiced the Heart Breath sufficiently to use it to connect with your High Self; you have learned how to recognize yourself as thoroughly present and held in the intelligent medium of love that will both keep you safe and inform you as you journey.

We will take three dives into the wave, with three different intentions.

First Dive

Our first dive will take us from our present position lagging just behind creation into the perspective of Isis, as the crest of the wave, as the entire wave, as all of creation itself. In this first dive, we witness physical reality from a new perspective. The more we practice this exercise, the stronger and the more at ease we become with the process, and the better prepared we will be for the more complex dives that follow.

EXERCISE

Instructions for the First Dive

The mechanics of the dive are simple. You are entering the deep ocean of creation with the purpose of gaining sufficient energy and momentum to generate and gather raw material for creation; the goal of the first dive is to allow the momentum achieved during the return to carry you past your physical body to the crest of the wave to be present and witness the moment of creation. By the time you get to the third dive, you will also be passing Isis as you surge up from the timeless realm of Ptah into and past the Now moment in all of creation.

As always, begin with the Heart Breath. Note that, for this work it is particularly important to connect with both the love aspect and the intelligence of Earth and Sky. Engaging the wisest aspect of yourself is imperative. Set your intention for this dive. . . . Then start a flow of energy through your body by raising kundalini, working with the breath and with whatever process you have practiced to get the flow of energy moving up through your body in a safe and grounded way. (Sometimes pelvic movement or squeezing and releasing the sphincter can help catalyze rising energy.) This energy that you raise is what attracts Sekhmet: she senses the flow, and her attention and enjoyment enhance it.

As the flow gains in power, you can release any blocks between you and source, and further amplify the current of energy. Now focus your intention as you direct this current into the depths of a great ocean, a bottomless ocean. You are about to dive from the warm current at the surface into the cold, dense reservoir underneath.

The excitement you generate as you dive reaches Ptah, the driving force in the cold, rich depth that is the source of everything. The excitement also stimulates a surge of additional creative material into your current. You are too buoyant to remain in the depths for long. As you lose momentum you change directions, now moving toward the surface. As you rise, picking up speed, you are one with this dense, rich surge that carries material substance you did not have with you when you were diving in. As you race to the surface, your thrust increases significantly and you approach and pass your physical body, which is holding space for you as you dive. Just before you pass yourself in your starting point, put out the request to Isis: May I join you?

Your consciousness gets swept past your senses, and you are now at the point of creation with Isis on the crest of the wave. The big bang is going on all about you; all creation is becoming manifest. . . . [*Pause.*]

You can only hang here for a moment, while all the new material you brought gets organized into the crest of the wave. Once the excess energy is spent, you fade back to your place behind the moment of creation.

Enjoy the contentment of knowing that you have shared the moment of creation—you have experienced a change in your perception of the wave with Isis.

Be sure to ground and center yourself. Linger for a moment in the embrace of the love that imbues the Heart Breath. . . .

Write in your journal and practice this first dive until you are comfortable with the shift in consciousness and perception that this part of the exercise offers.

Second Dive

The second dive carries the intention of exploring other vantage points, beginning anywhere on Earth and extending to galaxies without having to wait the light years for that information to come to us. Our goal for this journey is for you to experience how to observe the totality of creation so that you know what is going on along the length of the crest of the wave.

EXERCISE

Instructions for the Second Dive

When you become more accustomed to the possibilities associated with this second dive, you can direct yourself to specific places that you know about or want to learn about. For example, you might ask to explore a specific place or situation on Earth that is in need of repair or healing, or check out what Earth looks like from the moon or Mars. Perhaps you would like to study our galaxy from the perspective of another galaxy. Organize your intention during the initial Heart Breath while you are preparing for the dive so that it will be ready for delivery during your ascent.

As you enter this second dive (after becoming comfortable with the process by practicing the first), you should be able to gather more *prima matteria* and stay a little longer. The extra energy/matter will serve you well in fulfilling the potential of your task. Your request to Isis will be different, and a little more complex, as you seek to find a new point of perspective. Mark and I do not rely solely on words and proper English during moments like this if they will hold us back; rather, we transmit or broadcast our intention as focused and strongly as we can along with the few words that we need to convey our meaning.

As you are rushing upward from the dive toward Isis, send before you a strong and focused message that conveys the location you wish

---

to observe. You will not have much time: use thoughts and images, or simply clear intention to convey your request.

Take the time you need to explore the potential of this second dive. The opportunities are vast. As you learn to navigate with your intention and your requests, you will discover an encyclopedia of experience from a fresh perspective.

Third Dive

Now that you have some experience moving about within the depth and length of the wave, and now that you have plunged into the building blocks of the universe and have even ridden in a current you have created—you are ready for the third dive. This time as you come up from your dive, you are going to race past Isis beyond a moment of creation, with the goal of witnessing and perhaps altering that moment as it comes into existence.

One obvious use of the wave would be to interrupt or reverse the momentum of a growing tumor, as mentioned earlier. On a more planetary scale, you could look at the long-term consequences from open pit mining, rising water levels, shrinking glaciers, the weakening ozone layer, or the aftermath of wildfires, earthquakes, and nuclear and other disasters. Another example would be to address a dangerous and growing hurricane. For this situation, you could perhaps use the wave to create a shift that starves the storm of its energy, and changes its momentum from a building phase to one in which it is calming and shrinking. That is a logical solution, but what if the rain from the hurricane was much needed farther inland? The bigger picture might include the hurricane as part of the solution to a dangerous, prolonged draught. So here is the rub: when you invoke your more enlightened self, what is obvious and logical while in one frame of mind might change; your priorities and what you wish to create might change. This is the wire you will have to walk when you move from your personal will to co-creation with divinity.

You are moving here from the individual to the collective, from witness to participant. The logical brain can perhaps come up with resolutions; but nothing will happen at all without the participation of your wisest self in conjunction with divine intelligence. This dive will give you an opportunity to see possible solutions to the challenges we face as we race toward the potential future coming toward us in time.

EXERCISE
Instructions for the Third Dive

This time when you prepare to dive, you must be particularly mindful. What is motivating you to want to move forward on the wave and see what is coming? What would you like to accomplish in this journey? Are there particular planetary challenges or situations for which you would like to find solutions?

Your work with the Heart Breath and the medium of love is especially important in preparation for this dive. When you are centered and present and ready to fully engage with this process, take the dive. Raise the energy required and offer it to Sekhmet so that you and she can tickle an even stronger surge from Ptah. As you speed back up to the surface with this extra boost of momentum, know that it is okay to slip past Isis. You are the progeny of Isis, and more. It is with recognition that she witnesses you surge past her. Once past this moment in time, you can look back and get a clear sense of the potential of what we are facing in terms of your chosen subject—or you can ask for guidance to identify a problem of regional or global proportions, and the inspiration to deal with it. You perceive this before it solidifies into its manifest moment, and you can also see many parallel possibilities as you take in all the information that is available to you from this unique perspective....

Following is an example from Mark, just a little taste to tickle your pallet and make you hungry for more:

Floods and droughts, floods and droughts. For years I have been reading the same headlines, often with "All-Time Record Broken" attached, and often the flood will drain into the same river on one side while the drought-stricken area sits upstream on the other.

These observations and a life's collection of experiences and education had been sitting quietly in different parts of my brain; they had not found a connection until one grand moment during a class Nicki was teaching with the same name as this book.

It was during the third dive of "The Wave," as I was rushing toward Isis with my collection of unorganized energy that the question I had entered this exercise with came to the fore. "What can we do?" came out as a yearning filled with love and concern as I shot past the goddess and I was totally open to whatever subject I was about to be presented with. I was suddenly, dramatically, and absolutely immersed in the dire consequences of floods and droughts, and the steps, big and little, we can take to resolve them. The images came quickly, one on top of the other. They came with a powerful sense of comprehension. Knowledge accumulated from over the years combined with new insights and created a new body of knowledge that stayed with me and has stood the test of time. I have applied some of the insights to our seasonal stream, for instance, and now our water table does not fluctuate nearly as much, the force of the water leaving our property has stopped cutting a deeper gorge downstream, and we now store much of the rainwater, which allows it more time to enter and recharge the aquifer or to slowly flow away over a period of time following the rain event.

It is imperative that you are fully connected with your High Self in order to both appropriately ask your question, and receive the experience that will allow you to see solutions that you may never have imagined. If there is a world situation, environmental hazard, disease, or particular challenge that is on your mind, bring that into focus prior to entering the dive, so that you have your request in your heart when you enter the process.

Be sure to have your journal handy so that you can scribe the vision and any information you receive.

Ground and center yourself as soon as you return to your usual point of perception, using the Earth Breath part of the Heart Breath to anchor yourself back into your ordinary physical reality. Know that some things will never be the same, because each moment of creation begins a path that did not exit before.

26
Creating New Ideas

Before jumping into the question of where ideas come from and their importance to Creator, we need a brief recap of how the universe works, at least according to our theory, which meshes quite smoothly with the latest in quantum physics: the big bang is still going on, it has never stopped; it has only gotten bigger as the ongoing creation of all things material and energetic continues, and continues to expand. Measurable time is the sequential pulse as, moment by moment, everything in reality flickers into existence and dissolves into nothingness. Each successive moment contains all matter and energy, and then all matter and energy dissipates, as each moment is replaced by the next moment, which disappears and is replaced by the next, and the next, and so on.

These sequential moments comprise measurable time. The pace of time fluctuates, depending on certain variables, such as the presence of mass and the speed of objects. Since every iota of that piece of mass is flickering into existence and then back out continuously, heavy objects with greater mass create a drag on the flow of time.

As scientists have continued dissecting cells, and then molecules, and then atoms, ever searching for something that retains its material form in smaller and smaller units—just as they have kept looking for that which is not made of energy—they have discovered that the smallest points of matter have no mass! It is all energy!

Everything in existence is made up of unimaginable numbers of atoms that feel solid because of repelling forces. The electrons in our hand are repelled by the electrons in the table. Therefore we can rest our hand on the table and everything feels solid, but it is only energy repelling itself. Ultimately, the structure is made of and made by the energy. It takes a huge amount of energy to maintain the structure—energy generated by a complex of electrons, protons, and neutrons.

Time is a by-product of this ongoing event. Imagine the electron in orbit: it is not moving; it is merely flickering into existence a little ahead of the last place it flickered into existence. What it was before it flickered into existence is moving from a dimension that has no time; and for the moment that it exists before it is replaced by the next version of itself, there is a moment of time that follows the last moment the electron flickered into existence. All the electrons and all the molecules and all the quarks accumulated give us measurable time, even though the pace depends upon and differs according to the variables at play. The variables on the face of this Earth are pretty constant—our wristwatches work at the same pace everywhere, but time plays by different rules in other areas of the universe.

As we look at the components of our universe: time, space, energy, and matter, the question arises: Where does life fit in? More to the point, where does the intelligence and awareness we have evolved to fit in the puzzle? The universe could not exist without, for instance, time, but it could easily move along without us. The stars would continue to light the night sky. Their mere existence would be every bit as majestic whether or not we were here to unravel their mysteries, or just to gaze upon them. Is that why we are here? Does all of creation desire an appreciative audience? Or perhaps there is another raison d'etre, and it took a universe to bring us into being. After all, the bulk of our physical bodies was created in the core of long-gone stars, stars whose very existence would be lost but for the endeavors of the living intelligence they helped create.

Along with our ability to gather and interpret information, and perhaps to stand in awe as we learn more about the universe, is a quality and potential that may also be a reason for our existence—free will and creativity.

Imagine that! The only unpredictable thing in existence is us, except, of course, for all those self-aware, creative aliens. We know with some certainty the fate of our sun, but we cannot know how new art will be expressed. We can anticipate some of the scientific breakthroughs that are being worked on, although we will be surprised by how they get used. (Case in point: the touch screens on our smart phones incorporate technologies developed from quantum mechanics.)

Where do our ideas come from? New ideas are the divergence from Creator's creations, and are a path to our own creations. Neurologists have been mapping brain activity and the growing body of knowledge shows which areas are involved in certain activities, but we still do not know how a new and creative thought comes into being.

Once a thought is generated, it is our choice what to do with it. We can take up paper and pen and present it to others, we can put it into words and speak it, and we can shape it in clay. We can even simply hold it to ourselves. But thoughts have a way of accumulating. Historically, new thoughts have been influencing every aspect of our lives. They have also had an effect on physical changes in our evolving bodies. For instance, the loss of body hair coincides with the "invention" of clothes.

In order to prepare for the exercise that follows, we suggest the following steps:

1. We invite you to remember new ideas that you have had, and how everything led up to the specific moment of inspiration. Recall the satisfying, excited feeling that you had following that inspired moment. Remember, but be okay with, coming down from that moment. Compare that experience with any breakthroughs and epiphanies you have heard about that have changed the world. You may recall the scientists who ascertained the shape of DNA, or the machinist who, in a flash, discovered how to mass-produce something, or the biologist who discovered a cure. There are multiple types of excellent ideas, often the result of years of plodding through by trial and error and the process

of elimination. And then there are the intuitive discoveries that feel like divine intervention, but are they? They may simply be the result of everything coming together at the right moment and yielding inspiration.

2. Relax into a state of grace that allows inspiration. Of course this begs the question, are you waiting for Creator to whisper something in your ear? Or are you, at this moment, prepared to present Creator with something new? That leads to another interesting question: Can we know the difference between information from Creator and information that originates from within ourselves?

JOURNEY

For New Ideas

Have your journal handy before you enter this journey so that you can capture the details and breakthroughs as they present themselves.

Go within yourself, using the Heart Breath. Become less aware of your surroundings and more aware of your beating heart and your breath, and all the sensations within. Imagine that you are connected throughout time with everybody who has ever paused to think about their heartbeat and their breath. Go in further, as the connection to everyone through time becomes stronger, to the point where you can start sensing the eras some of these people were in, and glimpsing their surroundings, maybe even catching a whiff of the smells. There is a hint of a cabin with a fireplace, but the smell is reminiscent of the cave with the fire; the flickering around the fire is reminiscent of the little stove in the tower; and through it all your heart beats and you breathe in and out.

The other sense that you share with so many others is the process of deep thought. You and they have been pondering something that is beginning to make sense. It takes on a life of its own: the thought starts racing. . . . "But of course, if this, then this." Right now, enjoy that shared triumphant moment with everybody who has ever sat quietly observing their breath and heartbeat, and let the thoughts of those working on new ideas rise to the surface. Listen. . . . Listen for the guiding thoughts so that you may know what subjects are being tackled. . . . This is leading to that exquisite moment when the light turns on and absolute understanding allows for something new to emerge. Share in this moment, and look for clues as to what the guiding thoughts were expressing. . . . You will recognize the seminal thoughts by remembering moments from your life when you have had revelations or epiphanies. . . .

The connection with these others fades, and you are left in your present situation, listening to your heart, feeling your breath, and acknowledging the thoughts that have been fading in and out of focus—your own thoughts. Some are closer to those breakthrough moments than others. Pick one—one that you have been entertaining for a period of time, on again and off again. . . . Bring it up, into your focus. Look at it, and be comfortable with the concept that at any moment you may be struck by inspiration. Hold your thought lovingly. Mull it over, and put a wish out to the universe: "In the spirit of co-creation, I wish the fetters to be released, and the blinders to be dropped. I allow my bright and shining being to come forth now, or later, or in the middle of the night. I wish to participate in the art of creation. . . ."

Now as you sit there with your thoughts and your beating heart, once again (in recognition) share with all those others who have had this moment. Be there with them as they are with you. . . . [*Long pause.*]

And now begin the journey back into the here and now.

Ground and center, using the Earth Breath to help you connect with your physical body, fully grounded and centered. . . .

Be sure to write in your journal and get all the details down.

27
Celebrating a Peaceful Future

I was going over the edits for this book on my return from leading a group through Egypt, less than a month after the dramatic people's overthrow of the Mubarak regime. I have tasted first-hand the emotions of the Egyptians, whose peaceful tenacity resulted in the accomplishment of the impossible. Not even the youth at the root of this movement could have imagined that in eighteen days, with fear defeated, they would succeed in toppling a dictator who led such a corrupt and internally repressive regime for decades. The minister responsible for the violence against the demonstrators and the tragic loss of the lives of so many vibrant young people, is, along with several other extremely corrupt ministers, currently imprisoned.

How this will play out for Egypt and the many Middle Eastern countries that have followed Tunisia and Egypt to stand for freedom is a question that I do not think will have been answered by the time this book is published. That millions of Egyptians could stand together in peace against the perpetrators of violence was a miracle in itself and an example for all of us. Their celebration, their stories, and their joy, regardless of how their future unfolds, have paved the way for a new Middle East and a new world. The following journey stands as a tribute to the celebration of peace as we now know it can be.

Mark visioned the Journey to Celebrate Peace, which is the subject of this chapter, for the fourteenth annual Earthdance, a music festival that created an opportunity to "Give Peace a Dance." This one, in 2010, was to be the last of eight successive Earthdances to be held at the Black Oak Ranch in Laytonville, California—a venue that is close to my heart because it is the home of the Hog Farm community, one of the longest sustaining and always inspiring conscious communes that came out of the hippie movement, and of Camp Winnarainbow, a socially conscious summer camp that our children attended. What made this festival site special was its village atmosphere, and the opportunity to experience a wide range of musical and other entertainment on grounds that were cared for as sacred, with respect for the first peoples of the land. For a number of years, I was asked to be part of the Elders' Council, which includes a diverse array of wise elders from many traditions, mostly Native American, many of these from the local tribes still residing in the reservations and communities throughout Northern California.

The central event, which included the Prayer for Peace, happened on Saturday and was simultaneously being celebrated at 360 sites around the world, and also streaming live on the net. One of my contributions for the last four years had been to prepare the audience for the main prayer. Although my tradition was to use the Heart Breath to get everyone breathing together and in alignment for the prayer, I added a different empowerment each year. Because this was the last Earthdance to be produced at Black Oak Ranch, our journey gave thanks to the land and, in the spirit of reciprocity, offered back to the land the inspiration we had received there around peace and how to live it.

Here, we adapt that journey to cap this work on Planetary Healing because we think it is a powerful tool for remembering and creating the peace we desire in the world. Although this journey was written for Black Oak Ranch, you can translate the imaging to any place or festival where you wish to create this overlay of peace, using the exponential power of the numbers of celebrants to assist and empower the work.

JOURNEY

To Celebrate Peace

Use the Heart Breath to prepare yourself, and continue using it throughout. . . . Breathe with the intention of connecting your flame with the flames of others around the world who are engaged in meditating, praying for and celebrating peace.

In the light of your heart flame, imagine a beautiful valley covered with wild grasses and diverse plant life and graced with ancient black oaks, bay trees, and a meandering river. . . .

Imagine this valley before the roads and power lines and houses came into the landscape. Going back in time, imagine the huge black oaks that stand as giant sentinels in clusters, and watch them getting younger and smaller . . . keep going back before that. Notice the cycles within the years as they progress, like when the arrival of spawning fish attracts the eagles and bears to feast.

Sense the presence of the people who wandered through this valley throughout the millennia, including the ones who settled here and nearby for various periods of time.

Focus your attention on the tranquility and peaceful existence that was the norm for the Grass People, the people of this region, for thousands of years.

Once you discover that peaceful state of mind, know that it remains here. Tune in to it. . . . Harmonize with it. . . . Bring it into yourself. . . . And now amplify it back to the land. . . . Notice the similarities between that sense of peace, which resides within you, and the tranquility that was the way of life for generations upon generations of the Grass People. We are a continuation of the original harmony that existed in this valley.

Yes, there have been moments of disruption and conflict. Now is a time to overwhelm that discord with your tranquility and peaceful intentions. See the healing coming not only from here and now, but also from the ancestors, and the future generations. . . .

The predominance of peace and peaceful intentions we are now aligning with continues to flow through this valley like a river; and like a river, it continually washes away all those moments that were out of harmony. Know your connection to all past and future generations. Know the continuity of the peace and celebration that are here with you now.

Now we have an opportunity to empower the future. Feel the connection we have to the generations that are yet to come. Envision future generations who will also be here in peace and harmony, and in celebration.

Rekindle your Heart Breath and feed this vision with your love and with the powers of Earth and Sky. . . .

As you continue to focus your awareness on the predominance of peace in the generations that knew lifetimes of living in community and in balance with nature, expand your awareness. . . . Attune yourself with these peaceful people in other locations now—first, in other valleys nearby, and then out across the continent and beyond, and to islands in the Pacific. Your range spreads in every direction as you seek out the peaceful times that float to the surface. Sometimes you sense how the peaceful years were bracketed by war and distress. Bring your focus back to the peaceful times; tune in to that sense of well-being people get looking at their happy, well-fed, healthy children. Notice how easy it is to find that common sense of well-being as your focus expands to all the continents and all the countries around the globe—South America, Africa, Australia, and Europe; throughout the Middle East, India, and Asia. Move your awareness throughout all the lands, and throughout all the eras. . . . [Pause.]

Once again, kindle your Heart Breath, pouring love upon your flame and invoking the power of Earth and Sky. Bring this love and power to this shared awareness of well-being and tranquillity. Send it

to future generations while validating all that is good in the generations past, throughout the world.

Notice how, somewhere in the world, others are doing the same,
right now. Feel your natural state of joy as you acknowledge all that is
good and peaceful in the world.

As you focus with your expanded awareness through space and
time, notice how predominant the good is, and bring your attention
to the moments of celebration, of sharing happiness with others....

Now feel the throbbing pulse of the drums, and the feet on the
ground entraining with the rhythms. One pulse, in time with the danc-
ing ... It is growing.... Generations of celebration, and you are part
of it. Feel the shared joy of the heart reaching out to everything that
has ever been and everything that is yet to be. Feel the drumming, the
joy, the excitement. Every age group shares in their own way. Be part
of the universal smile, and the universal passion....

"As long as the rivers flow, and the grass grows,
may peace be with you."

Index

Page numbers in *italics* refer to illustrations.

About the Authors

NICKI SCULLY

Nicki Scully has been teaching healing and shamanic arts and the Egyptian Mysteries since 1983. Techniques from her Alchemical Healing form are used internationally by thousands of practitioners. She is a lineage holder in the Hermetic Tradition of Thoth and maintains the Lyceum of Shamanic Egypt. She is ordained as a priestess of Hathor by Lady Olivia Robertson, cofounder of the Fellowship of Isis.

During her first visit to Egypt with the Grateful Dead in 1978, Nicki experienced an epiphany on the top of the great pyramid and soon realized that her purpose in this life was to bring forth the hidden shamanic arts of Egypt. In the late 1980s, Nicki founded Shamanic Journeys, Ltd., and continues to guide inner journeys and spiritual pilgrimages to Egypt and other sacred sites. She is the author of *Alchemical Healing, Becoming an Oracle, Power Animal Meditations,* and coauthor with Linda Star Wolf of *The Anubis Oracle* and *Shamanic Mysteries of Egypt.* Nicki also has a series of CDs and DVDs available, which can be ordered directly on her storefront website, www.HathorsMirror.com.

Nicki lives in Eugene, Oregon, with her husband, coauthor Mark Hallert. She maintains a comprehensive healing and shamanic consulting practice and welcomes you to study with her at her beautiful garden center. For more information, please visit her website at

www.ShamanicJourneys.com

MARK HALLERT

Mark Hallert is an important member of Thoth's lineage. He is the visionary behind many of the teachings that Nicki presents to the public through her many forums. On occasion, he accompanies her on her travels and adds his unique articulation and clear sight to the work at hand, and he often cofacilitates her private sessions. Mark got a taste of Big Adventures when he was young and traveled the world in pursuit of them for many years. Little did he know in 1985, when he and Nicki found each other, that he was about to have the biggest adventure yet; a journey into the very fabric of the universe.

For additional interaction with the authors and other readers please visit
www.PlanetaryHealingBook.com

ALSO BY NICKI SCULLY

Becoming an Oracle
Connecting to the Divine Source for Information and Healing
A 7-CD audio learning course in 19 guided Oracular Journeys
Produced by Sounds True, 2009
For a sample journey visit www.BecomingAnOracle.com

The Anubis Oracle
A Journey into the Shamanic Mysteries of Egypt
Book with 35-card deck
Cowritten with Linda Star Wolf, illustrated by Kris Waldher
Bear & Company, 2008
For a sample reading visit www.TheAnubisOracle.com

Shamanic Mysteries of Egypt
Awakening the Healing Power of the Heart
Cowritten with Linda Star Wolf
Bear & Company, 2007

Alchemical Healing
A Guide to Spiritual, Physical, and Transformational Medicine
Bear & Company, 2003

Power Animal Meditations
Shamanic Journeys with Your Spirit Allies
Illustrated by Angela Werneke
Bear & Company, 2001

Alchemical Healing DVD
Experiences, Insights, and Empowerments
An interview DVD produced by Sacred Mysteries

CDS AVAILABLE FROM NICKI SCULLY

The first three of the following CDs can function as audio illustrations for *Power Animal Meditations.*

Journey for Healing with Kuan Yin
Nicki Scully with music by Roland Barker and Jerry Garcia
Track One: "Journey for Healing with Kuan Yin"
Track two: Music only
Proceeds from the sale of this CD go toward the production and distribution of more of these CDs to be *given away* to people with AIDS, leukemia, or cancer, or to centers and practitioners working with those diseases. Donations are tax deductible.

Awakening the Cobra
Nicki Scully with music by Roland Barker
Track one: "Journey with the Cobra for Clearing the Chakras and Awakening the Kundalini Energies"
Track two: Music only

Journey with Eagle & Elephant
Nicki Scully with music by Roland Barker
Track one: "Journey with Eagle & Elephant"
Track two: Music only

Tribal Alchemy
Nicki Scully with music produced and arranged by Roland Barker
Three journeys are available on this CD: *Renewal, Journey for Peace,* and *Animal Totems*

. . . And You Will Fly!
An Animal Circus Adventure
Written by Nicki Scully, Roland Barker, and Mark Hallert
Narrated by Nicki Scully
Music written and produced by Roland Barker

An Alchemical Healing story produced as a radio play for children of all ages to be given away free to any child suffering from a potentially terminal disease and to those hospitals and practitioners working with these children. Proceeds from the sale of this CD will go toward further production and distribution so that more can be given away. Donations are tax deductible.

To order, contact your local bookseller or
Nicki Scully
P.O. Box 5025
Eugene, OR 97405
www.shamanicjourneys.com
Online store: HathorsMirror.com

The *Making Spirit Medicine* CD

The *Making Spirit Medicine* CD includes a 39-minute guided visualization journey that is both shamanic and alchemical in nature. The text for this journey appears in chapter 5, "Making Spirit Medicine," and is one of the primary rites in the book. It is a ceremony in which the listener participates in creating a healing nectar that includes a powerful dose of love. The medicine we create in this journey heals at several levels: It heals the person that creates it; it is sent out to family, coworkers, and loved ones; and it can be sent out to places, situations, and communities throughout the world for Planetary Healing.

We originally visioned the ceremony for *Making Spirit Medicine* at the Women of Wisdom conference in 2004. My friend Alexa MacDonald, a song-writer/musician in Arizona, wrote a song for the ceremony and she and two friends worked on harmonies. As soon as we completed the ceremony, we knew we had to make a recording to make this powerful process more widely available.

Roland Barker, who lives in Hawaii, has produced a number of guided visualization CDs with me since the late 1980s, and he is the brilliant composer who brought this CD together with his computer magic. A number of musicians and vocalists added layers whenever Roland came to Oregon, to which he added his synthesized music to render a rich background for the journeys.

HOW TO USE THE
MAKING SPIRIT MEDICINE CD

Before listening, you might wish to prepare as if for any ceremony or rite of passage by smudging, setting up a small altar, or lighting a candle. Be sure that you are in a comfortable place and will have uninterrupted time within which to have the full experience.

The first part of the CD is a narrated guided journey that begins with the Heart Breath practice, which is fundamental for the work of Planetary Healing. Learning it from this CD at the outset of reading the book will be a great help for practicing all the exercises.

We are using this guided ceremonial journey to initiate readers into the Universal Life Force energy, the same current of energy used in most healing forms. Once this infinite source is accessed, you will be able to call upon it any time you use the Heart Breath, and it will always be available to you. You can direct it into almost every aspect of your life: into your food, your garden, your loved ones, your work of art or other creations, and anyone or any situation in need of healing.

The original Cauldron, to which we connect in this ritual, has been in existence for eons. Each time a person or circle invokes the Communal Cauldron, they connect to the energies of every person who has made Spirit Medicine in this way over time.

We have included a second track on the CD that is without narration or vocals. The music by itself is designed for journeying and can provide the background for many meditations, for other journeys in this book, or simply for your listening pleasure.

MAKING SPIRIT MEDICINE CREDITS

Journey: Written by Mark Hallert and Nicki Scully and narrated by Nicki Scully
Music: Roland Barker
Song and Lyrics, Vocals, Guitar: Alexa MacDonald
Chorus: Victoria Koch, Marcia J. Cutler, Martha Sherwood, Karen Stingle
Additional Vocals: Lisa Ashook
Additional Percussion, Srudi Box: Mz. Imani
Recorded at: Sprout City, Eugene, Oregon
CD label Artwork: Willow Arleana